THE
JIM PLUNKETT
STORY

Mom and I together during my senior year at Stanford. *(Painting by Gini Campbell Annis, photo courtesy of Ray DeAragon)*

THE JIM PLUNKETT STORY

*The Saga of a Man
Who Came Back*

By
JIM PLUNKETT
and
DAVE NEWHOUSE

ARBOR HOUSE
New York

To my family and friends.
                                    J.P.

To Patsy, Chad and Casey: my family, my friends and my life.
                                    D.N.

ACKNOWLEDGMENTS

IT'S difficult for me to talk about myself. For one thing, I'm a private person. And I look matter-of-factly at whatever success I have had in football.

Therefore, telling about my life hasn't been easy. Without the involvement of others—their anecdotes, insights and foresightedness—there couldn't have been as complete a book or even a book at all.

I owe considerable gratitude to:

My mother, Mrs. Carmen Plunkett, and my sisters, Mary Ann Plunkett and Veva Grijalva;

My friends—Jack Schultz, Jim Kauffman, Phill Passafuime, Dick Barrett, Jack Lasater, Nick Vlasoff, Bob Moore, Randy Vataha and Dave Olerich;

Special friends—Gerry Lavelle, Wayne Hooper, Jack Ditz and Gini Campbell Annis;

National Football League teammates, past and present—Delvin Williams, Dave Dalby and Raymond Chester;

Those who have coached me and coached against me—Al Cementina, John Ralston, Pat Lovell, Ken Castles, Tom Flores and Jim Sweeney;

Those who contributed material to the book—Will McDonough of *The Boston Globe*, Alan McAllaster of the *Oakland Tribune*, Gary Cavalli and Bob Rose of Stanford University's athletic department, Dave Winter-grass of the New England Patriots, Delia Newland of the San Francisco 49ers and, especially, Fran Connors of the NFL;

Editors John Porter and typist Lyn Heffernon;

Don Fine and Jared Kieling of Arbor House, two men who believed in this book before others and whose incredible patience makes Job look like a neurotic;

To agent Mike Franklin, an Englishman who had the prescience to ask after my second start at quarterback for the Oakland Raiders in October, 1980: "What if this bloke Plunkett leads the Raiders to the Super Bowl?"

Finally, to Dave Newhouse, who listened to Franklin, agreed there was a book and then helped me write it.

J.P.

CONTENTS

PROLOGUE

"GENTLEMEN . . . " The National Football League public relations man shouted above the noise in the post-game interview room at the Superdome. " . . . Jim Plunkett."

Heads turned toward the doorway. Moments later, Plunkett appeared, coal-black hair matted, rugged Diego Rivera features expressionless, injury-wracked body suffering with each step, silk shirt spotted with perspiration.

He seemed drained, unexcited, as he followed the public relations man to an empty platform. There wasn't even a trace of a smile. Plunkett pushed through the reporters crowded around the platform.

The questions came all at once. "Is this the greatest moment of your life?" . . . "Is your comeback the stuff of storybooks?" . . . "Talk about the two touchdown passes to Branch." . . . "Do you feel vindicated?"

His answers were composed. "This is my greatest moment as a professional, sure. The Rose Bowl happened when I was younger." . . . "It's a little bit of a comeback, but I've been ready for a while." . . . "The Eagles left Cliff alone on the first touchdown and he made a great play on the second." . . . "Vindication implies bitterness. I'm not bitter towards anybody. People don't always make the right choice."

New questions came with machine-gun rapidity and Plunkett calmly stood their fire. "Is this the happiest you've ever been? You don't look happy." . . . "What's bigger, the Super Bowl or the Heisman?" . . . "What was the lowest point of your football career?" . . . "How did you attack the Eagle secondary?"

Patiently, microphones jammed in his face, he responded. "I'm really happy. I don't express it, but I'm terribly happy." . . . "Winning the Super Bowl is bigger." . . . "Getting cut by the 49ers was the low point. I thought about quitting." . . . "Their defensive backs played off our receivers. We hit them underneath."

It was all happening fast. Too fast. One of the great sports stories and human dramas of recent times had unfolded, but the media had no time to appreciate it or slow it down. Deadlines had to be met. Readers, viewers and listeners in fifty states wanted to know how Plunkett lifted himself from the mud to touch the stars.

"I've been shooting for this all my life," he continued, finally forcing a smile. "I never thought I'd get here. . . . "

Jim Plunkett's ten-year road to the Super Bowl was bumpy, pockmarked and obstructed by detours and dead ends. Now he had made it after several wrong turns. The forgotten hero had led the Oakland Raiders to the Super Bowl XV championship. Written off as a second-string quarterback only four months earlier, Plunkett was named the game's Most Valuable Player after throwing three touchdown passes to destroy the Philadelphia Eagles, 27–10, in New Orleans.

Two years before, those who judge football talent for a living said that Plunkett was finished as a quarterback.

Damaged goods. Washed up. Two years before, he might have agreed with them.

"I felt I had failed," he recalled. "I had given up on myself. I thought maybe it was time to change professions."

He didn't, and fought his way back to the top instead. Those who know Plunkett would say it was characteristic. Life had been an endless series of obstacles for Plunkett, beginning with birth.

His parents were blind, Mexican and poor. William and Carmen Plunkett gave their three children love and a remarkably normal home life, and received vision and love in return.

James William Plunkett, their third child and only son, excelled in the classroom and on the playgrounds. He was an honor student and three-sport athlete at James Lick High School in San Jose, California. He was a standout pitcher and a .300 hitter in baseball. He was the first wrestler ever to win four consecutive Mount Hamilton Athletic League individual titles. He was even more celebrated in football, leading his school to a 17–1 record and two league championships.

Stanford University, twenty miles to the north, won the recruiting sweepstakes for this big, macho-looking teenager with the quiet, self-effacing personality. One month before he was to enroll as a freshman, Plunkett felt a lump at the base of his neck. It was a tumor. For two tense weeks, there was fear that not only was Plunkett's football career over at 18, but his life too.

He survived that ordeal, then faced another of less staggering magnitude, but distressing nonetheless to a young quarterback. Stanford wanted to make him a defensive end.

Plunkett resisted. Through hard work he became the greatest of Stanford's great quarterbacks. Plunkett broke numerous collegiate passing records. In 1970, he was named All-American and received the Maxwell Award and Heis-

man Trophy, both symbolic of the country's best college
football player. His crowning moment was leading Stanford
to a 27–17 victory over Ohio State in the Rose Bowl.

Boston Patriots Coach John Mazur watched from the
stands that New Year's Day in Pasadena. Witnessing Plunkett's humbling of Woody Hayes's greatest Ohio State team,
Mazur knew he had to have the strong-armed Stanford wun-
derkind. Because the Patriots had the first pick of the NFL's
1971 draft, Mazur got his man. Plunkett would be part of a
new face-lifting for the sagging Patriots, who were moving
into a new city (Foxboro) and a new stadium (Schaefer) with
a new name (New England).

"From what I've seen of Jim Plunkett," said George
Blanda, the Methuselah of quarterbacks, "he's fantastic, has
a great arm, looks like a leader, seems to have all the desire.
But if I were a coach, I wouldn't throw him in right away if
I had the choice. A rookie quarterback can learn faster and
make much better progress sitting on the bench and watching."

The Patriots had no choice. Plunkett played every
single down at quarterback in 1971—an NFL record—and
threw 19 touchdown passes. He directed the team to upsets
of Oakland, Miami and Baltimore. He was voted NFL
Rookie of the Year.

Then it all collapsed. Defeats began to pile up as the
Patriots failed to improve the following autumn. Plunkett
came under the media's scrutiny, the surgeon's scalpel and
the fans' contempt. He was booed loudly during introductions before the 1975 Dallas game, even though he was out
on the field trying to play with a plastic screw in his left
shoulder.

Plunkett asked New England to trade him to San
Francisco, an hour's drive from his home in San Jose. His
request was granted for a king's ransom. The 49ers mort-
gaged two future drafts—three No. 1 picks and a No. 2 choice

—plus quarterback Tom Owen to acquire Plunkett.

San Francisco started out strongly in 1976. Then, inexplicably, Plunkett began throwing like a semi-pro reject. He discovered that the home fans could boo in chorus too. Finally, in disgrace, he was benched for the first time in his life. The 49ers didn't make the playoffs, but the New England Patriots did, which didn't help Plunkett's already bruised ego.

His misfortunes continued in 1977 following an ownership change. Joe Thomas, who had built a reputation in the NFL as a top college scout, front-office troublemaker and an egotist, was brought in to run the 49er football operations. Amateurism took over on a professional level in San Francisco. Proven players were let go and replaced by unproven players. A qualified head coach (Monte Clark) was forced out and, in Plunkett's estimation, three unqualified head coaches (Ken Meyer, Pete McCulley and Fred O'Connor) then ran the 49ers.

Plunkett would not remain for the collapse of the 49ers and Joe Thomas. Not long after Plunkett threw 11 straight incompletions against Oakland in a 1978 pre-season game, he was cut by the team he had been brought home to save.

The vultures descended from the skies.

"He came out of Stanford, a passing school, so he was way ahead of most rookies in understanding the passing game," said an NFL personnel man who hid behind the mask of anonymity. "I think he looked better than he was. He was never more than an average athlete. He was not quick setting up or quick releasing the ball. He was very mechanical. So he could never get out of trouble. He took a lot of knocks and I think it's showing now.

"He still has a strong arm, but he never learned how to play quarterback. He was not a dedicated football player. He never studied films at night. He was not highly motivated. And he never learned the finesse parts of quarter-backing. He had a strong arm and he just tried to overpower defenses. He didn't learn to read them well, didn't learn to pick up second or third receivers, throw to the backs. He would just sit there and wait."

Jim Plunkett read this and cringed. He knew that he was a worker, a man who was motivated and dedicated to succeed at anything he set out to accomplish. He studied films at night; he kept a projector at home. He felt he could read defenses as well as any quarterback. He knew that he was a good athlete. What the personnel man failed to mention was that Plunkett, for the better part of his NFL career, was surrounded by average athletes. But back in 1978, with little meat left to his carcass and a once-proud reputation gone, Plunkett had absolutely no chance to defend himself. Who would have listened?

Three NFL teams contacted him almost immediately after the 49ers released him. Twenty-four teams didn't. Even the three who were interested—Baltimore, Green Bay and the New York Giants—weren't convinced Plunkett was anything more than a backup quarterback.

Then Al Davis called. Would Plunkett like to play in Oakland? Plunkett thought, "Why does he want me?" Now 30, he agreed only because he didn't want to move east. He had been east already. Plunkett joined the Raiders and didn't throw one pass in 1978 and just 15 passes in 1979.

Then Oakland quarterback Ken Stabler was traded to Houston for Dan Pastorini, which Plunkett misread as a ray of hope: Pastorini was handed the Raider quarter-back job without having to compete for it. Plunkett outplayed Pastorini during the 1980 pre-season. Even Pastorini said so, which required some effort because the two quarterbacks, longtime rivals, didn't care much for each other.

Five weeks into the regular season, Dino Mangiero,

a bulky, unknown nose tackle with the Kansas City Chiefs, landed on Pastorini's right leg, breaking it. Plunkett grabbed his helmet, ran on the field and promptly threw 5 interceptions.

The vultures hovered again.

Then the dark clouds that had trailed Plunkett dispersed and the sun appeared. In his first start in nearly three years, Plunkett knocked over San Diego. The following week, he threw three long touchdown passes as Oakland defeated Pittsburgh in a nationally televised Monday night game.

The Raiders, whose record was 2–3 after the Kansas City game, were on a roll. They won six successive games and nine of eleven to qualify for the playoffs. NFL personnel types looked at one another in bewilderment. "Jim Plunkett?"

Then, in a string of classic performances, Plunkett outpassed Ken Stabler in the sun, Brian Sipe in the snow, Dan Fouts in the rain and Ron Jaworski indoors. Oakland, a wild-card entry, became the first NFL team to win four games in the same post-season. Plunkett's 80-yard touchdown pass to Kenny King was a Super Bowl record.

Jim Plunkett had made his amazing comeback. The beaten-down, but never beaten, quarterback proved against overwhelming odds that he was a player and a winner. Then, with a demonstration of sportsmanship right out of the pages of Frank Merriwell, he refused to point the finger at those who doubted his ability and indestructibility, even though many thought he had every right.

"It's the American dream," Wayne Hooper, Plunkett's attorney, would later say. "It's the guy who gets up at the count of nine and knocks out the champion. It's a great story, a tremendous example for others who've been down, getting kicked, questioning whether they have any value in life, whether their life has been a waste.

"It's boy meets girl, boy loses girl, boy gets girl. Happy ending."

It's a one-of-a-kind story. It's Jim Plunkett's story, which he now tells for the first time in its entirety.

Dave Newhouse
June 1, 1980
Oakland, Calif.

Chapter One
THE MIND'S EYE

MY mother has never seen her three children. She has hugged us, scolded us, raised us and loved us, but she wouldn't know us by sight. My mother is totally blind. Typhoid fever seized her vision when she was 19. She has lived in a world of darkness ever since.

My father's world was blurred, like a man who spent his life swimming underwater. He was legally blind, though with the aid of thick glasses he could see well enough to work and get around on his own. His eyesight became progressively worse over the years, but his body deteriorated faster, and he died of a heart attack in 1969. He was 56.

They were born in New Mexico, my mother in Santa Fe and my father in Albuquerque, where they met at a school for the blind. Mom's given name is Carmen Blea. She is Mexican with a trace of Indian blood. Dad's full name was William Gutierrez Plunkett, though everyone knew him as Willie. He was Mexican with a few German and Irish

branches hanging on his side of the family tree. Plunkett is
an Irish name.

My parents came to California during World War II.
Dad got work in the Richmond shipyards across the bay
from San Francisco. By that time, my two sisters, Genevieve
and Mary Ann, had been born. I came along December 5,
1947, after the family moved to Santa Clara, where my father washed dishes in a restaurant. As rents increased, we
moved to San Jose, the adjacent town. We kept moving
across San Jose until we could find the cheapest low-cost
housing, which turned out to be on the east side.

My father had a new job by that time, running a
newsstand in a San Jose post office. The stand later was
moved to an employment office. Dad sold cigarettes, candy,
magazines and newspapers. He had problems counting
change because of his limited eyesight. Some customers
wouldn't bother telling him when he miscounted; they
pocketed the extra change and walked away, proud to have
fleeced a blind man.

Dad could barely see in his fifties, but he refused to
slow down. He would climb on the morning bus like any
other commuter and head across town to work. He refused
to use a cane or guide dog. So did my mother.

They didn't consider themselves handicapped.

Mom had four sets of eyes, really—dad's and the three
children's. My parents would go for walks, hand in hand.
Dad would tell mom what kind of day it was. He would
describe the flowers, the trees.

"How pretty they are," my mother would say.

My father delighted in coloring the day for my
mother.

The blind learn to substitute other senses for vision—
hearing, touching, smelling, tasting. I would bring a trophy
home. Mom moved her hand over it, touching its parts,
drawing a picture in her mind with her fingers.

"How pretty it is," she would tell me.

There is beauty in touching things just as there is beauty in seeing things. Helen Keller said: "I sometimes wonder if the hand is not more sensitive to the beauties of sculpture than the eye. I should think the wonderful rhythmical flow of lines and curves could be more subtly felt than seen."

Helen Keller couldn't see or hear. My mother can't see either, but she can perceive. And vision is what the mind perceives.

Mom doesn't need eyesight to sense moods. If she is in a room with people who are quiet, she knows something is wrong.

My mother can tell if it is a nice day by feeling the heat coming through a window against her face. She can sense shadows if a person or object comes between her and the sun, because her skin temperature goes down.

She also knows when my hair is too long. I'll bend down to kiss her and she will feel the hair on my neck.

"Jimmy, you better go see the barber," she'll say.

The blind are uncanny. They can "see" what is going on around them without seeing.

When I was a boy, I would bring friends over. Mom would be sitting on the front porch.

"Hi, Jimmy. Hi, kids."

She could hear the voices or footsteps of the other boys. She would know if there were two or three boys with me. "Hi, Mrs. Plunkett," my friends replied. They didn't even know she was blind until they went up to shake her hand.

My mother is incredible. She can clean, cook, sew, wash clothes . . . everything. I have two good eyes and I can't do all those things. She mentally records distances between objects by counting steps. We put items like salt, pepper and flour in containers and keep them in a certain order on the kitchen counter. She counts down the containers until she gets the one she wants.

Because of their own blindness, my parents were concerned about their children's eyesight. We would visit the
eye doctor twice a year instead of the dentist. All three
Plunkett children wear glasses, although our vision isn't that
far off from normal. I wore glasses more at Stanford than at
any time of my life to reduce the eye strain from long hours
of studying.

There are pro football fans in New England and San
Francisco who feel I should wear glasses all the time.

There is hereditary blindness on my mother's side.
My grandmother was totally blind. Yet there never was any
fear among my sisters and I that we would be blind.

As the years passed, mom began to burn herself a lot
while cooking or smoking. The cigarette ash would get low
before she realized it. She would reach for a frying pan on
the stove and touch a burner that was orange-hot. It got to
the point where she was burning away the feeling in her
fingers. We made her stop cooking. She stopped smoking on
her own, just cut if off the day my father died.

We couldn't have a fireplace in our house, not with
blind persons around. There was the danger of my mother's
dress catching on fire without her knowing it. If the house
caught on fire, and mom was alone, she could smell the
smoke and get out through several exits.

My mother now lives with Mary Ann. Each morning
before Mary Ann leaves for work at the computer company,
she makes breakfast for the two of them. Mary Ann also
prepares a lunch for mom. It might be a cold salad or something my mother can warm up in the microwave I gave her
as a Christmas gift. Mary Ann prepares dinner when she
comes home.

The world of the blind is trial and error mostly. They
learn by making mistakes. It takes some bumps and bruises,
for instance, before my mother gets used to rearranged furniture.

We love to kid mom when she gets lost in her own

house. She will be doing something, then forget the room
that she is in.

"Mary Ann, where am I?" she will holler.

It is hard every once in a while not to laugh at her
confusion. She laughs too. My mother is a good sport.

Mary Ann cuts mom's meat at dinner so that she
won't grab the blade of a knife by mistake. Mary Ann tells
her that the cup or glass is on her right, so she won't knock
it over.

You can't always avoid accidents with blind people,
however. We have had a lot of broken plates at home.

We used to buy talking clocks and chiming clocks for
mother. But she can get the time by telephone or on the
radio. She needs to know when it is 11 A.M., because that's
when "The Young and the Restless" is on television. At noon
it is "All My Children."

My mother sits in front of the TV set, picturing in her
mind the images that move on the screen before her sight-
less eyes. And she has a vivid imagination when it comes to
soap operas.

Mom is a remarkable person. Losing her eyesight in
her late teens certainly must have affected her more, psychologically, than if she had been blind all her life. Yet I've
never sensed any bitterness.

> *"I felt very bad when I became blind. I cried a lot. I
> used to ask my mother, 'Why did it happen to me when I was
> so young?' She said: 'Well, things happen.' There was noth-
> ing I could do about it. I asked my God to help me. He has
> helped me a lot. I am not sad anymore. I still have my kids.
> I have a good life. I am very happy in this world."*
> —Mrs. Carmen Plunkett

The mind's eye is everything to the blind. We take
my mother to the movies and explain what is happening on
the screen. She loves movies about the Bible. Her favorite

actors are Spanish, like the comedian Cantinflas, and she still remembers those old Shirley Temple movies.

My parents were blessed with creative minds and instincts. Dad loved to build wooden cabinets until money became a problem. Mom made rugs, pot holders and brooms at a San Jose blind center. Mary Ann or I would walk her to the center or we would take the bus. We would stay at the center or return later to pick her up. There were parties at the center and our whole family would attend.

My father and mother were very protective of each other. Mom would tell me to take care of dad and dad would tell me to take care of mom. They worried about each other, but didn't want the other to know.

My parents both liked gymnastics when they were children. And my mother likes to brag how she played baseball with the boys. When I was a youth, dad watched me play baseball or football in the street and described to mom how I was doing. Or he took her hand and they would walk to my Little League games a few blocks away. My father would tell her about the game. My mother saw with her ears and mind. She would nod her head at dad's play-by-play description and smile.

Except for blindness, mom has been in good health most of her life. Dad wasn't so fortunate. He had a hernia operation. He smoked quite a bit, so he coughed. With failing vision, razor blades became too dangerous and he bought an electric razor.

The blind do not require much sleep. One reason people with normal vision grow tired is that their eyes tire. The blind need maybe four or five hours' sleep because their eyes do not tire. Most blind people I know are keyed up, hyperactive. My father was like that.

A special memory I still have was getting up early in the morning to be with my father. He would awaken at 4 A.M., turn on the radio and get ready for work. Dad enjoyed listening to the latest news. I'd join him at the kitchen table and do my homework. He would ask me how school and sports were going. I would ask him about the newsstand. One of us would cook breakfast. It was our time together.

Dad did most of the cooking at home. It was mainly Mexican food, which my parents loved. The three kids learned to cook at an early age. We became independent at a time when most children our age were waited on hand and foot. If the Plunkett children wanted something done, they learned to do it themselves.

Veva—that's our nickname for Genevieve—is 16 years older than I, so she moved out of the house and was married before I entered school. Mary Ann is the middle child and 5 years older than I.

Our parents were not social people, yet they were sociable. They were quiet, family-oriented and preferred to stay at home. If I have learned anything about humbleness and perspective in life, it is because I had the very best training ground. I don't get angry very often, but I do have a temper. I received that at home too, from my father, who could erupt with the force of Mount St. Helens

My parents lacked education—they dropped out of school around the seventh grade—so they couldn't express themselves very well. When my father became upset, he would yell. He could be very physical. If I was told to come home right after school and didn't, I would get the belt. Dad dealt out the punishment because he was the only one who could see to catch us. He had an arm like a quarterback— a quick release and follow-through. I would rank him up there with the great spankers.

Dad would raise the belt over my exposed bottom and mom would yell: "Don't hit him!" My father didn't let that bother him. He knew I was my mother's son and that mom always tried to protect me. This would upset Mary Ann, so we fought a lot. But Mary Ann was her father's daughter, which upset me. So we fought some more.

Our parents received their greatest pleasure in life

from their three children, and a few headaches too. We were the light of their lives and, in mom's case, the light in her eyes.

Thinking back, I wonder how they managed it, raising us. They did an outstanding job. We thought our upbringing was pretty normal, except in one area.

Money. We didn't have much of it.

My father despaired over our financial plight. We were on state aid, though Mary Ann and I weren't aware of it as children. Dad apologized for not being able to give us money. We wouldn't understand the depth of his despair until much later. We just knew the Plunkett family lived frugally. The children didn't receive an allowance. If our parents had money, they would give it to us; if they didn't, they wouldn't. It was that simple.

I went off to grammar school with a quarter for lunch at the cafeteria. Or I would bring a bag lunch with a nickel for a half-pint of milk, just like the other kids on the block.

Not until junior high school did I begin to realize how bad things were at home. For one thing, we didn't have a car. Everyone we knew had a car. We walked or took the bus —everywhere. Veva and her husband Ruben would come by in their car, with their three children, and take our family along for picnics at Santa Cruz, Big Basin and Alum Rock Park. Those were big times.

I moved on to high school, but financially couldn't do all the things that teenagers do—formal dances, taking a date to the movies, going with the gang for burgers, fries and shakes. When I didn't have the $10 necessary to take out my girl, which was most of the time, I felt sorry for myself.

I was even embarrassed about where and how we lived in San Jose. Our houses, first on Oakland Avenue and later Emilie Street, weren't the nicest. Neither was our furniture. It was the best my parents could do, but our house hardly compared to the homes of some of my friends. I made it a point to visit my friends' homes instead of having them come over to my house.

"Jimmy," my mother would ask, "how come your friends don't come over anymore."

My parents enjoyed having my friends drop by. I made up all kinds of excuses until I couldn't think of any more. Eventually, I outgrew my embarrassment. I came to the conclusion that if you love someone, what difference does it make how much money is in the family bank account?

Athletics eased me through this awkward transitional stage in my behavior. Playing sports was usually free when I was a kid. If you had a bat and ball or a football, you had a game. Sports is something youngsters from all financial backgrounds can do regardless of whether their parents live like the Rockefellers or the Joad family in *The Grapes of Wrath.*

Mary Ann brought home the first athletic trophies. She played field hockey, volleyball and basketball in school, and later took up bowling. My mother has most of my trophies. The Heisman and Maxwell trophies sit next to a vase of flowers and a family picture on top of the TV set in her living room. There's the Heisman watching over—chaperoning?—"The Young and the Restless."

My parents couldn't attend many of my games once I was out of Little League. My high school games were mostly in the afternoon, when my father worked. Since Mary Ann also worked, there was no one to take my mother to the gym or field where I was in competition.

Dad's friends would make sure he knew about my progress in sports. That really perked him up. Willie Plunkett's son was doing well and others were aware of it.

I will never forget one night my senior year at James Lick High School. I was honored at a scholar-athlete dinner in San Francisco. My football coach, Al Cementina, came by

to pick up dad and me. It was one of the few times I saw my
father wear a coat and tie. You have never seen a prouder
man. Later that night, he told me: "I'm so proud of you, I
can hardly talk." After he said that, *I* could hardly talk.

My father would have been pleased at my later ac-
complishments in sports (he died after my first varsity football season at Stanford). However, my graduation from Stanford would have brought him the greatest joy, because I am
the only person from either side of the family to go through
college.

All of my grandparents were dead before I was 10,
which took a heavy toll on my parents. I believe it brought
them even closer to their own children. They did everything they possibly could for us, even if it meant self-sac-
rifice. Our parents wanted us to have what other kids had,
which wasn't always affordable. Getting a new bicycle or a
football was a special day. Even a new pair of jeans became
a major event.

If my mother needed a new dress or coat, which always seemed the case, she would consider us first. She would
wear the same old dress, but never complained. She would
have preferred to spoil us, which didn't take a whole lot.

Christmas was special for us because it was a family
time. We bought one another practical things, like clothes.
Mom's face sparkled when she unwrapped a present and
found the dress she needed but would never ask for. We
described the dress to her.

"How pretty it looks," she would say, listening to us.

I occasionally had money to buy gifts with, because I
worked as early as the third grade cleaning up in a gas
station after school. For a few hours' work, I would get a
couple of dollars. I'd put the money in my pocket, take it out
and stare at it, then put it back in my pocket. I'd do the same
thing over and over. The piddling sum of $2 looked like $200
to me.

I delivered newspapers until someone stole my bicycle. I had finally gotten a bicycle and it was stolen. I bagged groceries. I worked in the orchards of the Santa Clara Valley, picking apricots and cherries for one man's marmalade and another man's manhattan. For this I received blisters and 17¢ for every bucket I filled up.

One Christmas vacation, I hauled around footballs and equipment for the East team training at the University of Santa Clara for the annual East-West Shrine Football Game in San Francisco. I enjoyed being around college stars, although I wasn't much into hero worship as a youngster.

I worked mainly summers in high school, because I was playing sports from September to June. This should clear up stories I've read which said that I worked fifty hours a week during high school to help support the family. My coaches at James Lick would find that amusing because they were working me to death in practice after school. I barely had enough strength afterward to make it home, have dinner and collapse immediately into bed.

There are an amazing number of inaccuracies that have come out about my family. I'm partly to blame because I have protected and shielded them from what I feel would be media exploitation.

"We are basically private persons. We are happy for James and what he has accomplished in his life, but we want to live our own lives the way we always have. Normally. We don't want the spotlight."
—MARY ANN PLUNKETT

My mother gets very upset about articles that refer to her as handicapped. She is just the opposite.

"Mary Ann, where is the broom?" she will call out.

"Stay there, mom, I'll get it," Mary Ann will reply.

"No, I can get it myself," mom will insist. "Just tell me where it is."

Mom can get feisty. You don't want to make things too hard or too simple for her, because she doesn't like it either way. Mary Ann calls me if mom is giving her a hard time. I kid my mother about her feistiness.

I can get feisty too. When the Oakland Raiders went to the 1981 Super Bowl, three San Francisco television stations wanted to interview my mother. I said no three times. I sensed that all they were after was an exclusive interview with Jim Plunkett's mother. There was no need for that.

Nobody really asks me about my family unless they are doing an article. The guy on the streets says to me: "I read about your mother. She must feel proud of you." That kind of thing.

Mary Ann and my mother are more interested in my health and welfare than any dramatization of their own lives. They have each told me several times to quit football because of the injury factor. They are aware that I've had nine operations in fifteen years through the spring of 1981.

"I feel very bad when Jimmy gets hurt. He doesn't have to worry, but I do. I pray to God that he doesn't get hurt anymore. I have told Jimmy to get out of that football. He said he was. He didn't."
—MRS. CARMEN PLUNKETT

"James—I call him James when I want to talk to him seriously—will start feeling all those aches and pains when he gets older. He has had too much surgery. We don't want him to have any more."
—MARY ANN PLUNKETT

My mother is furious when negative things are said about me in the media, especially during my two seasons with the San Francisco 49ers.

"Why are the newspapers and fans saying these things?" she demanded to know.

"That's how things sometimes go in sports, mom," I told her.

"That's not right, Jimmy. That's no good."

I didn't have any problems with the media at Stanford. It started in New England, but I was 3,000 miles away and my mother wasn't aware of all the abuse.

Mom came to some of my games in college, and also in San Francisco and Oakland. I'm really not sure how many because I have never asked my sisters, who brought her to the games. If I knew beforehand that my mother was there, I would be nervous about her moving about in a crowded stadium.

It is bad enough in her own living room, sitting in front of the TV set, when the announcer says, "Plunkett is slow getting up. He could be hurt. . . . " When that happens, mom gets so nervous, she has to walk out of the room. After a while, she will calm down and return.

Mary Ann drove mom 400 miles to attend the Rose Bowl game my senior year at Stanford. My mother didn't go to the Oakland-Philadelphia Super Bowl in New Orleans. She had her 68th birthday in 1981 and it is too hard for her to fly now. She is much more comfortable at home—as long as I don't get hurt.

I phone her as much as I can, just to check on her. At the 1981 Super Bowl, I called her every day after practice. One day, out of the clear blue, she offered some motherly advice.

"Jimmy, hold on to the ball because they are going to try and take it away from you."

I almost dropped the phone. My mom! She was back with more advice the next day.

"Don't get nervous, Jimmy. Stay relaxed and you will throw better."

What is going on here!

"Mom, you have never coached me in my entire life. Why are you coaching me now?"

My mother actually has a pretty good feel for what goes on during a football game, like when a team should pass or kick. Obviously, she knew the magnitude of Super Bowl XV and what it meant to me after all I had been through in football. But, giving me advice? I had to laugh. We both did.

My mother, the coach.

I am continually astonished and impressed by people like my mother who can face adversity with strength, courage and humor instead of despondency and acridness.

My old political science professor at Stanford, James T. Watkins, had a leg amputated in 1981. Professor Watkins is a fine man who touched so many lives at Stanford. I visited him in the hospital and found a glass of sherry on his bed stand. His attitude was refreshing.

"Finding a way to get up the stairs on one leg will give me something to do," he told me. "This is a new adventure, and at 73, I can use a new adventure."

How can you not like a man with such a sunny perspective?

Harry Cordellos is a transit information officer in San Francisco. He also is blind. Harry has written an autobiography on his amazing life. He runs in marathons. He skis. He hang glides. Once he ran in a race while holding on to my arm. I felt bad because I slowed him down.

Joe Lazarus is a blind golfer. A caddy tells him what club to use and then lines him up. Lazarus does the rest. I played with him one day. He 3-putted only once or twice and shot in the 80's. I won't say how many 3-putt greens, or 4-putt greens, I had. And I'm not about to reveal my score either.

My junior high school wrestling team won the county championship. We met the California School for the Blind of Berkeley in an exhibition match. Out of twelve matches, we won one and tied one.

I lived in the same Stanford dormitory as a blind

student. He was carrying two majors. I was strug.
through one.

Who was handicapped?

Helen Keller graduated with honors from Radcliffe.
Mark Twain said the two most important persons of the
nineteenth century were Napoleon and Helen Keller.

Napoleon could see and hear.

I serve on the board of directors for a blind center in
Palo Alto, California. I accepted the position because it was
time to get involved in something that has been a big part
of my life. I've filmed a United Way commercial at the
center and raised $2,200 at a boat auction for the center, but
football prevents me from spending as much time on the
board as I would like.

My parents could read braille, though it wasn't necessary for my father, who could see, barely. As he got older,
dad sat closer and closer to the TV set and moved the newspaper until it was almost against his face.

Blindness wasn't a sensitive subject around our home.
It was treated sarcastically at times.

"How did you two meet in the first place if you
couldn't see each other?" we would ask our parents.

They knew we were having fun with them and not
making fun of them. This was just our relationship; we were
very hard on one another. It is a good thing my parents had
the ability to laugh.

There also was a lot of love in our family. We needed
it to hold the family together. There was this strong bond of
interdependence. It wasn't that our parents couldn't do
things by themselves, because they did. We children just felt
our parents needed us. And we sure needed them.

They insisted on three things from us: honesty,
proper manners and respect for older people. Our parents
were simple persons with simple, basic values. If we got out
of line, they would let us know. One way was dad's belt.

It wasn't until years later that I developed a complete
appreciation for my parents and the job they did bringing
up three children. They gave us love, encouragement and,
most importantly, a strong foundation.

Our family draws closer together each year. It has
become easier to tell one another "I love you." With only so
much time in life, there is no sense in not telling those you
love that you love them.

I have one regret. I have often wondered if I told my
father enough times that I loved him before I lost him.

I could have told him the last day of his life if I had
only known. . . .

For some strange reason, I awakened at 4 A.M. that
day. I was home between academic quarters at Stanford, so
I wasn't planning on getting up early. Not that early, anyway. Dad was in the kitchen as usual, listening to the news.
I joined him at the table, just like the old days. I cooked
breakfast for the two of us. We talked for a good while, then
I went off with some friends to play tennis. Mary Ann later
found dad on the floor and called an ambulance. He was
dead by the time I returned.

My mother was visiting relatives in New Mexico at
the time. Mary Ann and I wondered how we would get her
back home without frightening her. We called and said dad
wasn't feeling well, that we had to take him to a hospital. As
soon as mom arrived, she knew something was wrong.

It wasn't long after the funeral that the creditors
came. My father was in debt when he died. He never said
anything. I guess he was too proud. It wasn't thousands of
dollars, but it was a substantial sum. The creditors wanted
their money in a hurry. They weren't the friendliest of people.

Mary Ann had pride too—she is her father's daughter
—and set out to clear up those debts. She didn't want the
Plunkett family owing money. She worked extremely hard
to pay off as many bills as she could. I took out $2,000 in

government loans on top of my athletic scholarship to finish my last two years at Stanford. Whatever money I made working summers went toward those debts. After I signed my first professional football contract, I paid off the remaining money and reimbursed Mary Ann for all she had done.

I just wish my father could be here today. He died only a few years before the financial burden was lifted off the family's back. Dad could have stopped working. What had work gotten him, anyway, but deeper into debt.

He could be home now, with mom, relaxing. They could be enjoying their later years together, knowing that everything would be taken care of. Mom doesn't enjoy taking walks the way she did when dad was alive.

My mother has a comfortable home. Mary Ann and I made sure of that. When I signed with New England, I told Mary Ann to decorate the house any way she wanted. I would take care of the cost. Later, I bought them a nicer home. Mary Ann takes care of mother and I am in a position to make sure mom has a nice home.

Dad would have wanted that.

Chapter Two

PAIN IN THE NECK

HE wants to cut open my throat. The tests on the tumor were positive, the doctor says. He wants to operate right away.

It's cancer, right? Go ahead and say it, doc. I'm 18 years old and I've got the Big C.

I'm scared, really scared. First surgery of my life and it's a malignant growth. What am I supposed to do now, prepare for dying when I haven't really lived?

He must be wrong. Doctors aren't always right. I'll get a second opinion.

My God! The same diagnosis.

"At your age, Jim," this new doctor warns me, "it would be best to have the operation now. The longer you wait . . ."

A malignant tumor, he tells me, means that muscles from my neck and shoulder must be removed.

"You won't be able to play football again," he says, "but you can lead a normal life."

He says he performed the exact operation on another boy my age, also a football player. The boy now plays some tennis and golf by using other muscles to make up for those that were taken out.

If this is a normal life, then I don't want it. No operation. I'll take my chances. Not be able to play football, to compete, to win? I'm more afraid of that than losing my own life. No operation, I say. You hear me?

"With surgery, Jim," the second doctor stresses, "there is hope. Without surgery, there is little hope."

He is persistent. So is my family. They are breaking down my defenses.

OK, OK, you win. Operate. But I don't like it.

The doctors and nurses are looking down at me on the operating table. All those serious faces. I can only see their eyes. Who are these masked people? I don't even know all their names. My body—my life!—is in the hands of people I don't know.

"We're going to give you something to put you to sleep, Jim. It won't hurt. There, you see? When you wake up, you will feel . . ."

When I wake up . . . My God! There's a big patch over my neck. They must have taken out everything! I can't move my neck. It hurts to try. It's all over, I tell myself. Do I mean my football career or my life? It's so hard to think. I'm still groggy from the operation. . . .

"It's benign, Jim."

"Who . . . what was that?"

"The tumor is benign."

"Does that mean I can play football again?"

I don't even remember the doctor's answer. It didn't matter. I was going to play football no matter what he said.

Rod Rust. He was the Stanford assistant coach who recruited me. I remembered our phone conversation.

"Rod, I've got some bad news for you. I'm going to have surgery. I may never be able to play again."

"That's OK, Jim. We want you to come to Stanford anyway. The scholarship still is yours."

What a great guy! What a great school! But now I could play. I had better call Rod. I'm back!

It was a triple sense of relief. I had my health, my football career and no astronomical hospital bill. Because my family was receiving aid, the state of California paid for my medical expenses. Thank you, Sacramento!

There would be other crises in the months and years ahead, though nothing of *this* magnitude. It seems as if I was put on this earth to deal with crises. I have had so many, I've come to look upon them as temporary deterrents.

The crises all seem to have two recurring themes: people don't believe in me and/or people give up on me. I have spent my life proving myself to others.

Like that recreation director.

I was 8, in the third grade, and had not yet asserted myself in sports. I didn't even know how to hold a softball bat. The recreation leader handed me one and told me to stand in there at home plate.

He lobbed the ball in, I swung and missed badly. He lobbed the ball in again, I swung and missed by even a bigger margin.

"Now, kid," he said, "when I tell you to swing, you swing."

The third pitch was halfway to the plate when I heard "swing." I swung, far too early.

The recreation leader laughed at me. He deliberately made me look like a fool. The other kids laughed too. I dropped the bat and slunk from home plate.

It was at that moment I decided no one would ever make fun of me or embarrass me again in sports. I was determined to work so hard that I wouldn't fail.

I don't even remember that director's name, but he

indirectly instilled me with an inner drive to succeed. Since
that time I have competed against better natural athletes.
But by putting in the time, no matter how much time it
takes, I come out ahead of them in the end.

It wasn't long after that park incident that I could hit
a softball farther than kids my age. Pretty soon, I could
throw a football better too. I could thank that recreation
director, but I won't. You don't treat kids the way he treated
me. That was cruel!

When I was 9, our family moved from Santa Clara to
San Jose. I discovered a whole new way of life. In Santa
Clara, I was the only Mexican among my friends. In east San
Jose, it was a melting pot with Mexicans, blacks, Orientals
and whites attending the same schools. There were gangs,
which we didn't have in Santa Clara. You had to fend for
yourself, which I learned right away.

I was waiting in line for tetherball when some kid cut
in front of me.

"Hey, I'm next," I said.

"You're not anymore," he said.

"Get to the back of the line."

"Make me."

The next thing I knew, we were fighting. I got into a
lot of fights back then and didn't win too many. I wasn't very
aggressive. I hadn't encountered this kind of behavior before.

I was always the last kid picked for sports when they
chose up sides. This was because I was 9 and the kids I played
with were 11 and 12. I was big for my age, so I had to play
with older kids. Then I got smart. When I brought my own
ball, I was one of the first kids picked.

I was 10 years old when I saw my first college football
game, at Stanford. About a dozen kids from my fifth-grade
class made the trip. All I remember from that experience is
that Stanford lost. I don't even know which school beat
them.

Mr. Nanamura, who coached me in the fifth grade, caught me swearing one day during a game. He took me aside.

"Jim, swearing doesn't help an athlete's performance," he said. "You won't run faster, jump higher or hit a baseball farther by swearing. So why swear?"

He made a big impression on me. I gave up swearing. Well, almost.

That same year, 1958, I happened to see a football game on the family television set. I sat down to watch. I wasn't interested in TV sports at the time. I was more involved in playing games than watching them. But this was a classic—the first overtime game, between Baltimore and the New York Giants, which the Colts won for the NFL championship.

All I remember about that game is a quarterback named Unitas. I really didn't care who won. I didn't even read the sports pages then. But I loved sports.

It wasn't until five years later that a televised football game caught my interest. It was the 1963 Rose Bowl game between USC and Wisconsin, a wide-open and wild game won by the Trojans, 42–37.

"I want to do that someday," I thought. "I want to be there."

Eight years later, I was.

When I was 12, my knees began to trouble me for the first time. I had Osgood Slaughter's disease, which comes from growing so quickly that your ligaments and tendons don't have a chance to catch up to your bones. Because of my knees, I couldn't play sports that year.

I wound up getting into trouble.

I started hanging around with some bad apples. In no time, they had me down with them at the bottom of the barrel. They were good at stealing. They showed me how and soon I was into theft. Candy, cigarettes, gum . . . hey, this wasn't hard at all. I began smoking. We would steal cigarettes, then hide in the bushes and trade off drags.

It went on like this for a year until the day I was caught. Another kid and I took some stuff off a counter, even though I had the money to pay for it. Then we ducked in an elevator. When we got off a few floors later, a security guard was waiting for us. My mother was called. She came down to the store with my sister to get me. It was the most humiliating thing for my parents. My father really let me have it.

"How could you do this to your mother?" he yelled between whacks.

My stealing days were over. I dropped that gang and smoking at the same time. My knees started to come around and I got back into sports. I never got into mischief again. Well, except for the time Mary Ann bought that 1960 Chevrolet.

I didn't have a driver's license; I was only 14. The car sat there, invitingly, with the keys in the ignition, and I couldn't resist. I jumped in and went for a spin. I turned onto a street before realizing it was one-way and I was going the wrong way. Traffic was coming toward me and I panicked, swerving into a parked car. Most of the resulting damage was done to Mary Ann's car. She was furious. My parents got on me about that too, but I don't remember getting hit. Dad must have lost his belt.

My confidence as an athlete and student really grew when I was 13 and a student at Lee Mathson Junior High School. I was fairly composed for an athlete even then. If I did well in competition, I didn't brag. I have never been that way. I've always known what I could do in an athletic event, and I've never felt the need to tell someone else. If they didn't like what they saw, too bad.

Buck Shore helped build my confidence. He coached our junior high basketball team that was 15–0. Before a big game, Mr. Shore told me: "Take it to the bucket. Don't be afraid. They can't stop you." I followed his advice, scored a ton of points and we won easily.

I ran for student body president in junior high and was elected. President Plunkett.

Mr. Shore said something else to me later which didn't help my confidence.

"As soon as you lose your clumsiness, Jim, you will be a fine athlete."

Clumsiness? I didn't think I was clumsy. He was right, of course. I was so skinny, I looked like a goal post. I was 6'3", 160 pounds at the age of 14 during my freshman year at Overfelt High School.

My angular build is the reason why I chose wrestling over basketball as my winter sport. I wanted to strengthen myself for football, and felt cross-over toeholds would help me more than cross-under layups. I knew even then that football was my main sport and channeled most of my energy in that direction.

As a freshman wrestler, I beat out a senior at his weight position on the varsity. I tore a knee cartilage, but it was massaged back into place and I was back on the mat in a few days. I won the league 175-pound championship.

I was only at Overfelt for a year and a half before transferring to James Lick. Al Cementina, the Lick football coach for twenty-four years, was a big influence on me. When the college coaches started coming around, I needed someone for guidance. I couldn't go to my father because he really didn't understand all that was happening to me. Al was the buffer, the guy with the right answers. He helped with my decisions and I depended a lot on his advice. We became very close.

"There were two Jim Plunketts when he was growing up: Jim Plunkett the football player and Jim Plunkett the person. Jim compartmentalized himself. He didn't look upon the person as positively as the football player, proba-

bly because of his background. Jim had great confidence in his football ability, not by yelling or patting butts, but by getting the job done. The Stanford coaches questioned his ability to lead because he was so quiet. I told John Ralston and his assistant, Dick Vermeil: 'You don't understand the kid. He pulled out so many games for us. He'll do the same thing for you if you give him the chance.' "
—AL CEMENTINA, Plunkett's high school football coach

Al had one of the first pro-style passing attacks among Santa Clara Valley high schools. Chon Gallegos, who led the nation in passing at San Jose State, was one of our assistant coaches. Phill Passafuime, my tight end at Lick, told me that I learned to throw a soft, catchable ball from Chon. Possibly. All I remember is Lick's football team being so small, we had to go over them because we sure couldn't go through them.

We should have been called the Lick Lilliputians instead of the Lick Comets. One of our guards, Frank Lopez, weighed 137 pounds. I was 190 as a senior, the third biggest guy on the team. Dennis Sciba, our center, weighed 205. We had this big guy, Gonzalo Herrera, who weighed about 240 and played defense in short-yardage situations.

I was almost the biggest guy on the team my junior year. I ballooned to 220 pounds, looked like the Mexican Pillsbury Doughboy, and really had problems with my knees. We lost to Lincoln High of San Jose that year on the last play of the game, our only defeat in two seasons.

Cementina really got mad at the team in the championship game my junior season. Pioneer High was ahead at halftime. "Now is not the time to choke," Al told the team in a steely voice. With a little more than a minute left in the game, we drove the length of the field and I scored on a short run to win the game. I got a lot of mental toughness from Al.

We played Lincoln again my senior year and won, 20–2. We scored near the end of the game and I kicked off.

Ten of their players tried to "block" me. It is the only time I have ever been ejected from a game. I had to defend myself!

I wrestled my last year with another bad knee, though I got by the league level without any trouble. But there was this one guy I couldn't beat, Don Widmer of Manteca, who later played football for UCLA. We met in the semifinals of the northern California tournament my last two years and he beat me both times.

My knees gave me trouble in baseball; I had to give up catching because I couldn't stay down in a crouch. So I pitched and played the outfield. If I had concentrated on baseball, I feel I would have gotten a professional contract. I could hit for average and distance. I had a strong pitching arm and I could throw some junk stuff too.

"Jim had the potential to place in national tournaments had he dedicated himself to wrestling full-time. He had good range, strength, balance. And he was clever. He had a great head-and-ankle move where he pulled the opponent forward by the back of his neck. Jim would then reach across and grab the guy behind the knee, dropping him right on his butt. I knew Jim wouldn't wrestle in college; he was more interested in football."
—PAT LOVELL, Plunkett's high school wrestling coach, former National AAU champion and 1964 United States
Olympic team member

"I'm not sure how far Jim could have gone in baseball because he didn't spend his summers swinging a bat. He threw a football two or three hours a day. But Jim had a good pitching arm and great control. Once in a tournament, he pitched a full game Saturday, then worked in relief Monday and Tuesday to help us reach the finals. He kept saying: 'I'll throw, I'll throw, I'll throw.'"
—KEN CASTLES, Plunkett's high school baseball coach

High school classes were easy. They were basically memorization and I could memorize anything. I got A's and B's without too much trouble. In class I would sometimes daydream about the football game we were going to play that week. I'd picture myself throwing passes to Phill and our wide receivers, Dick Barrett and Don Frease, putting the ball where only they could catch it. I'd see the ball leave my hand, watch it spiral slowly through the air, the laces of the ball turning over and over. . . .

"Jim. Jim! Are you with us? Did you hear the question?"

"Question?"

"Yes, the four stages of cell division. Will you please give them to the class."

"Prophase, metaphase . . ."

Occasionally, I'd lapse into fantasy and see myself as Johnny Unitas or Bart Starr, the closest I ever got to having heroes. Unitas was the great passer and fearless leader, Starr the master strategist. I wanted to be a composite of the two, winning NFL championships as they had. Snapping out of dreamland, I knew this meant college first.

Cementina thought Stanford was the best school for me even though Stanford didn't show interest until my senior year. California, Santa Clara and Navy recruited me as a junior. George House, the Lick principal, had his fingers crossed that I would attend Santa Clara—he graduated from there—though he didn't try to influence my decision. I appreciated that.

Notre Dame wrote a letter, but by that time I had decided to stay on the West Coast. I eliminated Santa Clara because it didn't play major-college football. I rejected California because the Free Speech Movement was underway in Berkeley and I didn't want to be bothered by student protests. UCLA approached me, but it was too far away from home. The only coast school that didn't contact me was USC, but they had already landed Mike Holmgren of San Francisco, the first-team All-Northern California quarterback. I was named to the third team.

I knew all along that it would be Stanford, but I didn't want to miss out on visits to other campuses. Heck, I hadn't been on a plane before. I had hardly done any traveling. Every place I checked in, there was Don Parish. Maybe Don hadn't done any traveling either, because he also went to Stanford, and became an All-America linebacker.

I've heard of illegal recruiting offers—free cars, jobs for athletes' parents, automatic eligibility without attending classes—but none of that was ever offered to me. I wasn't interested anyway. Stanford was so brutally aboveboard, it wouldn't waive the required $30 entrance examination fee. My parents had to pay it.

Stanford won out mainly because I was a goal setter. The opportunity to attend a school of this caliber was something a person of my background couldn't afford to pass up. My father and mother accompanied me on one recruiting trip to Stanford. It was Parents Day. I saw my first rugby match. I was impressed by the Stanford Chapel, the Quad and Hoover Tower, named after a former Stanford football manager who became our country's thirty-first president and the subject of one of history's great bloopers ("Ladies and gentlemen, I give you the president of the United States, Hoobert Heever . . .").

The Steeford panple—er, Stanford people—were extremely nice to my parents. I am sure mom and dad wanted me to attend Stanford, though they never said anything. Following my conversations later on with Rod Rust, I was convinced I had made the correct choice.

My growing-up years in San Jose were special. I made friends for life—Al Cementina, Phill Passafuime, Dick Barrett—and I had mapped out my course in life. I know the way to San Jose, and I've returned many times over the years.

The City of San Jose held a day in my honor after I

graduated from Stanford. Ten years later, after Super Bowl XV, the city held a second day for me. At a dinner, my mother was introduced. She smiled and applauded for herself. Proceeds from the event went toward setting up a scholarship in my name for Mexican-American kids from San Jose.

A week before the second "Jim Plunkett Day," I received a call from someone connected with the NFL cheerleaders competition scheduled for Florida the morning after the San Jose event. The caller wanted me to fly back for the competition. I told him it was impossible because of the time conflict.

I thought that was the end of it until he phoned back again to say that he would hire a helicopter. This way I could leave the dinner early, take the helicopter to the airport and grab an all-night flight to Florida in time for all the pomp and pompons. I told him that I couldn't leave the dinner because it involved my family and friends.

"Look," he said, now exasperated, "what's more important, forty million television viewers or twenty-five hundred people in San Jose?"

"Twenty-five hundred people in San Jose," I told him, hanging up.

I enrolled as a Stanford freshman in September, 1966, less than three weeks after my tumor operation. I kept bugging the Stanford team doctors about when I could begin practicing football. They must have thought I had some wires loose somewhere.

I had these clamps on my neck at the time. The clamps were supposed to leave a smoother scar than stitches. But I must have looked like the Frankenstein monster to the Stanford coaching staff. Rust was accused of recruiting me in Transylvania.

The clamps stayed on for ten days. I had a four-inch scar at the part of my neck where I would knot a tie. I walked with my head down because the clamps wouldn't permit me to walk with my head up.

The doctors finally surrendered to my pestering and I started practice just a few days before the first freshman game. In 1966, freshmen played on the frosh team, not the varsity. Stanford played only a four-game frosh schedule, so there wasn't much time in which to impress the coaches.

I started back too soon. I was so eager to get going, I pulled a groin muscle and both hamstring muscles. I was a wreck, and played like one. I wore enough tape for football games to qualify as a mummy look-alike.

USC blew us out in the opener, but I played better than the other quarterbacks so I started the last three games. We beat San Jose State, then UCLA and California killed us. I impressed the coaches more with my running than with my throwing. It was an awful mini-season. I couldn't pass well, I couldn't produce . . . I couldn't play.

My performance didn't improve the following spring. Nothing I did was right. I kept asking myself, "What's wrong?" I didn't hear any answers. That whole freshman year was a total loss.

At the end of each spring practice, Coach John Ralston made it a point to meet with his players and discuss what training procedures they should use over the summer to prepare for the fall. John wouldn't face his players over a desk. Too authoritarian, he believed. John and his players sat in chairs near one another.

John is a very friendly person. But I could tell by the look on his face that this wasn't going to be a neighborly tête-à-tête.

"Jim, do you want to play this fall?"

"What, coach? Sure I want to play."

"Well, Jim, you're a fourth-string quarterback right now. It looks like a redshirt year and, honestly, you just don't throw the ball well on the run. If you're going to play this fall, it will have to be a different position."

"What . . . what position?"

"Defensive end."

Defensive end? I was crushed. Not again!

At the North-South High School Football Game, matching seniors from all over California, Holmgren was the North's quarterback. I was moved from quarterback to defensive end for the North. I played well and Ralston hadn't forgotten. Now he needed defensive ends and I was a perfect candidate. I could see it in his eyes as we looked at each other. He no longer thought of me as a quarterback.

I might have done all right as a college defensive end. I was tough, hard-nosed and experienced on defense. I played end, inside linebacker, corner and safety in high school. But I was a quarterback. Now I had to convince Ralston of that.

"Holmgren was twice as good as Plunkett back then. The North coaches didn't make a mistake. When I suggested to Jim that he consider a new position, his reply was 'I want to play quarterback. Tell me what I have to do.' I told him to get a sack of footballs, go home and throw as many passes as he could that summer. When he came back in the fall, you wouldn't have believed the difference. We sat there with egg on our faces."

—JOHN RALSTON, Plunkett's college football coach

I worked out every night that summer with Dick Barrett, who was playing for Cal Poly-San Luis Obispo. I worked hard at construction all day, while Dick had it easy. Dick worked at Sleepy Hollow Amusement Park. He wore a Jungle Jim outfit and drove kids around in a miniature train. I ran him ragged after work, though, as we practiced pass patterns until dark. I threw so many passes that I felt I could drop back, set up, throw with my eyes closed and Dick would be there.

Stanford had me come up that summer and work with its pass receivers too. Dick Vermeil, an offensive backfield coach, watched me throw footballs through tires and into nets. I hate throwing into nets, but I had no choice. I rolled out and sprinted out, left and right, again and again. When fall came, my throwing technique was back.

It was now apparent to everyone that I was the best quarterback in school. The other quarterbacks were aware of it too. Suddenly, I was treated like a blue-chip athlete.

A lot of good it did me. The other quarterbacks played that fall and I didn't. Not one single down. I was redshirted, a process which allowed me to sit out one football season and still have three varsity seasons left.

Ralston already had decided on Chuck Williams and Mark Marquess as his quarterbacks. Gene Washington was shifted from quarterback to wide receiver, a position at which he would receive all-pro honors with the San Francisco 49ers. Williams and Marquess started five games each in 1967 and Stanford finished with a 5–5 record.

I really caught the coaches off-guard when I came back ready to play. Ralston ran a sprintout-rollout offense then. Though I am primarily a dropback passer, I was thin then and could run well enough to quarterback that kind of system. If the coaches had any doubts about me, it was that I wasn't mature enough yet to play major-college football.

At least, they thought of me as a quarterback and not a defensive end. I had won that point. If they had persisted in shifting me to defense, I would have transferred to another school.

I came very close to losing that year's eligibility, because the coaches let me suit up the first three games. I warmed up on the sideline during the fourth quarter of the Kansas and San Jose State games. The Jayhawks and Spartans were driving for touchdowns. If either or both had scored, I would have been in the game. They didn't, as our defense held and we got out with two close victories.

Vermeil broke the news to me before the fourth game against USC. I was redshirted for the year and would not dress for any more varsity games. When Williams was injured with two games left, the coaches thought again about playing me. They wisely decided not to waste a year's eligibility on just two games. I was kept out of uniform.

When the team traveled, I listened to the games on the radio. When the team was at home, I sat in the stands with the rooting section. During the week, I practiced with the scout team—football's equivalent to a prison chain gang. Scout teams masquerade as the upcoming opponent. More accurately, they serve as dummies for the varsity and get their butts kicked. That redshirt year, I was Gary Beban the week we played UCLA and Steve Sogge when we prepared for USC.

"I turned out for freshman football and they sent us over to practice against the varsity. Some redshirts were working out with the varsity, but we didn't know anyone anyway. There was this guy throwing footballs against us. I hadn't seen anyone throw footballs like that in my life. There was nothing we could do to stop him. I asked someone: 'Who's that?' The guy said: 'Plunkett. He's a redshirt.' I said to myself: 'Redshirt! If he's this good, I've got to see the guy who's starting.'"
—JIM KAUFFMAN, one of Plunkett's teammates at Stanford

I wondered how Mike Holmgren was doing at USC. Not too well, I found out later. He was a dropback passer who went to a sprintout system that features the running game. Mike wasn't mobile enough to be the pass-run quarterback that USC prefers. Had he gone to a school with a pro-style attack, his career might have turned out differently. He wound up playing twenty-seven minutes in three years at USC. It isn't always easy to plan your life at 18.

I was having the same thoughts at Stanford my second year of school. My grades weren't good. I wasn't playing football, except on weekdays. And I felt out of place on campus.

I had this feeling that the rest of the students were smarter than I. Even when I got a ninety on a paper, it would only be a B grade. Others would get 95s and 97s. Even my best wasn't good enough, and I wasn't getting that many 90s as it was.

There are many bright people who attend Stanford, which is called "Harvard of the West." Maybe Harvard is the "Stanford of the East." My feeling was that the other students were getting more out of lectures than I. I studied hard, but got little in return.

I joined a fraternity, Delta Tau Delta, though I wasn't sure I wanted to or that they wanted me. I was very quiet and didn't socialize a lot. I went home every weekend to check up on the family. I didn't get involved much at Stanford my first two years. I missed out on a lot, but I wasn't sure I liked the school anyway.

Talk about feeling out of place: I was a poor, shy Mexican kid from east San Jose trying to mingle with the confident, intelligent scions of wealth who attend Stanford. Everyone else seemed to have a car. Everyone else seemed to have attended a fashionable prep school. The other male students seemed to have three Roman numerals after their names. I didn't fit in and so I stayed away, in San Jose. Many times I thought to myself: "Maybe, Jim, you belong someplace else."

Everything turned around my second spring quarter. Vermiel told me I would be Stanford's starting quarterback in 1968. My confidence, which had been battered, shot skyward. My grades began to improve. So did my entire outlook.

Stanford students no longer seemed so bad, and neither did Stanford. It had been my own depression from football, I realized, that had soured me on the whole campus.

I began to enjoy fraternity life. I felt wanted. I began making friendships that would last the rest of my life. I was no longer overwhelmed by the students around me. I knew they were interesting and had a lot to say. Now I felt that what I had to say was just as interesting.

Stanford drew me out as a person. One of the great things about the school isn't what you learn from books, but what you learn from others. Interaction between people is the most important thing I received from Stanford.

I went home that summer with a positive attitude. The cancer scare and the defensive end dilemma were behind me. Redshirting, I finally agreed, had been the best thing after all. Instead of creeping in the previous season and getting a starting position, I would begin a new season with some splash as the No. 1 quarterback.

Numero Uno. It sounded great.

The summer couldn't fly by fast enough. It had been two years since I played any real football—genuine, roll-the-camera, Saturday afternoon live, winning football—and I couldn't wait to get started.

I had looked good in spring practice. But I told myself: "Stanford, you haven't seen anything yet."

Chapter Three

BOUND FOR GLORY

"Jim Plunkett is the best college football player I have ever seen."
—JIM SWEENEY, Washington State football coach, 1970

"Jim Plunkett is still the best college football player I have ever seen."
—JIM SWEENEY, Fresno State football coach, 1981

I kept looking at the clock . . . 2:06 A.M. . . . 3:44 A.M. . . . 4:25 A.M. . . . 5:17 A.M. . . . 6:31 A.M. . . .

Sleep wouldn't come, though it certainly wasn't from lack of effort. I must have turned over ninety-five times, a National Collegiate Athletic Association record for a quarterback starting his first varsity game.

I have never been more nervous before a game, and I wasn't completely sure why. Sure I had waited a long time for this day, but I was ready. Was I ever! I knew the game plan so well that I could have recited it frontward, backward, in English or Arabic. I had watched so much film, the sound of a projector whirred in my brain.

Why was I tossing and turning then? The opponent was only San Jose State, not USC. Victory was certain, unless I forgot plays in the huddle, stuttered at the line of scrimmage, handed the ball off to one of our tackles. Lying in bed, eyes wide open, nerves jangled, I felt in danger of doing all three.

Things would be better, I kept telling myself, if I could sleep for more than five minutes at one stretch. Finally, as the sun peeked through the hotel room curtain, my head felt drowsy, my eyelids heavy and . . .

Riiiiinnnnnggggg!

"Good morning, this is your 7:30 wake-up call. The date is September 21, 1968. The weather is sunny with no clouds. The temperature outside is sixty-three degrees. Have a nice day."

I'm trying, operator, I'm trying.

I was hungry, but couldn't eat. My stomach sounded like a jackhammer: *tata-tata-tata-tata-tata* . . .

My Stanford coaches and teammates set another NCAA record for most "good lucks" spoken to a quarterback the morning of his first varsity start. Sixty-two.

"Good luck, Jim."

Sixty-three.

Everyone sounded so confident, though I knew what they were really thinking: "He looks good in practice, but what's he going to do under fire?"

Their apprehension was understandable. I hadn't done a darn thing yet.

Now it was 9:30 A.M. Final offensive meeting.

"Jim, San Jose's secondary likes to gamble at times. The cornerback will go single on Washington. We should be able to get Gene the bomb. Look for this."

Passing a locker room mirror, I caught a glimpse of myself. Jim Plunkett, No. 16, right? I found a bathroom and promptly threw up. Would it be like this every Saturday?

High noon. The team left the locker room and walked the quarter-mile to Stanford Stadium.

"Good luck, boys. Go get 'em."

The alumni were in full swing with their tailgate parties. Red blazers, peppermint striped ties, tomato-red Bloody Marys, red eyeballs. Check those sumptuous spreads. Tablecloths and candlelight too. Stanford must be the tailgate center of the West.

Getting closer: 12:35 P.M. San Jose State doesn't look too big. We aren't Paul Bunyans ourselves. Which one is the cornerback on Gene's side? There he is. . . .

Here we go, 1:05 P.M. Kickoff.

I overworried.

We ripped apart San Jose State, 68–20. Never again in my three seasons at Stanford would we score as many points. Never in Stanford history, at least through 1980, have there been more yards rolled up, 681. We scored the first four times we had the football and San Jose State had yet to make a first down. We led, 37–7, at half time, which was more points than a Stanford team had scored in an entire *game* in eight years.

The new quarterback in town threw 13 passes and completed 10 for 277 yards and four touchdowns. I would never throw with more explosiveness. Washington caught touchdown passes of 79, 51 and 10 yards, and Jack Lasater scored on a 68-yard reception; the coaches took me out in the third quarter. I was elated, but the biggest feeling I had was that of relief. Everyone knew now that I could play.

Although a starry-eyed kid, I was realistic enough to know that it wouldn't be this easy every week. San Jose State, the school in my hometown, has been a punching bag for Stanford for years. Stanford has won thirty-three games and lost four to the Spartans through 1980. San Jose's program is on the upswing now with Coach Jack Elway, father of Stanford quarterback John Elway. But from 1968–1970,

Stanford won three times over San Jose by a composite score of 165–44.

We ran off two more victories after the opener, over Oregon, 28–12, and the Air Force Academy, 24–13, before facing our first difficult test. The Trojan horse. USC was national champion the year before. Its big gun was O. J. Simpson. Stanford hadn't defeated USC since 1957, though their annual game had developed into a bitter rivalry.

The feud began when I was in high school. Stanford was warming up before the game when the USC team thundered onto the field and ran over everyone, including John Ralston, Stanford's coach. From that moment on, the battle lines were clearly drawn. However, USC has won most of the battles since.

Stanford and USC are the only private universities in the Pacific–10 Conference. In no other way do the two schools see themselves as similar. Stanford prides itself on being a great center of learning, and looks upon USC with all the respect one might show a trade school. USC produces doctors and lawyers too, though the school is recognized for 1,000-yard rushers and Heisman Trophy recipients. USC thinks of Stanford as a bunch of intellectual snobs. The Stanford rooting section and marching band love to make fun of USC during halftime routines. USC gets its revenge by making fun of Stanford on the football field. It is a never-ending cycle.

The bad blood between the schools reached its peak during the 1970s. Sam McDonald Road connects the locker rooms and Stanford Stadium; the road was named for a beloved Stanford groundskeeper. The USC team was walking along the road before a game when Coach John McKay claimed he was insulted repeatedly by Stanford students and followers.

USC won the game, but not by nearly a wide enough margin in McKay's mind.

"I'd like to beat Stanford by 2,000 points," he said.

Stanford Coach Jack Christiansen was asked for his reaction to McKay's comment.

"I refuse to get into a urinating match with a skunk," he said.

Supposedly, California is Stanford's big rival. Not if you asked Stanford students, however. They would say USC, and I would have to agree. We played the Trojans three times when I was there and lost twice in unbelievably exciting games.

The first defeat occurred during my sophomore season when O. J. beat us—with a pass. Gene Washington caught a 51-yard bomb on Stanford's first play, but we failed to score on that series or the next two because Steve Horowitz missed field goals of 28, 37 and 34 yards. Those misses would really chafe later.

The game heated up after a 10–10 first half. Simpson scored on runs of 45 and 4 yards. I called my first audible in college, which turned out to be a 27-yard touchdown pass to Lasater, and ran 10 yards for another touchdown. It was 24–24 entering the fourth quarter.

O. J. showed Stanford why he deserved the Heisman Trophy that season, carrying a phenomenal 47 times for 220 yards and 3 touchdowns. Not only was Simpson strong, fast and durable, but we found out he was a quick thinker too.

On a fourth down and short yardage play, O. J. found no holes in the line, so he broke out to his right and found another group of Stanford tacklers waiting for him. He spun around and dropped back deeper. O. J. was in deep trouble until he saw fullback Dan Scott standing by his lonesome on the sideline.

Now Dan Scott received a pass about as often as a circus fat lady. His job was strictly to block for Simpson. But Scott caught O. J.'s perfect spiral for 15 yards and a first down. USC kicker Ron Ayala, who would torment Stanford for two straight seasons, then drilled a 34-yard field goal and the Trojans won, 27–24.

It was a disheartening setback because we had to beat USC to reach the Rose Bowl. As it turned out, USC defeated us to reach the Rose Bowl. I saw Al Cementina after the game.

"Jim, I know you're upset. But O. J. is a heckuva back and you have to give him credit for making that play."

"I know, coach, but my job is to put more points on the scoreboard than the other team, and I didn't do it."

We went into a terrible tailspin after that game, tying Washington State, 21–21, and losing to UCLA, 20–17, and Oregon State, 29–7. We beat Washington the following week, but I had little to do with it, suffering a first-half rib injury. Sophomore Don Bunce replaced me and threw three touchdown passes, including an 80-yarder to Gene Washington. Bunce ran for a fourth score and we won, 35–20.

Bunce went back to the bench as I quarterbacked Stanford to shutout victories over the University of Pacific, 24–0, and California, 20–0, in the "Big Game." Stanford's 6–3–1 season matched the school's best record in seventeen years. It was a good year; beating USC might have made it a great year.

By now I had a sense of identity not only with my coaches, teammates and the Pacific–8 Conference (the Pacific–10 wasn't formed until 1978 when Arizona and Arizona State joined), but with the media and Stanford campus as well. The students began rallying around me, which was a lot better than having them rally against me.

I've handled media attention well from the beginning by trying to keep things in proper perspective. I've never been too excited about media attention and never tried to avoid it. When you are in the spotlight, which quarterbacks almost always are, the media seek quotes from you almost before anyone else. My opinion may not be any better than that of a center or tackle, but because they play a less glamorous position, they won't be asked. That really bugs me.

Seeking attention through TV interviews or newspaper stories is not my way. I love the game of football, and that is the only reason I've stayed with it through the agony as well as the ecstasy. As far as the glamor and the glory, you can unscrew the bulb out of the spotlight for all I care.

I would much rather spend the time with friends, mainly from Stanford, talking world politics, religion—anything. We'll stay up all night arguing some topic; we can get vociferous, but that makes us even closer. Or we might drop in at one of our old campus haunts.

Stanford is seldom ranked very high in football, but when it comes to college hangouts, Stanford is in the top ten.

The Oasis is a great place to have a beer and a burger. The "O" is located just outside the one-mile no-liquor-on-campus boundary. Students have carved their initials on walls and tables at the "O" for decades. When a table falls apart, it is nailed to a wall, and a new one is brought in to take its place. Students resume carving.

Other popular spots are The Dutch Goose and the Alpine Beer Garden, formerly known as Rossotti's and still referred to as Zots. *Sports Illustrated* held its own poll on favorite college watering holes a few years ago and included Zots, which is located in a rural setting three miles from campus. You just tie up your horse outside—which people have done for years—and go in and have a cold one. There's a parking lot for cars too.

Then there is "The Rat's." For some unexplained reason, Thursday night at The Rat's was a weekly event. The bar's real name was Souza's, but no one called it that. I still drop in occasionally for a burger, though not necessarily on Thursday nights.

It's funny how friendships begin. You celebrate with one another when times are good and help one another out when times are bad. My closest friends are Stanford-related. Jack Schultz, Bob Moore, Randy Vataha, Jack Lasater and Jim Kauffman were Stanford football teammates. Jack Ditz is a Stanford alumnus and staunch supporter who is in the construction business. I worked for him during summers while going through school. Jack turned 60 in 1981, but all of my friends regard him as one of the guys. Phill Passafuime also went from James Lick High to Stanford, played a little football. Nick Vlasoff didn't go to Stanford, but lived with a bunch of us one year. Nick then moved back to neighboring Menlo Park, where he has been ever since. He calls himself "Mr. Menlo Park."

"Jim Plunkett is what a lot of people aren't. He's a man's man. He's compassionate and he's competitive. He has never ever told a lie. He never even exaggerates. All the things I'm not, he is."

—NICK VLASOFF

"Jim has a real good sense of himself. He doesn't need to bounce himself off people. He is shy to the point where it was difficult for him to articulate when he first got to Stanford. He was so different from anyone else who went there. Jim knows his limitations, he knows his strengths. He can be moody. He told me that he is a victim of his moods. He doesn't like the image the public has of him as 'good, good, good.' He has faults like everyone else. The reason his friends like him is that he admits these faults."

—JIM KAUFFMAN

"Jim is extremely proud and very private. It is difficult to get close to him and I believe it's because he doesn't want to burden anyone. He enjoys making people happy. After I got married, he brought over a brass door knocker with 'Schultz' engraved on it. There was a painting Jim and I had seen and admired in New York. He had it crated and sent home. I know he wanted the painting, but in characteristic Jim Plunkett manner he said: 'Geez, Schultzie, I've got no room to hang this. You have it.'"

—JACK SCHULTZ

"In a lot of respects, Jim is just like he was as a Stanford freshman, shy and uncomfortable around strangers. It takes him awhile to know and trust people. I feel I know him now, but I couldn't have said that five years ago and I've known him fourteen years and we lived together one year. He is very loyal, and he is as honest and straightforward a person as I've ever met. There is no b.s. to the guy at all. Someone will throw out a cute comment at a social gathering. If it's inaccurate, most of us would say, 'Ah . . . ha . . . ha' and let it go. Not Jim. He'll say, 'That's not true.' He has this real sense of integrity."

                                         —BOB MOORE

"Plunk is squared away as a human being. When he retires, he won't have the problem of hearing the cheers anymore, like Mickey Mantle. Plunk never changes, never forgets old friends. In fact, he keeps getting better. He is the kind of person you go to your grave with. And that's a comforting feeling."

                               —PHILL PASSAFUIME

All my friends are different, but that's what makes the world go around. Passafuime and Lasater are attorneys. Moore is in law school and has served with the NFL Players Association. Vataha owns nine racquetball centers in Massachusetts. Schultz is vice president of a planning firm and Kauffman works for an organization that writes family histories and biographies. Vlasoff's line of work is the restaurant business.

Kauffman is an off-the-wall character. Stanford players were once required to wear coats and ties on trips. Kauffman would show up in these funny shirts and ties. I told him: "You bother me." It took me awhile to get to know him and to understand that football players get ready for games in different ways. There is no automatic way to put on your "game face."

The Stanford athlete is different, anyway, from athletes who attend other universities. Most Stanford lettermen, though they are talented athletes, aren't interested in professional sports. This isn't what they want out of life. They become doctors, lawyers, educators, corporate giants —even president.

I found Stanford co-eds are intelligent, serious-minded and interested in careers. I didn't date them, however, because I was going with Gini Campbell at the time. We went together in high school, through college, and my first two years with the New England Patriots, even though I was on the East Coast for six months each year and Gini was on the West Coast. She was an art major at San Jose State. She paints, sculpts and builds stained-glass windows. Gini would price her paintings so high, no one would buy them. The ones who did, she would then talk out of the sale. She hates to part with her work. She did a beautiful painting of my mother, me and our German shepherd. The painting still hangs in mom's living room.

The main reason I turned down the University of California was the student protest movement. Two years later, though, Stanford students were protesting too. The Vietnam War was on and young people were angry. Windows were broken at the R.O.T.C. building and other buildings on the Stanford campus. It cost six figures to repair the damage. Things were scary for awhile.

I was against the war. I have never been a volatile person. I can't see killing anyone, period. The United States didn't belong in Vietnam, which was just a toenail on the Asian continent and not a threat to anyone. It was a senseless war in a faraway country that we had no chance of winning or ending. Yet our young and strong were sent over there to die.

Stanford football teammates asked me to join a student strike movement. I read the protest statement, discussed it with them, but didn't sign it. I agreed with some

EARLY LIFE AND COLLEGE

My father, Willie Plunkett, in his twenties: a dashing young man. *(Mary Ann Plunkett)*

Mary Ann holds on to her 9-month-old baby brother. *(Mary Ann Plunkett)*

Dad and mom in Santa Clara.
(*Mary Ann Plunkett*)

Mary Ann gives me a hug, age 4.
(*Mary Ann Plunkett*)

Mary Ann, mom and me at age 7, in Santa Clara. *(Mary Ann Plunkett)*

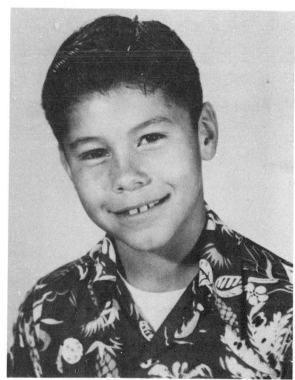

Growing up at age 9 in San Jose. *(Mary Ann Plunkett)*

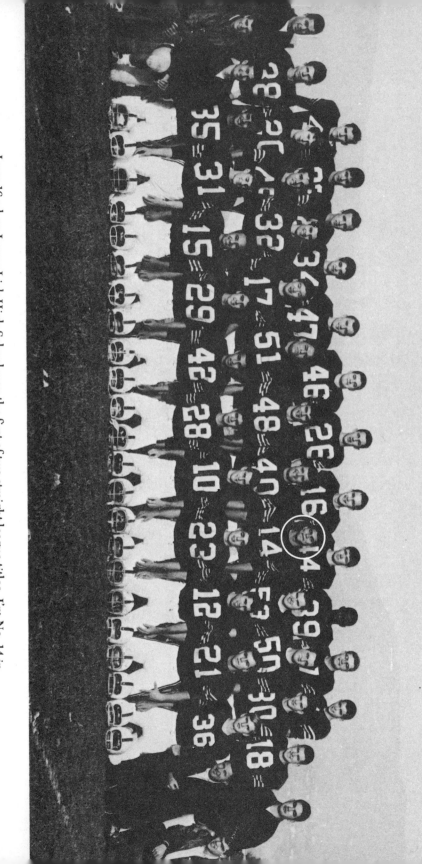

I was 16 when James Lick High School won the first of two straight league titles. I'm No. 14 in second row; Al Cementina is second from left in bottom row; Phill Passafuime (No. 32) and Dick Barrett (No. 18) are also in second row. (*Mary Ann Plunkett*)

Me, 11 years old, with dad on
our porch in San Jose.
(*Mary Ann Plunkett*)

The high school graduate.
(*Mary Ann Plunkett*)

My family today. Clockwise: Mary Ann, Veva, mom and me.
(*Mary Ann Plunkett*)

My Jim Thorpe pose. *(Stanford Athletic Department)*

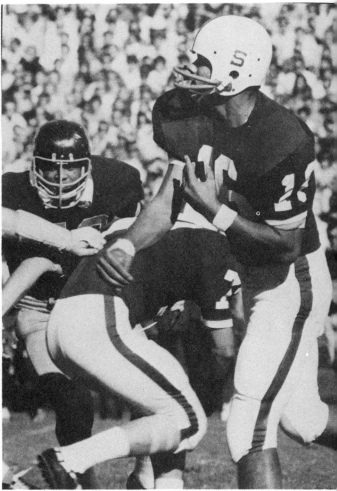

A touchdown bomb to Jack Lasater (No. 43) against Cal in the 1969 "Big Game." (*Russ Reed*)

Tight end Bob Moore (far right) tries for touchdown.
(*Russ Reed*)

Barking out signals.
(Russ Reed)

Dropping back to pass.
(Russ Reed)

Coach John Ralston, co-captains Jack Schultz and me. *(Stanford Athletic Department)*

Being chased by Purdue linemen. *(Stanford Athletic Department)*

Throwing from behind fullback
Hillary Shockley. *(Stanford
Athletic Department)*

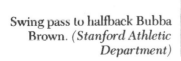

Swing pass to halfback Bubba
Brown. *(Stanford Athletic
Department)*

I remember this beautiful fall day on the Stanford campus in
1970. I had just been named National College Back of the Week
by The Associated Press. *(Stanford Athletic Department)*

Gini and me dressed up in style
for the Heisman Award dinner.
(Gini Campbell Annis)

Gini and me at a college party.
(Gini Campbell Annis)

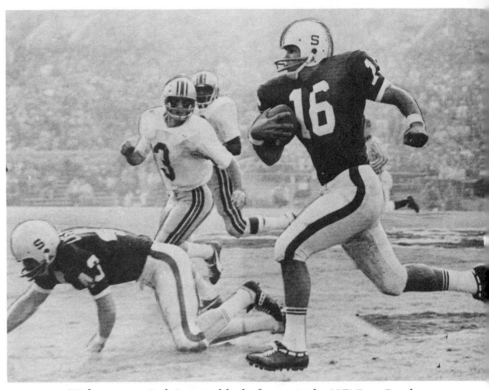

Wide receiver Jack Lasater blocks for me in the 1971 Rose Bowl
against Ohio State. *(Wide World Photos, Inc.)*

Quarterback Dan Pastorini, Coach Blanton Collier and me at
the College All-Star Game. *(Stanford Athletic Department)*

things they were protesting against, but they were attacking everything—Vietnam, Reagan and the imprisonment of Black Panther leader Huey Newton—and I couldn't buy all of it.

Protesting is one way of expressing yourself. People should be allowed to do that as long as it is done peacefully. I'm very much against violence and damaging property.

Standing on a soapbox is difficult for me even if I believe in the cause. But I might have led an anti-war rally after accompanying some other college athletes on a two-week trip to the Philippines before my last football season. We visited hospitals and talked to wounded soldiers who were flown from Vietnam to the Philippines for rehabilitation. They were shot up and didn't know why. One soldier needed 100 stitches in his body because of shrapnel. Another soldier had to have a colostomy. It turned out that he was an ex-Stanford student. I brought him up to date on campus life. A hospital official later told me: "He doesn't want to live." War is hell, even an undeclared war.

Getting back to football seemed so much safer.

Stanford switched to predominantly pro-style offense my junior year. I was dropping back more, rolling and sprinting out less. That 1969 team was the best I played on in college. We were stronger offensively, especially in the line. We had a good record, 7–2–1, but we failed to make the Rose Bowl again because of—you guessed it—USC.

We picked on poor San Jose State again, 63–21, in the opener, and then rolled over Oregon, 28–0. Next up: a titanic at Purdue.

It was a day for impressive statistics. Mine were very good and Mike Phipps's were better. It was my first 300-yard passing game in college—actually 355 yards and four touchdowns, plus 61 yards rushing for a Pacific–8 single-game total offense record. Phipps threw 5 touchdown passes and was an incredible 13–for–13 in the fourth quarter. Then he tossed a two-point conversion pass that gave Purdue a wild 36–35 victory. We still could have won the game, but I fumbled the football away on Purdue's 42 after a 17-yard run. Purdue ran out the clock. That was the first time I have ever cried after a football game.

An even more emotional finish awaited Stanford the following week in Los Angeles. For the second straight year, our kicking game got us into trouble against USC. An interception I threw didn't help matters either.

We started off quickly as Bob Moore caught a 3-yard touchdown pass. Steve Horowitz missed the conversion kick. Our fullback, Howie Williams, scored on a 12-yard pass to make it 12–0. We went for the two-point conversion but my pass just missed diving Bubba Brown.

USC then rubbed the sleep out of its eyes, yawned and became interested in the game. Mike Berry scored on a 4-yard run. I underthrew Brown on a halfback pass, Tyrone Hudson picked it off and had a free run down the sidelines. His 57-yard interception return gave USC a 14–12 halftime lead.

Horowitz had a field goal blocked before hammering through a 28-yarder that put Stanford back on top, 15–14. Not for long. Jimmy Jones flipped a 19-yard pass to tight end Gerry Mullins and the Trojans led again, 20–15, missing a two-point conversion try. We fought back. Brown plunged over from the 1. This time Horowitz didn't get the kick off because of a poor center snap, but at least we were in front, 21–20. It was short-lived. Ron Ayala drilled a 30-yard field goal and USC was in command again, 23–21, with 3:23 left.

We were really in a hole after I threw a pass. It was blocked and I caught the deflection for a substantial loss. Then we got lucky. I threw deep toward Randy Vataha. USC's Sandy Durko grabbed the ball, but Vataha ripped it out of his hands and continued upfield for a 67-yard gain. Horowitz kicked a 37-yard field goal and we had the lead for the third time in the half, 24–23, with only 1:03 left.

There was pandemonium in front of our bench. Players hugged, banged one another on the helmets, slapped hands. The Trojans were dead, we told ourselves.

Someone forgot to lock the coffin.

Jones coolly threw sideline passes to Mullins and Sam Dickerson. The Trojans, trying to beat the clock, moved 68 yards to our 17, managing to stop the timer with just seconds left.

The scene in front of me then began to move in slow motion in my mind. Ayala jogged onto the field, running as if his feet were stuck in tar. He marked off the steps to the ball, wiped his hands on a towel, then tossed it away, the towel fluttering to the ground. Eyes riveted to a spot on the ground, Ayala moved toward the football and swung his right foot six inches under his holder's extended fingers.

The ball left the natural green turf and began its ascent into the night air over the reaching fingers of Stanford linemen. The ball glistened in the stadium lights as it moved end-over-end toward the white uprights in the distance. The stadium was deathly silent for what seemed like minutes, as all heads turned to watch the ball's flight. A rumbling began to build from the USC rooting section, then it erupted into a roaring crescendo as the ball dipped between the posts. The scoreboard changed to USC 26, Stanford 24—and 0:00 on the clock.

Players were frozen in disbelief on the Stanford sideline as the USC bench emptied onto the field. Ayala was engulfed by teammates, then raised onto their shoulders. Ayala's fists waved triumphantly in the air as he was carried off toward the tunnel. The USC fight song was playing; it sounded like a dirge. Pat Preston and Rich Keller lay on the turf, pounding it in disbelief. Their fists came up slowly, then disappeared into the dewy grass. Once, twice, three times. They were Stanford seniors and would never beat USC.

I wanted to cry, but couldn't. I had told myself after Purdue that I wouldn't cry again.

Bob Murphy, Stanford's sports information director,

tried to lighten the mood a few days later.

"I wish USC would retire Ayala's number," he said, "with Ayala in it."

His remark drew laughs in Los Angeles, but not at Stanford. Somehow we recovered in time to play Washington State and manhandled the Cougars, 49–0. One week later, we had UCLA beaten at halftime, 17–3; the Bruins surged back to tie the score at 20–20. Horowitz lined up for a game-winning field goal, but it was blocked. The game ended in a tie. Stanford accepted it in the same way as a defeat.

As our team walked dejectedly out of the stadium, a hippie-type approached me. His body was in Stanford, but his mind was orbiting Jupiter.

"Hey, man," he said. "It's not you guys, man. It's Stanford."

He believed there was a hex on Stanford that prevented us from beating USC and UCLA. He wasn't alone on the Stanford campus, where football was hardly the most popular topic of conversation at the time. There was considerable talk about de-emphasizing football—cutting back the money spent, reducing the number of games and treating the sport in a low-key Ivy League manner. There was discussion about abolishing the sport. The 1960s were tough times for Stanford football.

Something happened in the locker room after the UCLA tie that ultimately would change the "hex" that Stanford associated with the two Los Angeles schools. After the coaches had their say and the media cleared out, ten Stanford players, all juniors, sat in a group: Lasater, Schultz, Kauffman, Ron Kadziel, Dave Tipton, Moore, myself and a few others. Moore started talking.

"Look, we've gone through two years of not beating USC and UCLA. We have just one chance left. We've got to do whatever it takes to beat those guys, even if it means staying around Stanford all summer and working out. Whatever sacrifices are necessary, we've got to make them. There has to be a commitment from all of us."

Back in the 1930s, some Stanford freshman team players watched the varsity lose to USC. Afterward, they vowed never to lose to USC. And they never did, hence becoming "Vow Boys." No one in our group vowed to beat USC and UCLA, but a pledge was made to be a better team in 1970. A bunch of hungry football lettermen remained on campus that summer.

We won our final four games my junior year against Oregon State, 33–0, Washington, 21–7, Air Force, 47–34, and California, 29–28. Cal made it very close on the passing of Dave Penhall, who never interested the pro scouts but always played against Stanford like a No. 1 pick. After the season, someone told me I had finished eighth in the Heisman Trophy voting, but I was happier about my Stanford athletic ring, which is awarded after a second year of varsity competition. That ring means a lot to me; I still wear it today.

"A group of touring football writers visited Stanford every year. They asked Jim before his senior season what was more important, the Heisman or the Rose Bowl? Now when someone asks a question like that, you might hesitate a bit because the immediate reaction usually is the individual thing. The question had hardly left the writer's mouth when Jim replied, 'The Rose Bowl, because I can do that with my team.' That tells you something about Jim Plunkett. Tears came to my eyes."

—JOHN RALSON

The Year of the Quarterback. That's how the 1970 college football season was promoted by someone who specialized in catchy phrases. Whoever he was, he was right. There were Archie Manning at Mississippi, Rex Kern at Ohio State, Joe Theismann at Notre Dame, Lynn Dickey at

Kansas State, Bill Montgomery at Arkansas, Dan Pastorini at Santa Clara and Ken Anderson at Augustana.

ABC-TV did a special before that season interviewing a number of quarterbacks, including me. When the topic of the Heisman was brought up, I tried to convey the feeling that if I won it, fine; if I didn't, fine. I hadn't come back my senior year because of the Heisman, though. I came back because I had three commitments: to myself, to Stanford and to youngsters. I've always preached the value of an education. How would it have looked to kids if I quit school without earning a degree?

Because of my redshirt season, I was eligible for the NFL draft in the winter of 1970, since my freshman class would graduate that June. It would be a lie to say that I wasn't thinking about ending my amateur standing then and there. Not to would mean turning down a lot of money, and money was something I didn't have.

There were a lot of people watching me to see what I would do, not only kids but people of my heritage. I have some impact on Mexican-Americans, judging from the letters I've received over the years telling me that I am setting a good example for all Mexican-Americans.

You hear professional athletes say: "If a kid wants an example, he should look to his father." I didn't agree with that thinking entirely. A kid can look up to his father and have other heroes as well. Why not an athlete? He is highly visible. He is big, strong, fast, daring. There can be heroes of science, industry and war. An athlete is just one more hero.

Athletes do set an exmaple, whether they realize it or not or wish to accept the responsibility. I feel they should set a good one.

I had a responsibility to fulfill in 1970, to my teammates and coaches as well. We were building for something: the Rose Bowl. How could I turn my back on them? The NFL draft would have to wait.

I had really become attached to Stanford. My classes were going well and I would graduate the following winter with a B average in political science. One class was particularly interesting—Chinese Foreign Policy, taught by Michel Oksenberg. He would come to class in a Mao jacket and carrying a little red book. He'd call us lackeys and imperialists. Professor Oksenberg dispelled the everyday drudgery of going to class.

President John F. Kennedy had inspired my interest in politics and government. Certainly he was a charismatic person—witty, intelligent, urbane, boyish-looking, articulate—but beyond that he was a man with vision and ideas, such as the Peace Corps and space exploration. Through him, I became interested in what was going on around the country.

I was a sophomore in high school when that dark day in Dallas turned an inspiration into a memory. I couldn't fathom that the killing of the president could happen in our country. Adults, kids . . . everyone broke down. I was stunned. "Why did he have to be killed?" I asked my teachers and friends. "Who would want to do something like that?" Thinking of Kennedy's widow and children convinced me that politics might be a course to study, but never an occupation to pursue.

Richard M. Nixon, on the other hand, didn't live up to our expectations that a president be a strong leader, a man who must make the right decisions and be able to carry them through Congress. Nixon went beyond his powers, if not his abilities, in the Watergate mess. It was hard to believe that a president would cover up or even be involved in such a scandal. The credibility gap was widened because the country didn't know whom to trust. Whom could we turn to for help if not our own president—our highest elected official?

Studying different governments at Stanford, however, I concluded that democracy was by far the best system.

Sure we have our serious problems, our shortcomings, our headaches, but democracy is the one system where the people can work from within. In other systems such as China's and the Soviet Union's, you don't have much say and your freedom of choice is limited. Democracy is still a happier place to be.

Speaking of China reminds me of an incident involving the Stanford marching band, which isn't your traditional college marching band. In fact, it lampoons that tradition. The Stanford band wears red blazers and black slacks that never seem to fit, plus crazy hats and shoes that don't match. Some of the instruments have been painted. The musicians are thoroughly rowdy, unabashed and as disorganized as a band can be and still be considered organized.

Once on national television, Chris Schenkel described a Stanford band halftime routine.

"The Stanford band is doing a salute to . . . Red . . . China. . . ."

Schenkel didn't say another word. The Stanford band has a way of leaving you speechless. You never know what it's going to do from week to week. Public sentiment for the band runs half and half. Half the public can live with the band, the other half wants to lynch it. I love that band.

I'm not sure what Leland Stanford would say about the band. He was a railroad builder (Central Pacific, Southern Pacific), a California governor and a United States senator. In 1885, he founded Stanford University in memory of his son, with a gift of land and securities. The legal name is Leland Stanford Junior University. The school was opened to students in 1891.

Stanford University is called "The Farm" because it sits in a lovely, rural location. Stanford Stadium fits perfectly in that pastoral setting, a rustic old stadium that seats 84,892 if the game is a sellout. On sunny California autumn afternoons, there was no better place to be than inside that stadium. It was home.

Fans are people who go to pro games. I don't think of those who attend Stanford games as fans per se. They're students, alumni or just followers of Stanford. Those who have played football at Stanford loved that walk along tree-shaded Sam McDonald Road past the tailgaters, especially after a victory—and if you weren't limping too badly from an injury. Family, friends, your girl, teammates and just students joined together on that walk. Walter Camp must have pictured college football this way at the turn of the century when the game was played with flying wedges and no helmets.

My high school years were great; my pro years have been so-so. But in college, I was growing up, finding out who I was, learning, making friends, having fun. College was the best time of my life.

I have donated money to the school's athletic department since my graduation, and in 1981 I set up a scholarship in my name at Stanford. I got a lot out of Stanford and wanted to give something back. I feel a part of the university; living about five minutes from campus, in Atherton, keeps me young. I help recruit athletes, telling prospects what Stanford can offer them as students. This is the important thing, because you don't know how far they'll go as athletes.

I will always be proud to be a Stanford Indian even though they became the Stanford Cardinals after I graduated. What is a Cardinal? Is it a bird, color or religious figure? Stanford students aren't sure themselves because their mascot is a tree. That's right, a tree! There was a campaign to change the nickname to a griffin, which is half-eagle and half-lion. It was defeated.

I can understand the American Indian Party's protest of an Indian as an athletic symbol. Prince Lightfoot, an actual Indian, waved a tomahawk and did a war dance during past Stanford football games, until the AIP stepped in. The AIP thought this was as defamatory as the cowboys who chased the Indians during those old Buffalo Bill Wild West shows.

I wouldn't like it if Stanford's nickname was the Chicanos. Imagine some guy running around in a sombrero and serape, waving a pistol like Pancho Villa and doing a hat dance around a Stanford helmet.

Nevertheless, without trying to defame or insult anyone, I'm still a Stanford Indian. I hope Stanford comes up with a nickname that is satisfactory and logical.

My redshirt season was a lonely time, so I can appreciate what Don Bunce went through in 1970. Don and I joined the varsity at the same time. A day hardly passed that Don didn't think he was a better quarterback than I was, which he reminded Coach John Ralston of constantly. Naturally, I felt I was better than Don, and I was playing. So he redshirted his last year and used the time for introspection. Don discovered football wasn't the most important thing in his life. He decided to attend medical school. Don came back in 1971 after I was gone and led Stanford to a second straight Rose Bowl victory. Today he is Dr. Don Bunce.

Don works closely with Stanford athletics. He is interested in sports medicine, a field that originated in Europe but has grown in popularity in the United States. Sports injuries are different from non-sports injuries because the athlete must be rehabilitated as fast as possible in order to play again, whereas the non-athlete is told to take some time off from work in order to let his injury heal.

A broken bone once meant that an athlete was, more often than not, through for the year. No longer. There are flexible protective casts or paddings that allow him to continue competing. Now it is possible to have surgery and play again the same season, as I have done more than once.

Sports medicine has become very advanced. There are clinics in hospitals or owned by private concerns that deal strictly in the strengthening and/or rebuilding of muscles and limbs. Thank heavens for sports medicine. Without it, my football career couldn't have lasted as long as it has.

Stanford opened the 1970 season on national television at Arkansas. Football fans in Little Rock are fanatical. How fanatical? Arkansas spring football practice is televised live. Razorback fans dress in red and scream "Soooooo-eeeeee" for their Hogs. I threw three interceptions that night, but completed eight third-down passes and audibled for our first two touchdowns. We got out of Little Rock with a 34–28 victory.

Soooooooeeeeee!

We shut down San Jose State for the third straight year, 34–3. I kidded Gini Campbell, my girl, about how bad the Spartans were. Gini went to San Jose State, but she didn't even know where the football stadium was. She wasn't one of your great football fans, but she came to see Stanford play because her boyfriend was the quarterback.

We had trouble the next week in Oregon, failing to score a point in the first half. Then we scored the first five times we had the football in the second half. I felt sheepish about one of those touchdowns, because it was a pass over Don Frease, who had gone to school with Gini and me at James Lick. Don switched from wide receiver, his high school position, to defensive back at Oregon. I threw for three touchdowns that day and ran for a fourth in a 33–10 victory.

We were 3–0 at this point with USC coming up in two weeks. The seniors couldn't wait for the Trojan game and neither could the coaches. Unfortunately, all of us forgot we had a game in between against Purdue. After each wind sprint in practice that week, Mike White, an assistant coach, would yell, "This one's for USC."

Purdue didn't look that impressive because Phipps was gone. The Boilermakers dumped us, 26–14. I threw 5 interceptions, one more than I had thrown in the previous 3 games. Ralston probably wished during the game that he hadn't redshirted Bunce. After my third interception, I came back to the bench frustrated. "That's all right," Ralston said, "keep throwing." So I went back in, threw another interception, returned to the sidelines even more frustrated. "That's all right," Ralston said again, "keep throwing." If we had played eight quarters that day instead of four, I might have thrown 15 interceptions. And after the 15th, John would have said, "That's all right. . . ."

About this time, I began having severe headaches. My head throbbed so badly one day during a lecture, I asked the professor if I could be excused. The doctors gave me a complete physical. The only thing they could determine was stress. We had lost to Purdue, and there were a number of big games coming up. The Heisman pressure was building; a day hardly passed that I wasn't asked about it by the media. The headaches lasted for weeks, then just disappeared.

Our fifth game was against USC at Stanford. The fourth-ranked Trojans were a touchdown favorite to defeat Stanford for the thirteenth straight year. Our seniors knew what was at stake. We reminded one another of our locker room pledge. Our last chance.

We jumped up quickly as Bob Moore caught a 50-yard touchdown pass. Sophomore Eric Cross returned a punt 47 yards to set up Jackie Brown's 1-yard run. We led 14–0, but USC closed it to 14–7 on Rod McNeill's 1-yard plunge in the third quarter.

Randy Vataha kept USC's secondary loose with 10 receptions for 120 yards. Vataha didn't score in the game, but his 34-yard catch set up another 1-yard run by Brown that made it 21–7.

Our defense was superb. USC banged on our goal line several times without getting a reply.

Mike Berry of USC dived over left tackle from a yard out and smacked into Larry Butler for no gain. USC was forced to give up the ball.

Trojan fullback Sam Cunningham became famous for his goal-line leaps into the end zone. He jumped over Ohio

State for 4 touchdowns in the Rose Bowl 2 years later. He must not have perfected his leap until after the 1970 season, because he jumped over the line twice against us and landed short of the goal. We were really inspired to play USC that day, but we were also lucky.

USC narrowed the margin, this time to 21–14 as Jimmy Jones hit Bob Chandler from 17 yards out. After USC marched to Stanford's 3, our defense saved us again. Jim Kauffman took some wild chances from his defensive back position that game. If Jones had been throwing, Jim would have been burned badly. But he guessed right every time. On fourth-and-one, Jones rolled around left end and Kauffman dropped him for a 2-yard loss.

Instead of a tied-up game, we still led by 7. Our offense then moved the football into position for Steve Horowitz's 36-yard field goal that finished off the Trojans, 24–14.

The Stanford seniors went berserk. We had done it. We had finally done it.

Afterward, McKay told Ralston amid the rubble of torn-down goal posts that the Indians were as well-prepared a team as he had ever faced. That took some doing for John McKay and showed some class.

There would be no immediate letdown. That would be a problem later in the season, but not now. We destroyed Washington State the next week, 63–16. Vataha caught a 96-yard touchdown pass to set a Stanford and conference record. I had my longest touchdown run ever, 39 yards, and finished the game as the NCAA's new all-time total offense leader. Not bad for someone who almost was a defensive end.

"I'll never forget Jim Plunkett against us up at Washington State. We put in a new defense one year where we doubled both their outside receivers, catching Stanford by surprise. The game wound up a 21–21 tie, but we would have won if Plunkett hadn't brought Stanford back with his run-

*ning. The kid could throw any kind of pass. And he was
strong. I've seen him hold off pass rushers with one arm and
complete the pass. I've seen him audibilize three times on
the same call and get the play off on time. When the going
got tough, he was the toughest. He was one tough hombre."*
—JIM SWEENEY

In three games against UCLA, we scored 3 points in
each of the second halves. We lost 1, tied 1, then won in my
senior year, 9–7. Horowitz, criticized at times for his kicking,
booted 3 field goals. Randy set up two of them with big
receptions. Our defense did the rest. USC and UCLA had
fallen in the same autumn.

We worked over Oregon State, 48–10, which meant
the following week's game with Washington was for the
Rose Bowl. It would be our Indians against their Indian.
Washington quarterback Sonny Sixkiller is a full-blooded
Cherokee.

Jim Krieg jolted us on the opening kickoff with a
95-yard touchdown return for the Huskies. I was pumped up
and threw first-quarter touchdown passes to Brown, Moore
and Lasater to put us ahead, 21–7.

Sixkiller threw a 1-yard pass to tight end John Brady,
then scored on a 9-yard run and flipped a 2-point conversion
pass to his other tight end, Ace Bulger. Washington led
again, 22–21, late in the third quarter.

Vataha caught a 15-yard touchdown pass and Brown
a 2-point conversion toss that put us back in front, 29–22.
Krieg got loose on another return, but we caught him after
47 yards and Stanford's defense stopped the Huskies at our
31. The 29–22 score held up and Stanford received its first
Rose Bowl invitation since 1951.

There was great excitement on the Stanford campus,
even among those who wanted to abolish football. The football players were on cloud nine. Unfortunately, we didn't
come down for two more weeks.

Ralston and his staff made a major mistake after the Washington game. They let up on us in practice, we lost our concentration, and then we lost to two teams we should have beaten. The Purdue experience hadn't taught us a lesson.

We traveled to Colorado Springs, and found a snowstorm had hit. The Air Force Academy then came down on us like an avalanche, 31–14. Our intensity was missing again in the Big Game when California, led by Dave Penhall, beat us, 22–14. The Cal players came across the field afterward to reclaim The Axe, symbolic of the Cal-Stanford rivalry. That was one of my worst experiences at Stanford, understanding the meaning of the Big Game when it was too late.

On that same day, in Columbus, Ohio, the Buckeyes of Ohio State defeated Michigan, 20–9, to clinch the Big Ten's Rose Bowl berth. Ohio State fullback John Brockington was asked about Stanford.

"Stanford?" he replied, sipping on a soft drink. "We're not worried about Stanford."

By this time, the Heisman votes were tabulated. Had they been mailed in after my last two games instead of before, I might not have won. That wouldn't have been catastrophic for me, though. Stanford was going to the Rose Bowl, and that was all that really mattered.

Don't misunderstand me. The Heisman Trophy is a wonderful award for a college athlete and should be given. Politics come into play, as it does in anything, and the Heisman isn't unique in this sense. Still, it's a great honor.

At the NCAA's sports information directors' convention in the summer of 1970, someone stood up and congratulated the Mississippi publicist for winning the Heisman Trophy for Archie Manning. Before the season!

Murphy was irate. He came home from the convention and fired off a letter to sportswriters around the country, saying, in effect, not to decide the Heisman race before it was run. This was all well and good, but Manning's Heisman campaign was off to a big head start.

Archie's campaign even included a song: "The Ballad of Archie Who." A Manning poster was disseminated to the media, showing Archie walking across campus on a puddly day. Some writers interpreted this to mean that Archie walked on water.

After Stanford's game at Washington State, Cavalli put together a Heisman brochure on me, and Murphy sent copies to the media. I was embarrassed by the Heisman attention and asked Gary and Bob if this was necessary. They explained that something was needed to slow down Manning. Stanford hadn't won a Heisman before either.

The Jim Plunkett Heisman campaign cost all of $200. These comments appeared in the brochure:

> *"Thus far, I believe, Jim Plunkett is the best college quarterback I have ever seen."*
> —BUD WILKINSON, ex-Oklahoma coach

> *"Plunkett is the best pro quarterback prospect I've ever seen."*
> —TOMMY PROTHRO, UCLA head coach

> *"Plunkett is big, strong and smart. He could play in the pros right now. He'll probably be the first guy selected in next year's draft."*
> —GIL BRANDT, Dallas Cowboys personnel director

> *"Plunkett is the strongest college quarterback I've ever seen. He's not just a dropback passer... he can half-roll, scramble, run when he's in trouble and get rid of the ball with guys hanging on him."*
> —JOHN MCKAY

Manning may have decided the Heisman outcome, unintentionally, by breaking his arm midway through the season. Stanford won the race.

I led the vote-getters in four sections—west, midwest, east, southeast—and tied with Archie in the south. Manning finished third overall, behind Joe Theismann of Notre Dame.

Theismann's name while growing up was pronounced "Theezemann." Roger Valdiserri, a Notre Dame sports publicist, knew that four Notre Dame quarterbacks had won the Heisman. He was looking for a fifth.

"From now on," Valdiserri told Joe, "your name is 'Thighsmann' as in Heisman."

The Heezeman, I mean Heisman, is obviously serious business.

When the announcement came, I was in New York to take part in the filming of the Kodak All-American show. Chris Schenkel, an announcer on that first TV game I saw between the Colts and Giants, broke the news to me. I was happy but didn't jump up and down and get all excited. I was rushed to the Downtown Athletic Club for a news conference. I called my mom and she was happy, although if you asked her today, she may not know what the Heisman represents.

I flew back from the Heisman announcement and a group of Stanford people were there at the airport—the band, cheerleaders, school officials. They were very happy for me. *That's* what made winning the Heisman special.

The Heisman dinner is done with great dignity. I really felt comfortable about the way the entire Stanford contingent was treated. John Ralston and his wife, assistant coach Jack Christiansen, Jack Schultz, Bob Murphy and my girlfriend, Gini Campbell, went back with me. It was only the second time in my life that I had worn a tuxedo. The other time was at the James Lick High School senior ball. I didn't have much of a wardrobe when I was a student. My last season at Stanford, I didn't have a suit to my name—just a sports coat. I borrowed a suit from Bob Moore to take back to New York.

"Tommy McDonald, the former NFL star, made a presentation of a painting to Jim at the Heisman dinner. Tommy said: 'I wish I could give my eyes to your mother for a couple of hours so she could be here to see this.' It was very touching. Then Jim got up and gave all the credit to his mother. How many athletes would do that? I've worked with a lot of athletes, but I've never enjoyed anyone more than Jim Plunkett because of his background and the kind of person he is."

—JOHN RALSTON

We stayed over in New York a few days after the dinner. Schultzie, his date, Gini and I all went to dinner at Ponte's Restaurant. The owners had a nephew who played for Ohio State. "You're going to get your clocks cleaned in the Rose Bowl," they kidded us. The restaurant was filled with lovely nude paintings, and the owners told us that if we were lucky enough to win the Rose Bowl, we had our choice of any painting. When I was in New York again after the Rose Bowl, I went to Ponte's and picked out a painting. I gave it to Schultzie because I had no place to hang it.

Ohio State was a 10-point favorite at Pasadena after compiling a 3-year record of 27–1. The Buckeyes' only defeat was to Michigan in the final game of the 1969 season when Ohio State couldn't go to the Rose Bowl because of the Big Ten's no-repeat rule, which was later rescinded. Ohio State had 6 first-team All-Americans: Brockington, tight end Jan White, middle guard Jim Stillwagon and defensive backs Jack Tatum, Tim Anderson and Mike Sensibaugh. Stanford had one: Plunkett.

The Buckeyes' impressive collection of talent was called Woody Hayes's finest team, and Hayes never disputed that. As good as they were, though, we had an edge. Ohio State didn't play passing teams in the Big Ten and we were one of the best. We thought we could pull it off in a one-game, all-or-nothing shot. In a 10-game series against the

Buckeyes, we might have lost 9.

Before the Rose Bowl, the two opponents are subjected to the pre-game publicity treatment—Disneyland, posing with the Rose Bowl queen and princesses, the "Beef Bowl" at a Los Angeles restaurant. At Disneyland the Stanford players ran around, eating cotton candy, having a good time. Then Ohio State arrived, virtually marching into Disneyland. Kauffman, Mr. Uninhibited, wore his Mickey Mouse ears, did cartwheels and took snapshots of the unsmiling, militaristic-looking Ohio State team.

The Buckeyes were upset about having to practice twice a day, but we had the same routine. Some Stanford players rebelled at this regimented life that included early curfew and off-limits on Rose Bowl courtesy cars provided by the two teams. Two players, Ron Kadziel and Demea Washington, came to see Schultzie and me because we were the co-captains. Schultzie and I would submit to anything, even regimentation, in order to win this game. But we agreed to talk to Ralston.

John said he wouldn't compromise his principles. He came down to the Rose Bowl to win, not to have a good time. He hadn't forgotten Purdue and the last two games, and he wasn't about to let that happen again. He did relent in one area. We got to use the Rose Bowl cars.

John Ralston is a very personable and positive man. With three Dale Carnegie degrees, he should be. John loves to come on with a big smile and hearty handshake. "Well, a very pleasant good afternoon, gentlemen," he'd tell the northern California football writers—win or lose—every Monday at their weekly luncheon. For awhile, I questioned whether John's manner was genuine. I found out he is well-meaning and sincere.

John was a Woody Hayes type when he came from Utah State to Stanford in 1963. He didn't allow long hair and beards. When John Haygood, a linebacker, showed up for spring practice with a goatee, Ralston was irate.

"I could almost hit you, John Haygood, for wearing that goatee," he snapped.

If Ralston had stuck to his rigid ways, he wouldn't have been successful. He noticed the shift in attitudes among students and changed his thinking. This helped him establish better rapport with his players, and it helped him win.

John was quite a sight on the football field. He was a head coach in perpetual motion. During his one-minute offense drill, he would blow the whistle, set the ball down, jump out of the way, blow the whistle, set the ball down . . . all the time shouting out the seconds on his stopwatch. John was a one-man show.

His rah-rah enthusiasm for the game hadn't changed since he was a Cal linebacker. John had all these sayings, like "If you think enthusiastic, you will be enthusiastic."

We had a lineman, Roger Cowan, a big, good-looking guy who wore shades—the whole Hollywood bit. We called him Hollywood Rog. He was in the whirlpool one day when Ralston spotted him.

"Roger, you can't make the club in the tub," John said.

"Coach, you can't take the field until you're healed," Hollywood Rog replied.

Ralston was flabbergasted.

We had to admire John, though. He survived tremendous pressure from alumni and media, who spent three years trying to get him fired. He persevered and won back-to-back Rose Bowl games, something no other Stanford coach—not even the legendary Pop Warner—had done.

Walking into the Rose Bowl the day before the game brought back memories. This was the same place that young kid in San Jose had seen one day on television. And here I was.

We were brought there for more publicity photos, then hurried over to the country club next door to watch

Schultzie on "The Dating Game." I was supposed to be on
the show, but Gini said no, so Schultzie took my place. He
and his date won a day in Vancouver, B.C. She was too
caught up with Hollywood, a modeling career and herself,
however. He wound up having more fun with the chaperone.

> *"I thought we were the superior team offensively and*
> *defensively, even though we hadn't seen a passer like Plun-*
> *kett. But if you don't watch it, a good team can be right back*
> *in your face and it's a fight to the finish. I supposed we*
> *looked like Goliath to them. They had all the enthusiasm in*
> *the world and their enthusiasm surpassed everything."*
> —TIM ANDERSON, Ohio State defensive back

Ralston was an innovative coach. He searched for
ways to keep the powerful Buckeyes on their heels. One way
was the flanker reverse, which Eric Cross sprang for 41 yards
on their very first play to the Ohio State 18. Then we un-
veiled surprise Number Two, the quarterback draw. I ran 4
that day for 49 yards. John Sande, our center, simply blocked
Stillwagon in the direction he was rushing and I ran the
other way. My first draw went for 13 yards and Jackie Brown
followed with a 1-yard touchdown run.

Horowitz kicked a 37-yard field goal on our next series and Stanford led, 10–0. Ohio State surged back to lead
at halftime, 14–10, on 1-yard smashes by Brockington. We
would give up 439 yards to Ohio State—364 on the ground
—but not many points because we stopped the Buckeyes
four times on fourth down. I'm not sure if Michigan has ever
done that in one game.

Horowitz set a Rose Bowl record with a 48-yard field
goal that narrowed the score to 14–13. Fred Schram's 32-
yarder raised Ohio State's margin back to 17–13.

Now it was time for the play Woody Hayes later
called "the mad dog pass."

Several times I had asked Moore to stay in and block on passing downs. I asked him once again with the ball at the Ohio State 37. For some reason as we broke the huddle, I said to Bob: "No, you better go out." The Buckeyes' pass rush forced me out of the pocket and to my right. I spotted Bob across the field. He jumped between two defenders to make a spectacular catch at the 2-yard line. Three plays later, Brown scored and we led, 20–17.

On the ensuing series, Schultzie intercepted a Rex Kern pass and ran it back to the Buckeyes' 25. They threw a safety blitz against us, but Vataha cut to the area the safety had vacated and caught the winning 21-yard touchdown pass. A dejected Jack Tatum dropped to his knees, his arms in the air after Randy's reception. The 27–17 upset was Stanford's first Rose Bowl victory in exactly thirty years.

It was bedlam on the field and in the locker room. I'm sure I cried, which I told myself never to do again. But everyone was crying, and laughing, and shouting, and loving every minute of it. I've never felt closer to a group of athletes than at that moment.

My college career ended perfectly. I accomplished what I had set out to do, what I had come back one more time to achieve.

I didn't drink at all until my last year at Stanford, and then it was only a beer or two with the guys at the Oasis or Zots. But I really got "blitzed" after the Rose Bowl, and I don't know what it was that even sacked me. The worst part of it was having to wake up. When I opened my eyes, barely, Bob Moore and John Sande were shaking me.

"C'mon, Jim, get packed. We've got to go."

"Pack? Go? The only place I'm going is back to sleep."

"Let's go, Jim. We've got to catch that flight to the Hula Bowl."

"Hula Bowl? What's a Hula Bowl? Whatever it is, it can bowl without me."

My stomach felt awful. My head felt worse. I just made it to the bathroom before getting sick. Somehow I climbed on that flight to Hawaii for the Hula Bowl.

It's hard to get serious about football in Hawaii. Ralston was our coach, so we used the Stanford system. We practiced one hour a day and went out every night. When the day of the game arrived, my shoulders were sore from surfing. I really felt guilty. I had been abusing myself. This was the first time I had not prepared for a game. I must have dissipated less than others for I was named the game's Most Valuable Player.

Flying back to the mainland, I played the Ohio State victory over in my mind for the umpteenth time. Thirty thousand feet over the Pacific, I was on top of the world. Schultzie, Lasater, Kauffman, Moore . . . we had accomplished the ultimate.

Nothing, I felt, could ever surpass winning the Rose Bowl.

Chapter Four

PATRIOT WITHOUT A HOME

"*Before the bowl games, we were uncertain as to which player we would draft. But after I saw Plunkett bring Stanford back against Ohio State—you could see him lifting his team up—there was no question in my mind that it would be Plunkett.*"
—JOHN MAZUR, Boston Patriots coach, January, 1971

I was in Miami with some other college football players to tape an All-America show. We heard the Dolphins were in town that day, so a bunch of us ran out to the Orange Bowl. Miami just killed Boston, 37–20. The Patriots were not a very good team. Suddenly, it flashed in my mind.

"Hey, I could be drafted by these guys."

The city of Boston offered an unusual surf-and-turf combination that fall—the finest lobster and the worst pro football in the country. The Patriots' 2–12 record put them at the bottom of the NFL, but guaranteed Boston the first pick of the 1971 college draft. This meant, if everything I read and heard was true, that I would be the Patriots' pick.

This would also mean Boston would have two Mexican quarterbacks from California. Joe Kapp was the Patriots' incumbent quarterback. Kapp was a fearless leader and a man of great charisma who could also negotiate a contract. Although 34 years old with a throwing arm that reminded no one of Sammy Baugh's, Kapp coaxed a 3-year $600,000 contract from Boston. Kapp's $200,000 salary was $75,000 more a year than what Joe Namath earned with the New York Jets.

Kapp was a take-charge guy when it came to quarterbacking as well. He led an average California football team to its last Rose Bowl (1959). He directed the British Columbia Lions to their first Grey Cup championship. He took Minnesota to its first Super Bowl.

If Kapp didn't think a tackle or linebacker was putting out in practice, Joe would invite the malingerer outside. Kapp was a tough individual with a thirst for winning and tequila.

However, during the 1970 season, he completed just 44.7 percent of his passes. He threw 3 touchdown passes and 17 interceptions. Depending on your arithmetic, that's roughly $66,667 a touchdown or $11,764 an interception. Either way, it didn't add up right for the Patriots, who began looking for another quarterback.

The first pick of the draft is the NFL's Hope Diamond: Everyone wants it and only one team has it. Boston possessed it and the rest of the NFL came to inquire about its cost. Mazur said he was interested in trading the No. 1 away. Dallas offered Bob Hayes, Baltimore dangled John Mackey and San Francisco tendered Ted Kwalick—all part of package deals and all rumors that were never substantiated.

Mazur was only testing the waters, however. He discovered there were piranha lurking and decided to keep the pick. Mazur wanted to select me, but Boston's 33-year-old boy general manager, Upton Bell, may have had other ideas.

"I love [Dan] Pastorini," Bell said before the draft. "He throws the ball as well as [Terry] Bradshaw and he's a great kicker, even though he's never worked at it."

Pastorini completed a great career at Santa Clara without the acclaim given quarterbacks from major universities. However, NFL scouts knew Pastorini was a tremendous prospect. So was Archie Manning of Ole Miss. It was almost certain that Manning, Pastorini and I would be the first three players drafted, although the order hadn't been confirmed.

If I had a choice of teams, it would have been the San Francisco 49ers. John Brodie, the 49ers' quarterback, was 35. I could see a future in San Francisco and I wouldn't have to leave home. However, there were two obstacles: the 49ers weren't drafting until 18th and I wouldn't have played right away in San Francisco.

I didn't want to sit around and learn a pro system for a few years. I wanted to start at once. New England, as things turned out, provided that opportunity.

First of all, I needed someone to represent me in contract negotiations. Stanford people had arranged for me to meet with several attorneys and agents. Out of the bunch, I liked Wayne Hooper, an Oakland attorney. I liked his straightforwardness and honesty. Hoop isn't a shark like some agents; if anything, he is more like a friendly dolphin. I told Hoop later that I chose him only because I felt sorry for him, a California graduate, living in the shadow of a great university like Stanford.

The thought of playing in New England pleased me. Hoop told me that if I didn't want to play for the Patriots, I could make my demands so high that they would have to trade me.

"No, Hoop, I'll play in New England. It will be a new challenge for me, a new experience."

I meant it. I had led a sheltered life up until then. The

only traveling I had done as a boy was by bus to New Mexico to visit relatives. At Stanford, there were a number of short trips to football games and award ceremonies. I hadn't really broadened my horizons, however, and was looking forward to living in a different part of the country, seeing a different life style. As it turned out, Boston is a lot like San Francisco, but without as many hills.

On January 28, 1971, the speculation ended. I became a Boston Patriot. Manning was taken second by New Orleans and Pastorini third by Houston. Mazur came out of the Patriots' drafting office and faced the media. He smiled.

"A Jim Plunkett comes along once in a great while," he said. "We believe he is the quarterback of the future—the Joe Namath of the future.

"Jim has a magnetism that few athletes have. Bobby Orr has it. So does Namath. I don't know what it is, but whatever it is, I want it."

Whatever it is, so do I. I've never considered myself magnetic. I'm not charismatic or, for that matter, phlegmatic. I'm somewhere in the middle. On draft days, you hear lots of things that aren't always true.

Billy Sullivan, the Patriots' owner, was ecstatic after the draft.

"We feel we helped solve our quarterback problems for the next ten years."

He was half-right.

The reference to Orr was puzzling for me, a Californian. When it came to hockey, I didn't know a puck from a check or a blue line from a red line.

I appeared at a promotion in Boston after the NFL draft. I was signing autographs when a little kid asked me:

"Do you know Derek?"

"Who's Derek?"

"Derek Sanderson."

"No, who's he?"

"He plays for the Bruins."

"UCLA?"

"No, the Bahstan Bruins."

If you live in Bahstan, you know about the Bruins. I learned about Orr and Sanderson and Phil Esposito in a hurry and became a big Bruins fan.

At my first press conference as a Patriot, I was asked if I had seen my new team play. Before I could reply, Kapp, who was in attendance, interrupted.

"The kid don't want to talk about no horror movies."

Wayne Hooper was a gunnery officer on a destroyer during World War II and visited Boston as part of the victory fleet. This all came up one night when Patriots owner Billy Sullivan and his wife, Upton Bell, Hoop and myself were having dinner in Boston.

"I love the seafood, the history, the community," Hoop said. "Boston's a great city."

"Well, you know it's the center of education in America," Mrs. Sullivan said.

"Yes, they do have some great universities here," Hoop said.

"We have the finest universities in the world," she went on.

"Well, we have a couple of fine universities on the West Coast called California and Stanford," Hoop said.

"Well, they are nothing like the schools in Boston," she said.

At this point, Billy Sullivan turned to his wife and said, "Why don't you shut up?"

Billy Sullivan is a gregarious person. He likes to be friendly, tell stories, be written about. But when it comes to the possibility of hampering contract negotiations before they begin, he isn't beyond telling his wife to button her lip.

Billy isn't much on directions, however. On my first trip to Boston, he decided to show me the Patriots' training camp at Curry College. Billy got lost. He had to stop and ask directions to the campsite where the team he owned trained every summer.

Hoop had a contract in mind comparable to those O. J. Simpson and Terry Bradshaw received when they were drafted. We should have asked for more than O. J. and Terry got; after all, how many NFL rookies have a horse race named after them? The Bay State Raceway of Foxboro held the Jim Plunkett Pacing Stakes that spring. Presumably, for plodders.

I didn't sign until July when I was at the College All-Star Game camp. My first salary was $25,000, which doesn't sound like much, but there was also a loan, a $75,000 bonus and incentives. I made more than $100,000 as a rookie.

Hoop felt bad about the 5-year contract a few days later when Kapp walked out of the Patriots camp and never returned. If we had known that the No. 1 quarterback was leaving, we could have negotiated for more money.

There were two games to get out of the way before I would launch my professional career—the Coaches All-America Game in Lubbock, Texas, and the College All-Star Game in Chicago.

Chuck Hixson of SMU and I quarterbacked the West team at Lubbock. At practice one day, someone told Hixson that he was throwing the football as well as I was.

"That's great," he said, "but I really didn't expect my mother and father to arrive this early for the game."

Chuck has a great sense of humor. And he was throwing the ball well.

I had been on the banquet circuit for about a month before Lubbock, but threw 3 touchdown passes in 11 minutes and called 4 quarterback sneaks on 1 drive, finally scoring from a yard out. I don't think I would have called as many running plays if Dick Butkus had been across the line smiling at me.

In Chicago, I completed 6 of 16 passes for 65 yards

against the Baltimore Colts, who won, 24–17. Pastorini also quarterbacked the College All-Stars that night, connecting on 2 of 9 passes for 13 yards. It was the first time we had ever been teammates, but it wouldn't be the last.

Mike Taliaferro was the Patriots' quarterback in 1969, the year before Kapp arrived. Now with Kapp gone, Taliaferro wanted the job back. I was his only competition.

I got to camp a few days before the pre-season opener, but over the next three weeks I began to play more and more. The terminology was new, but the mental approach to pro football didn't seem that difficult. I found out soon enough that the physical part of the game would be the problem.

The Boston Patriots were mavericks in their own hometown. They played at Boston College, Boston University, Fenway Park and Harvard Stadium before changing their name to the New England Patriots in the spring of 1971 and moving into $6.2 million Schaefer Stadium in Foxboro that summer. Patriot management wanted to present a completely new image, which included getting the No. 1 draft pick into the lineup right away. I started against Atlanta in the fifth pre-season game.

My debut was almost played before an empty stadium in Foxboro. There were sanitation problems at the stadium, the result of bad water pressure in the lavatories. The Patriots' executive committee had tentatively given approval to a game played without spectators, which would have meant refunding more than $450,000 in ticket sales, paying Atlanta more than $100,000, reimbursing advertisers, settling with the concessionaire who had made up 20,000 sandwiches, and so on. Only a 2–1 vote by Foxboro selectmen 16 hours before kickoff made it possible for the game to be played.

As it turned out, I would have felt more comfortable playing to an empty stadium than to the 48,631 fans who watched me take the beating of my life. John Zook sacked me 3 times and Claude Humphrey must have hit me more than that.

I called one play and Randy Vataha and I were the only ones to leave the huddle. I had called a Stanford formation. I was dinged pretty good by Humphrey and didn't know where I was.

The Falcons took a 38–7 lead, which meant I was passing every down. Humphrey would rush in, knock me down, pat me on the back and say, "I'll see you next play." And he did. We made the final score respectable, 45–35. Afterward Humphrey patted me on the rump and said: "Helluva game, Jim, helluva game."

Same to you, Claude, and thanks for the lumps.

We lost to the Jets, 38–9, in our pre-season finale. I yelled an audible, got confused and realized that I didn't know what I was yelling. I had to call a time out. Both sides were laughing at me. I felt like a fool. I was finding out that physical fatigue increases mental fatigue.

After the defeat, which made our record 1–5, someone asked Namath what he liked about me.

"His knees," Joe replied.

Mike Montler, one of our offensive tackles, was leaving the locker room following the game when a sportscaster approached him.

"Hey, Jim, got time for a short interview?" the sportscaster said.

Montler thought a moment, smiled, then said, "Sure."

Montler did a ten-minute radio interview posing as Jim Plunkett. He was continually mistaken for me, even though he outweighed me by 40 pounds. Mike complained to the media that he was always signing "Jim Plunkett" autographs. I know for a fact that Mike got a lot of free drinks and some dinners from people who thought he was Jim Plunkett and picked up his tabs.

I never received one free drink or meal from anyone who thought I was Mike Montler.

New England picked up Vataha midway through the pre-season. Randy was drafted in the 17th round by the Rams, who then cut him. Mazur and Sam Rutigliano, one of our assistant coaches, asked me how good was Randy as a receiver.

"He's better than anyone we've got," I told them.

The Patriots had difficulty finding Randy. He was down on a southern California beach, drinking beer, figuring his football career was over. He joined the Patriots and caught 51 passes, 9 for touchdowns. Over 6 seasons in New England, he would catch 178 passes, 23 for touchdowns and average 17.2 yards per reception. Not bad for a last-round discard who was thought to be too small to play with the big boys.

Vataha and I got an apartment in Brookline our first year. Brookline is close to Boston and somewhat noisy because of the traffic. Randy was married before our second season, so I rented in Chestnut Hill, which is halfway between Boston and Foxboro. Chestnut Hill is a nice area, a fairly well to do, quiet section. There are tree-lined streets and a number of brick houses. You see a lot of brick in New England because of the hard winters.

I lived in Chestnut Hill my last four years in the East, probably because it reminded me most of the area around Stanford. When I went out in Boston, it usually was to functions or sometimes Daisy Buchanan's, a bar where a lot of the professional athletes in Boston hang out. I didn't meet many of my neighbors in Chestnut Hill. Like I said, it was a quiet area, and I'm a quiet person.

While practicing at Schaefer Stadium for the 1971 regular-season opener, Tom Neville, our other offensive tackle, nudged me.

"See those box seats?" he said, pointing. "Those are the people paying your salary. The people in the seats up high are paying mine."

My teammates told me not to worry about our pre-season record, that the summer months were just for getting into shape, not knocking down mountains.

Mt. Everest was our first opponent.

The Oakland Raiders have won more games than any pro football team over the last two decades. Now the Raiders were coming to Foxboro. So was the Stanford football team.

Stanford belted Army, 38–3, the day before at West Point, then flew up for the Oakland-New England game. There must have been 125 people in the Stanford party. It was an exciting day for Randy and me, and for the Patriots.

We made very few mistakes and Oakland made a lot. Fred Biletnikoff, of all people, dropped a few passes. Oakland fumbled a PAT snap and George Blanda missed a field goal. The Patriots players received a standing ovation at halftime—and we were losing, 6–0! What would they do, I wondered, if we won? I found out soon enough.

The Patriots started rolling in the second half, and the Raiders couldn't slow us down. I threw one touchdown pass to Ron Sellers and another to a tight end whose name I can't remember. Wait a minute. Moss. Something Moss. Roland Moss. That's it.

After our 20–6 victory, it seemed like the Rose Bowl all over again. Then the Stanford entourage flew back to its side of the continent and Randy and I remained on our side.

After beating Oakland, I was out to conquer the galaxies. I thought to myself, "If this is all it takes, we've got it made."

I learned my lesson in a hurry.

Detroit demolished us the next week, 34–7. The Lions changed their pass coverages all day. I was never so baffled in my life. Baltimore rode into Foxboro the following Sunday and drove us into the ground, 23–3.

Now that reality had returned, I realized I wasn't getting much in the way of pass protection or coaching preparation. I liked John Mazur a lot. He was a gentleman and a hard worker. He just wasn't the best head coach in the world, but he didn't have a lot to work with either.

I didn't learn a lot from a coaching standpoint my first year. Things were simplified. I didn't have to read the linebackers; if they blitzed, our running backs picked them up. I'm sure the coaches were trying to help me out, because I was getting enough pressure as it was from defensive linemen whose eyes were red with fury. But some games, the bench wouldn't send in one play. Talk about leaving a rookie quarterback by himself in the wilderness!

My biggest enemy wasn't the coaching staff or the defensive linemen, however. It was the free safety. In college, the free safety is instructed to play as deep as possible, so that no one will get behind him. The professional free safety is paid to take chances. So he watches my eyes in an attempt to pick up a sign where the ball is going. You try to look him off, but it's hard. NFL free safeties would never lose a staring contest.

I played recklessly and fearlessly my first year, running when I had to, throwing on the run. I was 6' 3", 200 pounds and not about to shy away from anyone. I was young and tough and could take it. If I had to run for a first down, I'd do it without a second thought and wouldn't back off from collisions either. I didn't slide when a tackler approached. Sliding is for base stealers, not quarterbacks. I took them all on, regardless of size.

It took me a while to learn.

A quarterback who runs too often is just plain asking for trouble. That's trouble with a capital "T" and it rhymes with knee, and that means surgery.

Running is too dangerous. Give the defense a chance to get one in and they'll get one in. Late shots, early shots, they all hurt. I discovered that there are two things wrong with me as a running quarterback. I'm not a punishing runner; I'm the one who gets punished. And I can't run fast enough to get out of bounds. I started backing away from collisions after spending several off-seasons on operating tables.

I slide all the time now. I've got a slide for every occasion.

You'd think I was Lou Brock.

"Jim really took a beating his first three years with the Patriots. He looked like Carmen Basilio."
—WILL MCDONOUGH, *Boston Globe* sportswriter

I took some real shots as a rookie. One time I was running and a Miami linebacker just knocked the crap out of me. My head was spinning and I got up out of pride more than anything else. I didn't want the Dolphins or their fans to think I couldn't take it.

Later, against Buffalo, I threw 4 touchdown passes and we won, 38–33. On one throw, a bomb to Randy, Al Cowlings knocked the hell out of me. I don't know how I made it to my knees, let alone my feet and back to the huddle. When I got there, I was almost begging.

"Please, someone, block Cowlings."

Over a 5-week stretch, I was sacked 24 times, including 7 by Miami and 5 by Dallas on successive weeks. As bad as I was being run over, I wouldn't come out of the game. I wanted to learn by playing, not observing. If I had started right away for Dallas, there wouldn't have been the same punishment. The Patriots just weren't a very good team, that's all.

The seventh week of the season, we traveled to San Francisco to play the 49ers. Because it was a homecoming of sorts, I used all my influence with Patriots teammates to come up with 75 tickets. Vataha helped too. We hoped to sweep the Bay Area teams—the Raiders and 49ers—in the same year. It didn't turn out that way.

Randy scored a touchdown on a crossing pattern and

we trailed the 49ers 13–10 in the third quarter. Then we fumbled away 2 punts. Forrest Blue, the 49er center, picked one up and ran it in. We lost, 27–10, in a game remembered more for trivia than anything else. It was the only time in NFL history where ex-Stanford quarterbacks on opposing teams threw touchdown passes to Stanford receivers. John Brodie tossed one to Gene Washington for San Francisco.

Steve Kiner, one of our linebackers, intercepted 2 passes in that game. Afterward, a reporter approached him for an interview.

"Not right now, man," Kiner said, "I must have taken a thousand beans."

Kiner was a good football player who was in another world most of the time. Definitely a first-team All-Twilight Zone selection. Kiner left Florida for training camp one summer without any money. So he ran all the toll booths. He was caught.

We played Houston in 1973. Ron Bolton, one of our cornerbacks, intercepted an Oiler pass and started to run it back. He crossed the field and reversed direction again before he was tackled. Bolton was mobbed by teammates. Then they started off the field. All this time, Kiner hadn't moved from his original stance. You can see the whole thing on film. Only after the other defensive players passed by him did he move. Kiner began to clap his hands. Clap . . . clap . . . clap . . . clap . . .

Steve cleaned up his act later and played some great football for the Oilers, who traded for him.

The Patriots had other characters, like Hubie Bryant, who was known as "Fashion Plate." Hubie believed in stylin', I think the term goes. He saw himself as the Frenchy Fuqua of Foxboro. Hubie showed up for practice one day in red tennis shoes that came all the way up to his knees. The players got a kick out of it, but Mazur really was angry and sent Hubie back to the locker room.

Hubie returned punts for us. One game he caught 2,

retreated both times and was tackled for losses. Afterward, some writers asked him why he was moving in reverse and not forward. Daryl Johnson, dressing next to Hubie, answered the question.

"Hey, you guys don't understand. Hubie was in there to run back punts. And that's what he was doing, running them *back!*"

Then there was Ron Sellers. He was the Patriots' first draft pick in 1969, a 6–4 wide receiver who didn't like to practice or catch balls over the middle.

Every so often, Ron would catch a "cold" and stay home from practice. The rest of the team would send him flowers.

Sellers complained that my passes were coming in at his knees. I told him I couldn't help it, because those same passes hit Randy in the chest.

Boston has several sports talk shows on radio that are acid in tone and sarcastic in nature. "If you send in so many box tops from such-and-such cereal," a talk show host said one night, "we'll send you your very own glossy of Ron Sellers dropping a pass."

Carl Garrett was a fine halfback, but a wild guy. He still owes me money. Are you reading this, Carl? He was in the military reserve and his unit would meet during the week, which meant Carl was excused from practice. One day his unit called the Patriots and wanted to know if Carl was at the practice field, because he sure wasn't at reserve. Carl couldn't be found. The Patriots tried to suspend Garrett, then wound up trading him for Duane Thomas.

Thomas was only in New England one or two days. He really was strange. You'd say hello to him and he wanted to know what you meant by it. Mazur asked him to get down in a running back's stance and Thomas refused. He fought everything, so Mazur sent him back to Dallas and Garrett came back to us.

Thomas wasted a great amount of talent. But you

judge greatness on more than just ability. Longevity and
desire must be considered. Thomas just didn't have all it
takes to succeed.

Boston fans can't get enough of sports. The local
newspapers cover the teams well and there are the sports
talk shows. The Boston area is more up on sports than any
section of the country I have been in. Boston fans can be
callous, however.

The positiveness following our victory over Oakland
turned into negativeness after we lost 5 of our first 7 games.
"Plunkett, you stink! Go back to Stanfahd."

Everything was positive again down the stretch of the
1971 season. Super Bowl-bound Miami came into Foxboro.
Mercury Morris returned the opening kickoff for a Dolphin
touchdown. Then we laid into them. Vataha caught touchdown passes of 26 and 25 yards, setting up one of those
scores with a 51-yard bomb. Randy had his 23rd birthday the
day before the game and I turned 24 the day of the game.
The 61,457 at Schaefer sang happy birthday to us. The Patriots whipped the Dolphins, 34–13.

We closed out the season in Baltimore, which was
exciting for me, getting to see Johnny Unitas in the town he
made famous. Watching Unitas on television is an experience; watching him up close is an education. He still had the
master's touch even in his third decade in the NFL.

New England was hanging onto a 14–10 lead in the
second half when we pulled off a daring play, a Unitas play.
The Patriots were third-and-eleven back on our 12-yard line.
I decided to go for it all.

Walking up to the line, I was really shaking. I kept
thinking that we ran the same play earlier and I overthrew
Randy. This one seemed overthrown too but Randy ran
under it and we had an 88-yard touchdown play, the longest
pass in Patriot history. We beat the Colts, 21–17.

Unitas, my boyhood hero, told me, "Nice game." It
was the ultimate compliment.

The bomb to Randy was my 19th touchdown pass of the season, 3 behind the NFL record for rookies held by Charlie Conerly of the New York Giants.

My playing every down that season not only set an NFL record, but cost Taliaferro $7,500. Mike's contract specified that he only had to play 1 down to get the bonus. He accused the Patriots of deliberately not playing him. I wish they had, for selfish reasons: I was tired of taking all the pounding.

Six wins and 8 defeats isn't a winning season, but it was the best the Patriots had had in 5 years. We knocked Oakland out of the playoff picture, Baltimore out of first place and we beat the powerful Dolphins.

A writer asked me if playing on artificial surface bothered me, since Stanford's football field is the kind you mow, not sweep. I told him that I would play on a sandlot to quarterback an NFL winner. And I felt the Patriots were on the road to winning.

My rookie year taught me that there is a big difference between the college game and the pro game in terms of preparation. The morning of a game in college, everything is quiet and still. There isn't much talking at all in the hotel and the pre-game meal is eaten in almost total silence. You don't even turn your head from side to side—you look straight ahead. The pros go out the night before a game, have dinner, fool around a bit, relax. Even the morning of a game, there's still a lot of talk going on, people joking and listening to rock music. Jim Kauffman could wear his Mickey Mouse ears in an NFL locker room Sunday morning and no one would think it odd.

The locker room is a kaleidoscope of life. New players come in, old players leave. Friendships are made and broken with regularity. A player getting dressed across from you wasn't there yesterday and won't be there tomorrow. For those with talent, the locker room is a second home. For those with marginal talent, it's a bus stop.

All ranges of moods can be found in a locker room: laughter, tears, anger, elation, dejection, alienation, fraternity, friction. Confidence and despair are often only a locker apart. Players' relationships change from happiness to hostility and back to happiness within a matter of minutes. Strong bodies go out from the locker room and broken bodies return. Some grown men tremble with fear—the fear of pain, of the opponent, of the future. Other grown men fear nothing . . . even when they should.

The locker room is a melting pot and a meeting place. Blacks, whites and even an occasional Mexican come from different parts of the United States, and different life styles, to band together for one common purpose: to beat the other guys. Racists and militants join with those who have devoted their lives to God and those who are devoted to a life of raising hell.

A locker room has its own personality and its own scent. Helmets and uniforms hang in lockers, with a pile of football shoes at the bottom of each one. Players have a special language—"male language"—they wouldn't use at home. Guys lift weights, sit in whirlpools, play cards, talk on the phone, kibitz, pull practical jokes, get taped by the trainer, get taped by the media, drink Gatorade, smoke, chew tobacco, get to know one another.

The locker room is like the office you work in or the store you run. When the work day is over, it's time to leave. After practice is finished, I'm one of the first players to shower and get out. I spend most of my life in a locker room, and I don't want to spend any more. A lot of guys like to sit back after practice, light up a cigarette and relax. To me it's a job. I work hard when I'm there. When the work is done, I go home.

When I first came into the NFL, there was considerable talk about the game being dehumanizing. Chip Oliver and Dave Meggysey, former pro linebackers, alluded to this in books on their lives. I've never believed it. Sometimes

things are a little cruel, but it isn't dehumanizing. Someone
gets hurt in practice and the trainers take care of him while
you continue practicing. That happens in high school and
college too. Ignoring a teammate who is being treated while
you are practicing doesn't mean you don't care about him.
I'm sure he'd feel the same way if I was hurt and he went
on practicing. Broken bones and torn muscles go with the
job, which isn't the case when you work in a bank. Those in
pro football who think the sport is dehumanizing have the
right to leave. A few have, but most don't. Meggysey
coaches high school football now in California. I wonder if
he finds the game less dehumanizing.

John Mazur told me I was on a 3-year quarterback
plan. I was being brought along slowly in order to pay divi-
dends later.

Mazur wouldn't be around for the fulfillment of that
plan.

Because we finished strongly in 1971, the coaches and
management believed we had the material to keep on winning in 1972. We didn't make any off-season improvements.
I can't remember one new player in '72. That was the start
of our downfall.

Cincinnati left us in a heap, 31–7, in the opener. We
scraped by Atlanta, 21–20, and Washington, 24–23, then the
levee broke and our season washed away. We lost 9 straight
games. Not once in that span did we hold a team under 24
points. Twice we didn't score a point. From 6–8, we plum-
meted to 3–11. We were lucky to win the three.

The physical abuse was worse the second year. My
sacks increased from 36 to 39. It took me a lot longer to get
up after I was hit. My rookie year, we played one quarter of
catch-up. My second year, we played 3 quarters of catch-up.
This meant I was passing on every down and getting hit
almost every down. Defensive linemen used me as a blocking dummy. I would need a knee operation after the season.

Dwight White drove a forearm under my facemask in Pittsburgh, closing one eye and puffing up a lip.

I started smoking, something I had tried, then given up as a kid. For the first time in my life, the media were really on me. Instead of cheers from the fans, I now heard jeers. I picked up the phone and called Hoop.

"Jim, remember one thing," he said, "those aren't Stanford alumni out there. Those are professional football fans who feel they own the team. You have to accept that."

I couldn't. I took the booing and the media comments personally. I stopped smoking, but the only time I was happy, if you could call it that, was when we played away. Then I wouldn't have to face the New England fans.

My touchdown passes dropped horribly from 19 to 8 and my interceptions climbed embarrassingly from 16 to 25. I ranked dead-last in the NFL's passing statistics. Over a 6-game stretch, I threw no touchdown passes. Sure, the defense made it rough on me. We gave up 446 points, the only team in the league to give up more than 400. But I made it rough on the defense by forcing passes.

One of my favorite passes over the years has been the hook pattern. I threw it a lot in college and during my rookie season. In 1972, opponents took that pass away from me by mixing up coverages. They forced me to look for other ways to complete passes, but I was slow adjusting. I was young, stubborn and still tried to get the ball to my hooking receivers. The ball never got there. It took 25 interceptions before I realized the extent of my bullheadedness.

Mazur yanked me from the Jets and Miami games. We were taking a bad beating. No longer was I the aggressive, big-play thrower. I had become a defensive quarterback. Instead of one foot behind the other, looking for receivers, my feet were squared, ready to run at the first glimpse of enemy colors.

I knew the pocket would break down and I would have to run for my life. There was no place to go with my speed. I was Jim Plunkett, not Fran Tarkenton. One time at Three Rivers Stadium, the day Dwight White nailed me good, I was hit so many times (6 sacks) that I felt like a condemned building being beaten on by a wrecker's ball. A band at Three Rivers captured the feeling of the afternoon by playing the "Anvil Chorus."

I wasn't the only wreck on the Patriots. With each defeat, Mazur put more hours in, slept more in his office. The carnage lay all around him. He failed to see that he soon would be part of it.

Upton Bell made it clear before the start of the season that Mazur wasn't his kind of coach. Only a vote of confidence by the players insured that Mazur would be back in 1972. Bell was pinned in a corner.

The ninth week of that disastrous season, Miami got even for the previous year's defeat by breaking the Patriots into little pieces, 52–0. Everyone knew what that meant. Mazur was gone. Phil Bengtson was named interim coach, but he was in a suicidal situation, just as he had been replacing Lombardi in Green Bay. Bengtson was let go after the season, and so was Bell.

Upton's dream was to own a football team. His father, Bert Bell, had been NFL commissioner before Pete Rozelle. Upton's critics carped that he became a general manager in his early thirties only because of his father's good name. Upton then got into the radio talk-show game.

What happened to us in 1972 wasn't entirely John Mazur's fault. Let's face it: There wasn't much foresight shown in the general manager's office.

My birthday came around again late in '72. Some reporters asked me if I expected the fans to sing happy birthday to Randy and me again.

"They may sing something," I responded, "but it won't be happy birthday."

For the first time in my life, I couldn't wait for the season to end.

"The biggest problem was that Jim was billed as The Franchise from the start. People believed that, especially after his first year. The next two years were bad years. It soon became obvious everything that happened to the Patriots, good or bad, was attributed to Jim. I absolutely maintain that no quarterback, I don't care who he is, can look good without the support. After 1974, everyone's expectations were high again. In '75, Jim got hurt, came back, got hurt, came back, got hurt again. The frustrations of the fans hit a peak. 'Plunkett's never going to take the team anywhere . . . he doesn't hit his secondary receivers . . . he doesn't throw the ball quickly enough . . . he's not this, he's not that.' I don't think the whole thing really hit Jim until the day the fans booed him in unison before the Dallas game. There will always be a little scar in him from that day."
        —RANDY VATAHA

The Patriots received front-office resuscitation in 1973 when Chuck Fairbanks was named general manager-head coach. He was a big winner at the University of Oklahoma, but a man who didn't talk much. You needed pliers to pull the words out. The players had to pay close attention because he spoke softly, slowly and infrequently.

One thing he told me, though, rang like church bells. He promised more pass protection by holding in the backs to block and relying on three-man patterns.

Fairbanks's strong suit was that he knew talent. His first three New England draft picks in '73 were Alabama guard John Hannah, USC fullback Sam Cunningham and Purdue wide receiver Darryl Stingley.

Bill Nelsen was named quarterback coach. He was a former quarterback with brittle knees. He lasted 10 years in the NFL by dropping back quickly and getting rid of the football before the pass rush got to him. He taught me the same strategy.

We became a better team. Our hopes began to rise again.

The Patriots' record improved to 5–9. My touchdown passes increased moderately from 8 to 13 and my interceptions dropped approvingly from 25 to 17. I moved from last to 16th on the NFL passing chart. Our offense improved its points scored by 66 and our defense cut down its points surrendered by 146. The sickly Patriots were getting well again.

Green Bay sacked me just once and I threw for 348 yards and 2 touchdowns and ran for a third.

"Funny," Bob Windsor, our tight end, said after the game, "it makes a big difference if you're not throwing from a prone position."

So true, so true.

The media weren't as hard on me in '73, though I became the No. 1 Boston talk-show target after Eddie Kasko was relieved of the Red Sox manager's job. At Foxboro, the fans were taking out their frustrations against me in a different way that fall. I called my favorite attorney.

"Hoop, I've solved the booing, but now they're throwing things."

"Jim, catch everything that's edible."

Thanks a lot, Hoop.

The 1973 season was harder on me from a personal standpoint. Gini and I broke off our relationship. We always thought we would get married. The time I asked her to marry me, she said no. Other times, I said no.

I've always been shy around girls anyway. I'd be afraid to kiss a girl good night sometimes. I was always a gentleman, overly cordial in fact, which could have been partly the result of shyness. I'm not as shy around people now, because I've continued to grow in confidence as a person.

I didn't date much in Boston while Gini and I were on opposite sides of the map. I already had a girlfriend and I didn't care to get to know other girls closely. All that does is complicate things.

Gini was a big part of my life and I love her to this day in a special way. She is a wonderful woman, the greatest person I have known in my life.

"I met Jim in English class our senior year. I was impressed with his physical appearance, then found out that he was quiet, shy, a nice person. There are so many aspects to Jim; he is not an easy person to describe. What impressed me about him was his inner strength and his close relationship with his family. What intrigued me about him was that he had a lot of boyishness in him—a sparkle in the eye, a little giggle. One of the special things about our relationship was that I didn't know what football was. This has been a problem for Jim, wondering if people like him because of him or because he is a football star. Jim always has known that I liked him because of him. I was a dependent person at the time we dated, very dependent on Jim. Having him away in New England, was forcing me to grow up too. I had to find out about myself, what I needed in life to be happy. It was bad timing all the way around. Jim will always have a special place in my heart."
                                        —GINI CAMPBELL ANNIS

During the 1973 season, Fairbanks decided to call all the plays. After the season, I flew from California to Fairbanks's summer home in Michigan specifically to talk about play-calling. I was adamant. If I couldn't call my own plays, Fairbanks should trade me. He agreed to let me call the plays. I left feeling a whole lot better.

Near the end of the '74 season, Fairbanks began calling the plays again.

Fairbanks thought like a college coach even though

he no longer was one. He insisted on using the quarterback option—a college play—on the pro level. In the option, the quarterback takes the snap from the center and runs left or right along the line of scrimmage. It's a deceptive play in that the defense isn't sure whether the quarterback will keep the ball or pitch it to a trailing back. It's a very effective play on the goal line or in short-yardage situations. But it can get a quarterback hurt.

The option's main weakness is that you must have enough quarterbacks to make it through the season, because a quarterback will absorb much more punishment running the option than he will dropping back and standing in the pass pocket. One guy might hit you in the pocket, but a number of guys will hit you if you're running. Just ask me. I'm living proof.

Fairbanks traded for Jack Mildren, who ran the option for him at Oklahoma. The Patriots listed Mildren as a safety, but every day after practice there would be Mildren at quarterback working on the option with the offensive coaches.

Once Fairbanks installed the option, Patriot players feared that he would go one step beyond and put in the Wishbone offense, which is also as much a part of college football as cheerleaders and card stunts. The Wishbone is a run-oriented offense with three backs lined up in a "V" behind the quarterback. I knew Fairbanks wouldn't use it, although he gave the impression that he might. There wasn't enough time to coach the Wishbone, option, drop-back and everything else.

I believe Fairbanks's main reason for using the option was plain stubbornness. He wanted to prove a point, that a college play could make it on the professional level. I have the surgical scars to show that it can't.

The Patriots started out with a blaze in 1974—coming within 5 points of winning their first 8 games. But our season ended in a puff of smoke.

Miami, the New York Giants, Los Angeles, Baltimore and the New York Jets fell to make us 5–0. Then came two disappointing losses to Buffalo, 30–28 and 29–28, sandwiched around a courageous 17–14 victory at Minnesota.

Courageous, as in Bob Windsor. There were only seconds left to play when Windsor caught a pass near the Viking goal line. He was hit as he made the catch, tearing knee ligaments. Somehow, and I'll never know how, Bob fought his way into the end zone for the winning touchdown. Patriot players were out of their minds with excitement. We didn't even know Bob was hurt. He was lying there in excruciating pain. The injury finished his career, even though he tried to play one more year. His teammates will never forget how he said farewell.

Over the last half of '74, we resembled a fife-and-drum corps, bandaged and battered. We lost our other tight end, Bob Adams. Cunningham and Hannah suffered broken legs. Reggie Rucker broke his wrist and Vataha had a deep thigh bruise. I managed to last out the season playing with a torn hamstring, torn knee cartilage and a sore throwing shoulder that required cortisone shots before each game.

We lost 6 of our last 7 games because we simply ran out of people. We had no depth. John Tanner played tight end and defensive end in our final game, a 34–27 defeat at Miami that evened our record at 7–7.

Without the injuries, we felt we would have made the playoffs. We planned on making them in 1975.

Meanwhile, Wayne Hooper met with the Patriots in November, 1974, to discuss a 5-year contract extension that Hoop believed would make me the highest-paid NFL player, surpassing Namath's $250,000 annual salary with the Jets. Despite the hard times in Foxboro, the Patriots believed in me and my future. We never got close enough to finalize a deal, but there didn't seem to be any hurry. I still had one year to go on my first contract.

The Patriots were concerned for awhile that I might

jump to the World Football League, which prompted New England's attempt to renegotiate my contract in '74. The Portland Storm of the WFL drafted me first in a selection pool of NFL players. I talked to Ron Mix, the Storm's general manager, who offered me a one-million-dollar package. I wasn't interested. The league looked shaky to me financially. Its chances of lasting permanently were about as good at the Pet Rock.

It was fun coming home to California after the 1974 season, although California is a nice place to be at any time of the year. The scenery is great, so is the weather, and so are my friends. The whole thing is idyllic, really.

One favorite place is Lake Tahoe, half of which is in California and the other half in Nevada. Even in June, there's a little snow on the mountain, yet the weather is warm. It's a gorgeous setting, and the beauty of it draws me back again and again.

When I get an invitation to play in the Harrah's Celebrity Golf Tournament at Lake Tahoe, it takes me all of a half-second to say yes. I used to shoot ducks when I first played golf at Stanford. Then I began taking lessons and found that I could hit the greens just as easily as I could geese. My game dropped down into the eighties, sometimes the low eighties.

I always have a good time at celebrity tournaments, whether it is golf or tennis, because I enjoy meeting people. The only thing I don't like are the cocktail parties. You answer the same questions all night. I try to gravitate toward someone I haven't met who might have something interesting to say, but that kind of person isn't always there at a cocktail party. So sometimes it's a drag until we leave for one of the shows playing at the numerous casinos at Lake Tahoe.

There are many beautiful parts to California, including the Monterey-Carmel area. Carmel is a charming,

ocean-side town with quaint shops and restaurants. There is
the picturesque Seventeen-Mile Drive and Pebble Beach,
where Bing Crosby decided to hold a golf tournament forty
years ago. I also enjoy Monterey and eating along Steinbeck's Cannery Row. I've been to the Monterey-Carmel
area a hundred times, and it is as alluring as the first time I
saw it.

California's wine country, which is centered in the
lovely Napa Valley, is just as inviting. There are wineries
throughout the valley ranging from internationally recognized vintners to little mom-and-pop places where the
wines are often just as good. I enjoy a good bottle of wine
with dinner as long as it's dry, and prefer Cabernet Sauvig-
non for a red. Although I like California wines over French
wines, I do like a Puligny-Montrachet or a Pouilly-Fuissé for
a white.

How can you beat California? You can't. The rocky
coast, the smooth beaches, skiing in the Sierra Nevada or
picnicking in the wine country. You can enjoy them all on
the same weekend. California weather also offers a variety
of choices, such as jogging in a t-shirt in February. Try this
in the Midwest and they'll need an ice pick to find you.

I don't want to sound like a snob, though, because I
do enjoy other parts of the United States. Hayden Lake in
Idaho is breathtaking, a miniature Lake Tahoe. I don't often
get that laid back. I enjoy that kind of living, but only for a
little while. I like the excitement of being around people and
games, and that means California, which is home. I don't
ever want to be too far away.

Though the Patriots wanted me for five more years,
I wouldn't last that long if I kept running the option. The
1975 season bore this out.

It was the final pre-season game against San Diego
when I became part of a Bacon-and-quarterback sandwich.
Charger defensive end Coy Bacon grabbed me from behind

while I was running, pinned my arms and threw me down on the Astroturf. Bacon's 280 pounds landed on top of me. My left shoulder was separated.

"If you'd have seen it happen, you'd have said, 'That's it. The kid's through for the season.'"
—WILL McDONOUGH

Our injuries were mounting already. Besides myself, offensive tackle Tom Neville, defensive tackle Arthur Moore and defensive end Julius Adams wouldn't play in the opener.

I didn't know when I would be ready. The decision was made to put a plastic screw in my left shoulder to speed the healing process and get me back in the lineup as soon as possible. That would be six weeks.

Fairbanks remained positive for public purposes. "You don't shoot all the dogs because one gets hurt. We'll have to go with what we have." Neil Graff took over for this dog while a young pup, Steve Grogan, waited for his chance.

New England played four games and lost all four. The wolves in the stands began howling at the dogs down below. The team was losing and the coaches wanted me back in the lineup. Like a fool, I came back.

I'm a player, not a sitter, and if the team says it needs me, I'm going to play. The shoulder wasn't strong or close to being healed. The doctors strapped on a harness with a chain that prevented me from lifting my left arm more than six inches away from my body. I started against the 49ers.

Twice in the first quarter I ran the option—the play remained in the game plan, injured quarterback or not—and pitched the ball to halfback Andy Johnson. 49er linebacker Dave Washington taunted me.

"You ought not to be running like that," he warned, "because you're going to get hurt."

He was right. Three plays later, I took off on another

option to my right. 49er defensive end Tommy Hart
stepped into the path of the trailing back. There was nothing
for me to do but turn upfield, exposing my left shoulder. I
didn't see Washington hit me, but I sure felt him. The shoulder gave out again.

I went back into surgery to have the plastic screw
removed. Washington's hit had dislodged it. I experienced
considerable pain from the incision where the pin was taken
out. Doctors said taking it out cost me about 25 percent of
the progress I had made.

Grogan replaced me in the San Francisco game and
threw 2 touchdown passes to spark the Patriots' 24–16 victory. Grogan became an instant hero in Foxboro. I read all
about it in my hospital room.

The coaches called the play on which I was hurt
against the 49ers. On short-yardage situations, they called all
the plays. I told reporters afterward that I would have called
the play on which I was hurt, and for a reason. It was part
of the New England offensive system and I wasn't going to
work against the system.

My only complaint is that if your quarterback keeps
getting hurt by the system, why not change, or at least alter,
the system? It makes a lot more sense than continually
changing quarterbacks. Fairbanks wouldn't do this. He
knew I would continue running the option even at the risk
of further injury. What choice did I have? In my mind, this
whole thing didn't speak well of Fairbanks or his judgment.

Three weeks after the 49er game, I started against
Dallas. Fairbanks asked me how I felt. I said "fine." So he
started me. Ask a player with a broken leg how he feels and
he'll say "fine." Sometimes, for his own safety, a player
should be held out of the lineup, but right or wrong, this is
the exception, not the rule. The Patriots were having a bad
season, it was Fairbanks's third year and the wolves were
howling. I was thrown to them.

New England fans may be the most vocal, and opinionated, of all NFL fans. Win a couple of games and they start talking Super Bowl, lose a couple and they are ready to join a vigilante mob.

I expected to be booed before the Dallas game. Grogan had played well the week before in the 33–19 victory over San Diego. He was the new hero of the moment. I was used to scattered booing, so I was ready. I thought.

"At quarterback, No. 16 from Stanford, Jim Plunk—"

The public address announcer was drowned out by a sonic boo. Five years of frustration were welled up in one long deafening, thundering, stadium-shaking boooo . . .

OK, maybe I was partly to blame for the problem. But it wasn't just me. The Patriots were losers before I got there. No one booed Billy Sullivan. No one booed Chuck Fairbanks. No one booed the rest of the players.

Well, the whipping boy was through with being whipped. There would be no more booing this quarterback in Foxboro after December. If Patriot fans had given up on me, I had also given up on them.

I had to do well against the Cowboys that day or things would only get worse. And they did, physically. The Cowboys sacked me 6 times. On the first sack, something gave in my right knee. I wasn't going to come out and let the wolves feast on me again. I stayed in the game.

I threw for 3 touchdowns and scored a fourth. We lost, 34–31. I strained ligaments in the knee. I never played again for the New England Patriots.

"You know what I think?" center Bill Lenkaitis told writers after the Dallas game. "I think what they (the fans) did to Jim Plunkett today is bull—"

Lenkaitis is a good man. Dr. Bill Lenkaitis. He is a practicing dentist in the off-season. Drills on his teammates' teeth. The other Patriots are nice to Bill or he might drill without first giving them novocaine.

Bill is the one who first introduced me to Gerry Lavelle at a party not long after the Dallas game. Gerry is from Cleveland and was a buyer of bridal gowns for a Boston store. She and I started talking. She asked me to dance. I said, "No way." My knee wasn't in the best of shape, but I don't dance well or often as it is—no confidence, Gerry told me. She got me to dance anyway.

You never know what it is that attracts people to one another. Gerry and I just hit it off. The way my football career was going in New England, this wasn't a particularly good point of my life. But Gerry and I began to date, which kept that autumn from becoming a total disaster.

The Patriots lost their last five games of the 1975 season to finish a deflating 3–11. The '75 Patriots highlight film should be titled: "Déjà Vu: Remember '72."

I was in no way threatened by Steve Grogan. My situation had nothing to do with Grogan's potential, which everyone could see was excellent. Y. A. Tittle gave me some good advice a long time ago that I have never forgotten.

"They always want the quarterback who isn't playing."

He meant the fans, and he was 100 percent right. When Tittle was a young quarterback with the 49ers, the fans wanted the old quarterback, Frankie Albert, off the field. When John Brodie was a young quarterback with the 49ers, the fans wanted the old quarterback, Tittle, off the field.

When Grogam fumbled the ball away a couple of times against Buffalo after I hurt the knee, the fans chanted: "We want Plunkett."

No more. You've had me. No more.

It was during the tail end of the '75 season that I made up my mind to leave New England. It had been a traumatic five years and now it was time to say good-bye.

It wasn't Boston, the city. Walking down the Freedom Trail past the Old State House, the Old North Church and Paul Revere's house, I felt a sense of history in Boston.

It is a great city, with great culture and charm.

I was treated well in Boston away from the football field. I liked wearing tuxedoes to all kinds of gala events. And I enjoyed being the toast of the town, even though I often got burned on both sides.

I wasn't leaving because of a need to be near my mother, which Billy Sullivan would later say was the heart of the problem. It *is* true I wanted to play on the West Coast, however.

But I would have stayed in New England if not for Chuck Fairbanks. He was the main reason I wanted to leave.

It was impossible to talk to the man. He improved the franchise, made the Patriots a playoff team in 1976. But I needed someone to communicate with and Fairbanks wasn't the kind of person that I or anyone else could communicate with very well.

Fairbanks wouldn't talk. He just wouldn't talk. And if someone won't talk to you, it is hard to work out problems —like the quarterback option and who should call the plays.

Hoop and I had a contract session with Fairbanks and Patriot executive Peter Hadhazy. Fairbanks addressed Hoop.

"Well . . . Wayne . . . it's . . . nice . . . that you could . . . come all the way . . . across the country . . . to . . . talk about . . . Jim . . . "

"My God, Jim," Hoop told me later, "at the rate of speed Fairbanks was talking, I thought we were going to be in there for days."

I told Hoop that Fairbanks was in one of his faster talking moods.

Three years after I left New England, Fairbanks was suspended by Billy Sullivan for the last game of the season. The reason: Fairbanks was recruiting assistant coaches and high school prospects for a coaching job he was planning to take with the University of Colorado. Not only hadn't he told Sullivan about his leaving, but Fairbanks supposedly was preparing the Patriots for the playoffs. I'm sure the New England players felt let down. It was a very underhanded thing to do.

You can make light of it, but as soon as Fairbanks left Oklahoma, the school went on probation. As soon as he got to Colorado, the school went on probation. I'm not saying that he was responsible in either case, but some bad things have been following him around.

The Patriots had no alternative but to trade me to the team of my choice. I had the leverage, the "hole card." If they attempted to deal me to a team I didn't prefer, I'd tell that team: "Look, I'll play for you in '76, but then I'll play out my option and won't be back in '77."

Money wasn't even a determining factor. The Patriots offered me more money to stay in New England than what the 49ers eventually paid me to play in San Francisco. That was okay; playing in San Francisco was the important thing.

I considered two other clubs, Los Angeles and Denver, though not strongly. John Ralston was Denver's head coach and he later told me, "If I had gotten you, I'd still be the head coach."

Denver offered running back Otis Armstrong and defensive end Barney Chavous for me. Los Angeles was ready to part with defensive tackle Larry Brooks and free safety Bill Simpson. Fairbanks was interested more in draft picks, because he didn't want players who were established in other cities and who might be unhappy in New England. Fairbanks wanted college players who didn't know any better, like Jim Plunkett in 1971.

The bartering between San Francisco and New England was back and forth, give and take, across 3,000 miles. The 49ers gave me a physical and I was pronounced fit. It was finally decided that San Francisco would relinquish its first two choices in the 1976 draft and its first two choices in the 1977 draft, plus quarterback Tom Owen. I was a 49er.

Just before the trade was consummated, Larry Claflin, *Boston Herald American* sports columnist, made this comment:

"Plunkett never wanted to play in Boston in the first place, but he took it like a gentleman and made the best of it. Now, as he seems certain to leave, he is still the gentleman. The fans who booed him out of town should wish him nothing but the best."

Those were nice words. I will always remember Boston as a positive experience. There were some rough times, but I hope we parted friends.

On April 5, 1976, the 49ers' new quarterback met the media at San Francisco's Fairmont Hotel. I was all smiles. Coming back home, playing in front of the hometown crowd . . . I was filled with excitement and anticipation. I would help make the 49ers a winner again, get them into the playoffs, get me into the playoffs—

I was primed for my greatest success.

Chapter Five

NO ORDINARY JOE

"If the Nick Buoniconti deal was the worst one we ever made, this [Plunkett] one is the best—by just as wide a margin."
                —PAT HORNE, New England Patriots official,
                                        September, 1977

Will Rogers wouldn't have liked Joe Thomas.

Thomas is the one person in my life that I have come the closest to hating. I don't dislike Chuck Fairbanks; we had our differences, that's all. But I can't see one good side to Joe Thomas.

He had a perfect 2-year record in San Francisco—he treated the 49er players, the fans and the media all the same. Badly. Thomas destroyed the 49er franchise, just before he destroyed himself in San Francisco.

Thomas came to the 49ers after creating chaos on the Baltimore Colts. He then drove Monte Clark, a qualified head coach, out of San Francisco.

Qualified head coaches wouldn't work for Thomas, not after what happened in Baltimore. So he hired three unqualified 49er head coaches, wouldn't let them do anything, and all three were gone in twenty-one months.

Thomas was still at war in Baltimore with his head coach, Ted Marchibroda, when I was traded to the 49ers. If Thomas had already been in San Francisco in 1976, I would have gone to Denver or Los Angeles instead. But with Monte Clark running both the 49er front office and the coaching office, I felt in good hands. Monte was interested in my safety, which was more than I could say for Chuck Fairbanks.

Monte Clark promised me that I wouldn't have to run the option in San Francisco. We both believed in an old football saying: There are a number of young running quarterbacks and a number of young passing quarterbacks, but there are no old running quarterbacks.

Clark defended the trade for me that cost the 49ers the front end of two drafts. "Jim is a premier quarterback . . . " he told the media. "There are no quarterbacks like that in the draft. This [trade] is a cornerstone, though we are more than one or two players away from what we want to achieve. While the 49er name doesn't have a ring to it now, in time we hope to be the best in the business."

Six months later, though, Clark began to doubt the trade. He felt like he had given up a Mercedes for Jack Benny's Maxwell: a sometimes starter with a habit of sputtering and breaking down.

The 49ers, since John Brodie's retirement in 1973, had changed quarterbacks faster than Lily Tomlin changed characters. Steve Spurrier, Joe Reed, Dennis Morrison, Norm Snead and Tom Owen had all started in a 2-year period. Dick Nolan tried to get Billy Kilmer from Washington, but the 49er front office vetoed the trade. Nolan's failure to find a replacement for Brodie led to his firing as head coach. Monte Clark was then brought in to run the football operations, and he put together the deal with the Patriots for me.

The spring of 1976 was a time of promise for the 49ers, Monte and me. Everything looked so good. The Golden Gate Bridge was never more majestic, the sourdough at Fisherman's Wharf never tasted better, the cable cars never clanged as happily.

I was home. Really home.

I signed a 3-year contract calling for a $200,000-a-year base salary plus a percentage of increased ticket sales (51,-284) over the previous season.

Money never has been the driving force in my life, even though I spent my first twenty-three years without it. I have made good money in comparison to what quarterbacks are making—some earn more, some less—but I haven't gone overboard to make it. If money were all I was interested in, I would fill up my personal calendar with appearances. I do some of that—especially if it involves charity—but I'd rather have the free time to myself.

To me, money is security, and I'm lucky to be in the position where I can apply it toward my future and not hospital bills. I'm getting paid well, but I've paid too—with my body.

It's probably my background, but I'm a believer in frugality. I don't buy the first item I see. I will look around and compare prices if it means saving money.

This doesn't mean I'm cheap. Even when I didn't have money, if it was my turn to buy a round for the guys, I bought it and worried later where the money was coming from.

I can still remember holding that $75,000 bonus check and looking at it. I couldn't believe that such a small piece of paper could be worth so much money. I was happy and excited all at once. I wanted to put it in the bank and do something constructive with it, like having my mother's house remodeled.

By the time I returned to San Francisco as a 49er, my tastes in material possessions were developed. I selected things that were functional, comfortable and economical.

I'm a little like my 1973 BMW automobile. I'm functional, I don't like much nonsense and I like to get things done. I've kept the car all these years because it handles well, it is comfortable and I like it—it's my toy.

I'm not like some athletes who want a new car every year. I have one other car, a 1978 Mercedes sedan. I don't like small cars because I don't fit in them well. And I don't want to get mangled if I hit a tree. I like to have a lot of metal around me. My two cars fit me fine. If they keep doing the job, I'll keep driving them.

My house in Atherton, which I bought while playing for the 49ers, is functional too. It's fairly small for a house, nothing elaborate. I could have bought a more showy house, but this one is out of the way and you can't see it from the road. It has a sense of privacy, and I'm a private person.

The house sits on one and a half acres, not far from Stanford University. I had a tennis court built, because I love to play the game and the court adds to the value of the property. So does the swimming pool I use to stay in shape.

I dress functionally too, wearing jeans and corduroy pants most of the time. I've taken to wearing cowboy boots. I suppose it's the "Urban Cowboy" influence, but the boots are comfortable and give good wear. I take pride in the way I dress, though I don't think I'm that great a dresser. My clothing is conservative but comfortable—fashionable enough to wear in San Francisco's financial district. Comfort in clothing is important when your collar size is seventeen and a half and your shoe size thirteen. My biggest concern about clothes is finding them.

My tastes in food are easier to satisfy, because I will eat anything. I grew up on a basic Mexican diet, but I like

Japanese food, Chinese food, French food, Persian food . . . all foods. That's a problem of mine: I love to eat.

I chose Atherton as a place to live, because it's safe and comfortable. It has an affluent population of about 8,000, and people tend to keep to themselves, making it a quiet location. People who live there are extremely interesting because they've traveled to different parts of the world, met famous people. I'm a football player, but no one in Atherton is awed by it. I like that.

Celebrity status hasn't unduly affected me or my relationships with others. I'm courteous and friendly toward people I know or have just met, but I have always been like that. I'm an extension of what I am, not something fame has made me.

I enjoy talking to people, so being asked for my autograph isn't usually an imposition. I almost always sign. I don't mind, and it is more trouble to say no. Some athletes don't like to, and will try to explain their reasons to people holding out autograph books and pens. They could sign and be on their way in half the time it takes them to get out their explanation. Besides, I wouldn't want to be a kid and have an athlete turn me down. That would be so depressing for a youngster who probably mustered every ounce of courage he had just to ask for a signature.

I will say no to autograph seekers if I am having dinner. I'll ask them if they will wait until I have finished eating. Once in a while, I get a smart reply. I might go tit-for-tat and give the person a smart reply in return. But that doesn't happen often because I generally go out to places where people already know who I am and don't think it's a big deal that I'm there.

Now, though I have more money than most of my friends, I'm happy to say that they act the same toward me. We all take turns picking up the check. However, if we go to an expensive restaurant, and I feel the bill will be a problem for them financially, I'll grab it.

This doesn't bother me. They do nice things for me too. We've always been comfortable around one another. I think my friends, if you talk to them, would agree that money and whatever success I've had haven't changed me. If they felt the opposite, it would really bother me.

"Jim's a model in a society where athletes are paid well and the media exposure is tremendous. He is portrayed, unrealistically, as a . . . Superman. He is a two-personality guy. With the media, he has usual, normal answers. With us, he'll lean over and punch a guy in the arm. It makes me grin."
—DAVE OLERICH, former NFL player and friend of Jim
Plunkett

"I don't think anything has ever gone to Jim's head. He's never forgotten where he came from, never gone too far one way or the other. He's always had a good perspective about the success he achieved and what it means in relation to him as a person. He always has been Jim. He's a breath of fresh air in the whole pro football business."
—RANDY VATAHA

The 49ers were 11 defensive players in search of an offense when I got there. San Francisco had a great front four in Cedrick Hardman, Cleveland Elam, Jimmy Webb and Tommy Hart; the 49ers set a club record of 61 sacks in 1976. This foursome had a flamboyant side and a quiet side.

Hardman was colorful and quotable, a tremendous pass rusher who designed his own clothes and had designs on a movie career. Forty-Niner teammates dubbed Cedrick "Fontana Wagonwheel, the next cowboy star" and built a wooden horse, "Sugar," which they hitched to Cedrick's locker. Hart, the other end, was a man of few words who saved his money with the same determination that Cedrick spent his. Webb wanted to be a veterinarian. Elam, like Garbo, *vanted* to be left alone. Every time Cleveland was interviewed, he played poorly the next week. He had few interviews—and fewer bad games—in 1976–77, and he made the Pro Bowl each year. Elam's career fell apart in 1978 when Joe Thomas switched him from tackle to end.

We had talented linebackers. Dave Washington felt bad about taunting me in Foxboro; he is a nice person, very religious. Willie Harper came out of a Toledo ghetto, Skip Vanderbundt out of the California Mother Lode. Frank Nunley was called "Fudgehammer," because he was as soft as fudge and hit like a hammer.

The cornerbacks were Bruce Taylor and Jimmy Johnson. Usually it's the quarterbacks who bring out the wrath of fans, but in San Francisco, Taylor was the fans' target. Bruce was a good player, but he happened to play the same position as Johnson, one of football's all-time great cornerbacks. Johnson was beaten on the bomb just once his final season, 1976, at the age of 38.

The safeties were Mel Phillips, one of the toughest and most underrated players in the game. Phillips once played with two broken arms. He'd walk through airport security and alarm bells would start to chime. He'd empty his pockets, take off his watch, and the chiming continued. It turned out the problem was the metal plates inside his arms.

Ralph McGill, the free safety, was once kicked in the head by placekicker Tom Dempsey while attempting to block a conversion kick against Los Angeles. "I thought he was dead," a Rams player said later. After some time in the hospital, McGill was back at safety.

This defense gave up just 190 points in 1976—only 2 teams, Pittsburgh (138) and Minnesota (176), gave up fewer. The Steelers and Vikings made the playoffs that season; the 49ers didn't, although we gave every indication that we would by winning 6 of our first 7 games.

My first league pass as a 49er was run back for a touchdown by Packers safety Johnnie Gray. Great beginning! I recovered to throw 2 touchdown passes to Willie McGee and we took the season opener, 26–14, in Green Bay. The Clark regime was off to a successful start.

The following week, though, was anything but a happy homecoming for me and the team. The Chicago Bears nearly drove us into San Francisco Bay in a 19–12 defeat for us that was as bad a 7-point thrashing as a team can receive. The Bears overpowered us. I was sacked 6 times and thought to myself, "Oh, no, not again." A 13-yard touchdown pass to Delvin Williams with 90 seconds left made the final score look close, but both teams knew differently.

The booing started in fragments, but by the second half it was cascading down on us from the upper deck at Candlestick Park.

Welcome home, Jim.

Booing, I learned to my chagrin, is a national and not a regional affliction.

A quarterback's life was even less safe behind the 49er offensive line, a patched-up unit called the "Soup Line." Everybody's rejects, it seemed, came to San Francisco to play offensive guard. Woody Peoples and John Watson, the two starters, were out with injuries, Peoples for the year. Steve Lawson was brought in from Minnesota and Andy Maurer from Atlanta to play guard. Castoffs Rocky Rasley, Mark Nordquist and Dick Enderle spent time at guard too. None of the five lasted more than a season. The center was a rookie, Randy Cross, and the tackles, Keith Fahnhorst and Jean Barrett, were very young.

Despite the line's transient look, it pieced together well, but it wasn't the kind of forward wall that would inspire confidence in a quarterback who remembered just such a line in New England. After 14 sacks my first preseason in San Francisco, I realized I was still on the run.

My statistics against the Bears weren't bad—19 for 29 and 173 yards—though it would be written that I played poorly.

Delvin Williams rushed 16 times for 25 yards in the same game. When something like that happens, it's the poor blocking of the offensive line. But if the quarterback passes badly, he is the only one at fault.

Gene Washington pointed out the contradiction after the Chicago game, but I wonder how many caught it.

"Jim's the best passer in football," said Washington. "He's throwing the ball as well as he has ever thrown it, but he has got to have some support. Not even Bob Griese could do any better without proper support. It's got to be a team effort."

A quarterback is one-eleventh of his offense. If the other ten parts aren't functioning properly, the quarterback won't either. It's very simple. Yet a reporter came up to me after the Chicago defeat and said, "Now be honest, you didn't have a very good game." I hated that reference to being honest. If he didn't think I was honest, he shouldn't have asked me the question.

It is questions of this tone that breed general distrust of the media among athletes. I've always tried to be honest with reporters, even though it sometimes hurts to admit your failings. Because if you're going to stand up and talk about the glory, you also have to stand up and talk about the grime.

The media sometimes enjoy making fun of an athlete, ripping him to shreds. Athletes are human beings with human feelings. A writer who may not know what in the hell really goes on on a football field will say a player has no guts, no character, or that he's a quitter. This is almost character assassination. An athlete thinks to himself, "What if my family reads this?"

The media tend to put athletes in general categories. Terry Bradshaw was called dumb. How would the media

know if he's dumb or not? Reporters who don't have anything to write about some days create an analysis of the
team. If they are inaccurate, which sometimes happens,
does anyone call *them* dumb? Next to inaccuracy, this
categorizing is the biggest complaint athletes have of the
media.

There are reporters who are serious about their work
and do excellent jobs, and for the most part, I've been
treated fairly by the media. If something bad is written
about me, I don't hate the guy who wrote it. But I do get
angry at times, like before the 1980 American Conference
championship game in San Diego. Some reporters from
Washington, D.C., asked for a half-hour interview. The Raiders had just flown into town. I was tired and wanted to catch
some sleep before a team meeting that night. So I told them
no.

Those same writers told a reporter I know: "Jim
wouldn't give us an interview. We always thought he was a
nice guy." That really bugged me. Most of the time I bend
over backward to give interviews. The one time I didn't,
they got all over me.

A reporter asked me after the 1981 Super Bowl if it
was the greatest moment of my life. Every five minutes he
would ask me the same question. I tried to be patient, but
after the fourth time I shouted: "I DON'T KNOW IF THIS
IS THE GREATEST MOMENT OF MY LIFE!"

Give me a break, guys.

The 49ers recovered from the Chicago disaster to win
the next 5 games, including a 4-game string where the defense recorded 2 shutouts and held opponents to 9 points.
The highlight was a 16–0 Monday night victory over the
Rams in Los Angeles. Tommy Hart may have played the
greatest game ever by a defensive end, with 6 sacks, 2 forced
fumbles and 1 recovery.

At the halfway point of the season, the surprising
49ers were the leaders of the NFC's Western Division, and
the talk of pro football. We were moving ahead with a full
head of steam when, inexplicably, the steam went out of my
throwing arm.

Quarterbacks, like hitters in baseball, have slumps. I
had a horrible, unexplainable slump over the last half of the
1976 season. I still don't have the answer on what happened.
There were a lot of assumptions, but no concrete explana-
tions. There was nothing wrong with me physically. It might
have been a mental problem—lack of confidence in my line,
plus a fear for my health renewed from New England—that
led to problems of technique in my throwing motion.

Throwing a football is comparable to painting a canvas or playing a piano. You have to practice often enough to
stay at a high performance level. The difference is that Beethoven didn't play the *Moonlight Sonata* and van Gogh
didn't paint *The Potato Eaters* with Mean Joe Greene charg-
ing at them from the blind side. And van Gogh's canvas and
Beethoven's piano weren't moving targets like pass receivers.

I know one thing: I lost my throwing rhythm in 1976.
I wasn't getting enough time to pass, whether real or imagined, so I would throw the ball quicker than I should have.
This meant I was throwing off my back foot instead of stepping into the throw. Consequently, one pass would be high,
another low, another off-target completely. I was inconsis-
tent.

Quarterbacks, like pitchers, also get sore shoulders
and elbows. Football elbow is like tennis elbow. My elbow
bothered me part of the 1976 season and also in 1980. I
cleared it up each time with exercises.

In any event, I lost my throwing touch in 1976 at an
inopportune time, with the 49ers facing a tougher schedule
over the second half of the season.

I noticed the difference in my passing at St. Louis the

eighth week of the season. I was missing receivers who were open. I thought, "That can't be me." The problem continued and there was nothing I could do to stop it.

We lost that game 23–20, in overtime. A freak thing happened at the start. Our kickoff return men, Anthony Leonard and Paul Hofer, both ran up to block. No one fielded the kick, which St. Louis gladly recovered for a gift touchdown. Near the end of regulation play, Steve Mike-Mayer missed a close-range field goal that would have given us the victory.

I felt pressure building on me to regain our earlier momentum. I became cautious, afraid to make a mistake. I called more running plays, dumped off to my backs more, took off running out of the pocket before giving my receivers a chance to get open. I'm a mentally tough guy, but I was no longer the aggressor. And it showed in my throwing, which became timid, half-certain and off the mark.

I always felt I was the best thrower in football; this is nothing more than my confidence speaking out. I looked at a football as just an extension of my arm. I could get the ball anywhere, long or short. I've lost that feeling only twice in my life—in 1972 and the last half of 1976.

So many things can throw a quarterback off. It's a vulnerable position. You can hold on to the ball too long or not long enough. You can hold your ground in the pocket too long or not long enough. The receiver slips on a wet spot and goes down, and you've got to find another receiver in a hurry because there's a defensive tackle two steps away from putting his helmet right under your chin.

A quarterback who is pounded-on a lot begins to watch for and fear flashes of colors in the corner of his eye, which means the enemy is near. Most quarterbacks have experienced this fear. (One who hasn't is Ken Stabler. He is amazing; he stays so unfazed.) So many things can happen to a quarterback, which explains why it is difficult for a quarterback to be consistent year in and year out.

Quarterbacks are unique. That's why I defend them so religiously. They take the snaps, they make the handoffs, they drop back and find receivers, they throw the completion that wins the game, they throw the interception that loses it. On third-and-one, the quarterback hands to a running back who gains only a half-yard. Maybe there was a breakdown in the offensive line, but the quarterback—in the minds of the fans and coaches—should have called a better play.

Only the center and quarterback touch the ball every play, except in kicking situations. Once the center gets rid of the ball, he's through with it. He has to find his man to block. If he misses the block, it's not noticed. If the quarterback misses the pass, it is.

Like I say, it's a unique position. It's the only one I want to play.

It didn't help matters in 1976 that Willie McGee broke his leg midway through the year. McGee and Washington gave us two deep threats. When McGee went down, we traded to Minnesota for Jim Lash, a good receiver, but not fast. Defenses saw this and began doubling Washington, who was playing with a broken wrist as it was. From that point on, the 49ers went to a control passing game with a quarterback whose passing was out of control.

Delvin Williams was something special over the last half of that season. He rushed for a team-record 194 yards in St. Louis, then came back with 180 more against Washington the next week. We combined on an 85-yard touchdown pass, the longest in 49er history up to that point, but we lost 24–21 when Mike-Mayer missed a makable field goal down the stretch.

Things deteriorated further in Atlanta. The players were ready to play, or so they thought. Monte Clark said he had never seen a team so excited before a game. It was only make-believe. We were flat and the Falcons left us flatter, 21–16. Three straight losses.

"Jim Plunkett is one of the two most talented quarter-backs in the league," Rams coach Chuck Knox said a few days later. He didn't say who the other quarterback was. Knox may have re-evaluated his thinking after I completed only 6 of 18 passes against Los Angeles for 35 yards, no touchdowns and 2 interceptions, one of which was returned for a touchdown by a Ram. Los Angeles flung us around like rag dolls, 23–3. Four straight losses.

By now the 49er coaches were worried. I was lifted from the Rams game and replaced by Marty Domres. Clark and Doug Gerhart, the 49ers passing game coach, were openly critical of my performance, joining a growing cast of thousands.

"Psychologically, it didn't help [Plunkett] when we had offensive linemen meeting for the first time when they got to the line of scrimmage during exhibition games," Clark was quoted. "The knowledge of that and what his protection would be like both started in Jim's mind. But we've made progress up front. Look where we came from. Our quarter-backs have been sacked about on the average in our conference."

Clark was right. I would be sacked 26 times in each of my two seasons in San Francisco. The abuse was far worse in New England. I may have left the Patriots behind, but not the memories. Only now things had deteriorated to the point where I feared the *idea* of being sacked. I was a fidgety quarterback who was ready to run at a moment's notice— running from myself as much as the defense.

Gerhart told the media, "Jim's more of a set-up thrower, but he couldn't get into the groove of a nice set-up because of the pass rush. I'm thinking now of studying some old films on Jim. He's like a Jack Nicklaus who is off his game. Jim's always been a big-play guy who never really established himself as a percentage passer. I'm trying to help him be consistent. It also looks to me like he has lost some snap and strength in his arm."

It wasn't my arm. I had been lifting weights, and my passing arm was as strong as ever. Gerhart was nearly all theory. He'd tell the quarterbacks: "If you read this key, you go there." That's great, but if the guy is covered, what do you do then? He didn't tell us that.

Percentage passing isn't my game. You can complete 5 or 6 in a row and not get a touchdown. On the other hand, you can hit 1 or 2 long ones and they might break a team's back. Terry Bradshaw and I are alike. We're not high-percentage passers, but we come up with the big play because we look for it and because we can also run.

Gerhart was correct in one regard. I was off my game. And everyone but Jack Nicklaus was offering suggestions on how I could straighten out. Nothing seemed to work.

"Wayne Hooper talked to Monte Clark, who said the way Jim was wandering around, he didn't think Jim cared that much about football. That's an incredible thing to hear. He cares about football more than anything in his life with the exception of his family. I don't think there is a quarterback in the league who works as hard as Jim. In the off-season, he runs five to six miles a day, plays three or four sets of tennis, then will throw the football for as long as you want. The problem with Jim in San Francisco was that he put too much pressure on himself. No one expected as much from him as he expected from himself. He made himself out to be the savior. That was the horror of the whole thing."
—BOB MOORE

Monte Clark's system was fairly simple. It was the same system Miami used when Monte was offensive line coach under Don Shula. The Dolphins had a quick back in Mercury Morris and a big back in Larry Csonka. Williams was our speed back and Wilbur Jackson our fullback, though Jackson looked like a skinny colt next to the bullish Csonka. We'd line Delvin up in the I-formation and run him behind

Wilbur, who was a good blocker. We also were run-oriented. There was one difference. We didn't have Miami's line.

Monte is a big man. He stands 6' 6", which makes him taller than all NFL head coaches and most of his players too. He is an imposing figure, weighing 260 pounds, and he uses his largeness as a coaching device. He knows how to get on people. He will scare you because he screams and yells a lot. Monte coaches by using fear and it works.

He gets a lot out of his players, even those who are given up on by previous clubs. "Monte is like a street fighter," Hardman said. Monte is articulate and humorous with the media, but he's no-nonsense on a football field. He'll come down on a player in a second if he doesn't think the player is doing the job.

This is what happened between us: He was critical of me in the press. We played an exhibition game in Los Angeles and the Rams' front four worked me over. In a statement to the press, Monte said, "A lot of times, Jim had the time to throw. . . ."

That really upset me and I told Clark so.

I banged up my ribs against the Rams later in the year during our fourth straight defeat and couldn't play in a Monday night game against Minnesota. Rookie Scott Bull of Arkansas replaced me. He only had to throw a half-dozen or so passes because Jackson ran for 156 yards and Williams added 153. San Francisco beat the Vikings, 20–16, to make its record 2–0 that fall on Monday night.

The coaches didn't say it publicly, but I knew they were gaining confidence in Bull and losing confidence in me. I was healthy enough to start in San Diego when I found out just how much confidence Monte had in me.

Clark started calling the plays for the first time that season.

This time, I wasn't bothered by the idea. It had happened so many times in my career that perhaps I was now conditioned. If it was temporary and would help the team, then fine. We needed help.

A coach's calling the plays on a consistent basis isn't necessarily a good idea, though Tom Landry in Dallas would disagree. My feeling is that the ball should be kept moving —the players moving quickly in and out of the huddle—for one reason: defensive linemen get tired. If the plays are shuttled in from the sidelines, it takes longer and gives the defensive linemen extra time to catch their breath.

The 49ers and Chargers played to a scoreless tie for three quarters. I heard that a sportswriter in the press box stood up in the third quarter and "gonged" this boring offensive show.

The pressure was worse than ever—I was more cautious, more defensive, more off-target. One pass to Delvin was overthrown by 5 yards and intercepted. I hit on 7 of 13 passes for 55 yards and couldn't get the team anywhere near the Chargers' end zone.

Monte had finally had enough. He took me out with 1:13 left in the third quarter and started screaming at me. He was feeling the pressure too and he really let me have it. I wasn't used to that and I sure as heck didn't like it.

Most quarterbacks are emotional and sensitive. It's the nature of the beast. What we go through, only a quarterback can appreciate. I feel problems between a coach and player should be kept private anyway. If a coach yells at you in front of the team, teammates could lose confidence in you.

Let's face it, whether you are an athlete, bus driver, lawyer or secretary, everyone needs a pat on the back once in a while. We all need positive feedback. I don't crave it; it's just nice to have.

When Monte started yelling at me, I was stunned, then stung, then angry. Things were bad enough on the field. He acted as if I were deliberately trying to screw things up.

I didn't lash back. I folded my arms, bore my resentment silently and stared across the field. All I could see was red.

Bull ducked a Charger blitz and dumped the ball off to Hofer, who valiantly fought his way for a touchdown. The Chargers eventually won in overtime, 13–7, and Monte was really angry with Mike-Mayer, who had missed 11 of his last 15 field goals, costing us 3 possible victories and a playoff berth. Mike-Mayer hadn't signed his 1976 contract and there was only one game left.

"We've got to get better in our kicking," said Clark. "Either he [Mike-Mayer] does it or we'll have to get someone who can. It's the same law of survival for both of us."

Ironically, neither Mike-Mayer nor Clark would return in 1977.

Monte said after the loss to San Diego—our fifth in six games—that I was still the No. 1 quarterback. By Tuesday, I was No. 2.

Bull would start the season finale in New Orleans. When Monte told me the news, I was really upset. He tried to explain that I was under stress and that it would be better if Scott played. I knew Monte's responsibility was to the team, not one player. He had to do what was needed to win. However, I tried to convince him that I was OK, that I should start. He genuinely felt the 49ers had a better chance of winning without me.

I was benched.

Meanwhile, the Patriots had made the playoffs with Steve Grogan at quarterback. New England used the 49ers' first two 1976 draft picks and selected Colorado center Pete Brock and Ohio State free safety Tim Fox. With San Francisco's first two choices in '77, the Patriots drafted Texas cornerback Raymond Clayborn and Oklahoma running back Horace Ivory.

At the halfway point of the '76 season, the 49ers were 6–1 and the Patriots 5–2. There was talk in New England about a 49er-Patriot Super Bowl. Then after the 49ers faded, all of New England—the Patriot organization, the media, the fans—was gloating over the rise of the Patriots and the fall of Jim Plunkett.

But I was pulling for the Patriots in the '76 playoffs, mainly for Randy Vataha, Bill Lenkaitis and Julius Adams, the guys I had played with who had worked so hard and survived all kinds of adversity to get there.

I wanted to be in the playoffs too, only with San Francisco, not New England.

One thing you learn in football: if you aren't playing, you aren't part of the team. Coaches talk a lot about football being a "team game." What they really mean is the guys who are playing. Those who aren't playing don't count. I've never been on special teams; I don't hold for placekicks.

So when I didn't play for the 49ers that final week in New Orleans, I was just a body.

A useless body.

Bull led the 49ers to a 27–7 victory. I received less exercise than anyone in the Superdome that day. I waited on the sideline for someone to yell, "Plunkett, warm up!" No one yelled.

It was an awful way to end the season. Heck, it would be an awful way to start. Once again, I was glad it was an away game.

Clark made it appear after the 8–6 season that I was very much in his plans for 1977, though he also made it clear that my hold on the 49er quarterback job was no longer firm.

"Don't write Jim off," Clark told a reporter. "Everything is there. He just needs to get his confidence. I don't think the story is over yet. To count Jim out now, you're not giving credit to the tremendous competitive nature that brought him to where he was. I'm counting on Jim coming back next year. But he has to do it. I can't."

In my mind, all that was needed was to find out what

went wrong in '76 and work out the flaws. I would be better than ever in '77 and we would be a definite playoff contender.

My '76 season statistics were average—51.9 percent on completions, 13 touchdowns, 16 interceptions—which placed me 17th among NFL passers. However, I sat out 2 games.

"Statistics are like loose women," said Monte in my defense. "Once you've got them, you can do anything you want with them."

The same thing applies to head coaches who find themselves in the hands of new ownership.

The following spring, Edward J. DeBartolo, a shopping mall and race track magnate from Youngstown, Ohio, peeled a measly $17 million off his $460 million bankroll and bought the 49ers from the Morabito ladies, at that time the only female owners of an NFL team.

The 49er ownership prior to the sale had consisted of three general partners—Josephine Morabito and Jane Morabito, widows of previous 49er owners, and the club president Lou Spadia—and nine limited partners, including ex-49er quarterback and head coach Frankie Albert and Golden State Warriors owner Franklin Mieuli.

The 49er owners had tried to sell the team before, without success. In desperation, they looked across the bay to Al Davis, the Oakland Raiders' managing general partner. In an unusual business arrangement, Davis agreed to find an owner for the team that was in competition with the Raiders for the same Bay Area sports dollar. Davis came through and received a "finder's fee" worth six figures. Some say $100,-000, some say more. Davis hasn't said.

Joe Thomas knew the DeBartolo family. Al Davis knew Joe Thomas, who had traded him a washed-up Bubba Smith for a young racehorse named Raymond Chester. Edward J. DeBartolo talked with Al Davis. Soon a deal was struck with the 49ers.

Monte Clark wouldn't be part of it. He wasn't about to work for Joe Thomas.

The two knew each other from Miami, where Thomas was eminently successful as a college scout. The two didn't like each other, which wasn't too surprising. Thomas wasn't easy to like.

Joe Thomas had first tracked the bushes for Baltimore, where he gained some clout by convincing the Colts to take Wisconsin fullback Alan "The Horse" Ameche over Georgia Tech linebacker Larry Morris in the first round of the 1955 draft. Ameche scored the winning touchdown in that 1958 overtime game with the Giants.

Thomas moved on to Minnesota and then Miami. Wherever he lent his Midas touch, his employers were as good as gold in talented rookies.

In 1967, Thomas was prepared to do a dastardly thing in Miami that would create controversy from Sonesta Beach to the alligator swamps. He was going to pass over Florida's Steve Spurrier, a state hero and Heisman Trophy winner, and draft Purdue's Bob Griese. The 49ers took Thomas off the hook by trading with Atlanta and grabbing Spurrier one spot ahead of Miami's turn in the first round. Thomas breathed a sigh of relief.

Spurrier never wrested the job from Brodie in San Francisco, though he kept the club in the 1972 playoff hunt while Brodie mended from an injury. Griese directed Miami to three straight Super Bowls, including two victories, and a perfect 17–0 season in 1972. Thomas had done it again.

Thomas worked his way up to Colts general manager in 1972 in an interesting sleight-of-hand shuffling of franchises. Robert Irsay bought the Los Angeles Rams and then completed football's most expensive "trade" by swapping ownerships with Baltimore's Carroll Rosenbloom. Irsay named Thomas to run his football operations.

Thomas believed his magic touch would cure all ills in the front office just as it had in the personnel department. After sending Johnny Unitas off to San Diego, Thomas bushwhacked New Orleans on draft day, 1973. The Saints gave up their No. 1 pick for Colts defensive end Billy Newsome and a No. 4 draft pick. Thomas used that choice to snare Bert Jones, who quarterbacked the Colts to the playoffs in 1975–76–77. Newsome played two years in New Orleans and was gone.

Outside of a boundless ego, Thomas's biggest problem is that he is an incurable meddler. Three months after assuming power, he fired Colts coach Don McCafferty and replaced him with John Sandusky. Four months later, Thomas hired Howard Schnellenberger as head coach. That relationship lasted 19 months before Thomas fired Schnellenberger and named himself head coach. Thomas won 2 games, lost 9 and the Colts finished 2–12, their worst record in history.

Ted Marchibroda was chosen head coach for 1975 and directed the Colts from last place to first in the AFC East. Thomas tried to fire Marchibroda in '76, but the Colts' players came out in support of their head coach. The hostility between the general manager and coach reached such a pitch that Irsay stepped in, sided with Marchibroda and fired Thomas.

The DeBartolo regime officially took over in San Francisco on March 31, 1977. Edward J. DeBartolo, Jr., 31, became principal owner and team president, with Mieuli and Jane Morabito the limited partners. Eddie, as the young owner likes to be known, preferred to stay in Youngstown, leaving the 49ers under the control of Thomas as the general manager.

Control was the operative word. Clark had control of the 49er football operations, which meant drafting, trading and coaching. Thomas wanted control of the first two, relinquishing the third grudgingly. He had tried to do all three in Baltimore and it hadn't worked out.

Monte refused to give up his power. He knew what he was doing. Thomas fired him, which meant the DeBartolos were stuck with the remaining four years of Clark's contract.

Thomas named Los Angeles assistant Ken Meyer as head coach. Meyer's system was similar to that of the Rams, with the fullback running off-tackle. This system was feasible in Los Angeles with Lawrence McCutcheon and a strong forward wall, but not in San Francisco where the line wasn't that strong.

Meyer found himself in instant trouble. He was working for a new ownership determined to become an instant success in San Francisco. Meyer also was hired late, which meant there would be no veterans' mini-camp in which to learn his system. The playbooks arrived late.

If you are a good football team, all of this may not be a problem. If you were the San Francisco 49ers of 1977, it was.

Joe Thomas is an egocentric. We all have an ego; he just let his get in his way. His ego definitely clouds his judgment. He is too caught up in Joe Thomas to see things clearly.

He enjoys telling everyone he meets about what he's done in Minnesota, Miami and Baltimore, leaving out the friction he created in Baltimore. Thomas never mentions the bad things, just the good he has done, the players he has drafted. Getting Bert Jones was no big deal; any general manager would have made that trade. New Orleans was dumb enough to make it.

I've talked to other people who have known and worked with Thomas. Their opinion is that Thomas hasn't done nearly all the things he has claimed, yet he has taken the credit and bragged about it from ocean to ocean.

Thomas loves to tell how he kicked Johnny Unitas out of Baltimore, without even giving Unitas the credit he deserves for making the Colts a great franchise. Thomas is so proud of getting rid of Unitas. He brings up the story all the time, without anyone's asking.

Monte Clark has the respect of the 49er players. None of the three head coaches Joe Thomas hired in San Francisco had the players' respect. Pete McCulley, who replaced Meyer in 1978, wouldn't even be a good assistant coach. Fred O'Connor, a 49er assistant who replaced McCulley halfway through the '78 season, was a guy with a Napoleonic complex who yelled and screamed a lot. O'Connor was let go after the season.

These are the men Joe Thomas hired—the only men he could get.

The 49ers lost 9 straight in 1978 after I had left the team. Following one defeat, Thomas barged into the dressing room and screamed: "If you guys do this to me, I'm going to take you down with me."

Thomas told one veteran who refused to sign his contract: "How would you like to play in Green Bay?" Delvin Williams also threatened to become a free agent, then signed his contract. Thomas traded him anyway, to Miami.

"Joe Thomas destroyed the mold of the 49ers and a winning attitude built up by Monte Clark. Thomas got rid of me, Dave Washington, Cleveland Elam and Tommy Hart, all Pro Bowl players in '76. All Joe did was create a low-base salary. In letting quality players go, he didn't put any quality players back. He traded me away as I was going into my fourth season and brought in O. J. Simpson, who was going into his tenth season. That doesn't make sense."
—DELVIN WILLIAMS

Some coaches are more interested in fat content than how you play the game of football. Meyer is one of these men. I feel 215 is my best weight. He wanted me down to 207 to help my ability. (The Patriot coaches wanted me that light in '72 and I had a bad season then too.) My weight dropped to below 200 in San Francisco because I was on a salad diet. When I get too light, I get hurt. All the weight comes off my upper body because I'm too bottom-heavy. I was thinner and faster in '77, but my ribs had no protection and it was only a matter of time before they were broken.

Meyer not only took away my red meat, he took away my plays. He called the plays over our first 5 games, and we lost all 5. Then he let me call the plays and we won 5 of the next 6. Still, we didn't exactly overwhelm people. After Monte left, we just weren't very well prepared.

I broke some of my ribs against Atlanta in the fourth game. My throwing was affected. I told Meyer that I didn't want to hurt the team and if he wanted to start Bull, it was OK with me. Meyer replied that even though I was injured, I wasn't hurting the club with the kind of offensive errors a younger quarterback might make. He would appreciate it if I stayed in the lineup. I told him I would.

Three weeks later the pain was so bad that I told Nick Vlasoff I wanted to quit the game. I didn't think it was worth it. I had trouble raising my throwing arm. The only reason I could was that I was shot up before our games. Ribs are a painful injury. When you laugh you cry. When you cough you almost die. Imagine what it's like when you get sacked!

"Jim had two broken ribs and another one cracked. But he's a company man. If he signs something, he plays. I saw him in a gym. He took off his shirt and I couldn't believe it. His whole side was black with all these holes in it from being shot up. It looked awful."
—NICK VLASOFF

"I felt sorry for Jim playing behind a makeshift line. If your tackle can't handle the defensive end on the blind side, the quarterback has to think about that. Then Jim got the broken ribs. He took his shot before the game, went out and played. He never said a thing to the media, his teammates, no one. I really admire Jim."
—DELVIN WILLIAMS

I completed 51.6 percent of my passes in 1977. Playing for my third head coach and third new system in 3 seasons, I threw 9 touchdown passes and 14 interceptions.

Those aren't great statistics, but statistics sometimes lie. As the quality of the team you play for increases, so do your statistics. The 49ers then were a bad team. We finished 5–9 in '77, losing 8 of the 9 games by margins of 1 touchdown or less.

We were just good enough to lose.

I had spent 7 NFL seasons, all on non-winning teams. New England and San Francisco, when I was there, had to play at a high performance level in order to stand a chance of winning.

If we went up against a Dallas or Pittsburgh, we were in awe. We'd say among ourselves: "Let's make this game close."

In Oakland, it is different. The players say: "Let's beat these guys." The Raiders have instilled in their players the belief that they can't lose, that somehow they will find a way to win.

Certainly the difference in winning is talent, but attitudes and combinations also play a part. New England, Dallas, Pittsburgh and Los Angeles generally were considered the most viable Super Bowl candidates before the 1980 season. None of the four made it. Talent on paper isn't as important as talent on the field. Oakland found the right combination of talent in 1980, blended it together with a positive attitude and didn't stop improving as a team until it captured the Super Bowl.

The single most important facet of winning football is being able to keep the game close enough so that you can win. If you throw a 95-yard pass that cuts the opponent's lead to 35–7, no one cares. If you throw a 95-yard pass that breaks open a tight game and helps your team win, everyone notices.

I played a lot of fine games in New England, but no one remembers because we lost. In San Francisco, I threw 4 touchdown passes and ran for a fifth score against Dallas. Who remembers? We lost.

We had the Vikings beaten, 27–7, late in the third quarter, but lost, 28–27, when Tommy Kramer threw a long touchdown pass against a "prevent defense," which is specifically designed to stop the long pass. It was ridiculous.

Seattle had Oakland down, 17–7, in the fourth quarter in 1980. I threw a 50-yard pass to Derrick Ramsey at the Seahawks' 1-yard line. People remember that pass because it meant something—it was on Monday night TV, it helped us win the game, get to the playoffs and make the Super Bowl. It was an important pass. Yet I threw similar passes in New England and San Francisco, and all they helped us do was lose by a more respectable margin.

Football must be played well to enjoy the game. When you lose, it isn't fun. You're getting knocked around and have nothing to show for it except a body that goes "clink" in the night when you try to sleep. When you win, the pain isn't so bad. It almost seems worth it.

I remember a football game from junior high school when I was really having fun. I was running, passing, throwing blocks, having a great time. I was also smiling. Our school principal told me later that he couldn't believe I was smiling. But I was enjoying the game. It was a close game and the adrenalin was really flowing.

When you get in games like this, you're too excited to be nervous. It's a great experience. I'd rather play in a close game any day than win 45–0. It's not fun beating someone 45–0 every week. If I went out and beat Bjorn Borg 6–0, 6–0 in tennis I would really be disappointed. I want to hustle and run and get to the ball, make some great shots. I want my opponent to do the same thing.

This is what sports are all about—close hard-fought competition. Struggling, rallying, come-from-behind. Big games. Championship games.

This where you show your stuff.

That feeling was there in high school and at Stanford, but not in New England and San Francisco. And I couldn't see things getting any better with the 49ers—as long as Joe Thomas was there.

For the first time I began to doubt that I would ever achieve the same end result in pro football—the Super Bowl —that I achieved in college football—the Rose Bowl. The Super Bowl now looked as far off as Shangri-la and about as attainable.

With each defeat in 1977, I drew further within my-self. Normally I like to separate football from my private life, to get away, clear my head. But I stayed home more and more in San Francisco. These were tough years; people didn't let me forget. Someone might make a smart remark toward me in a restaurant; if I wasn't in a good mood, which I wasn't most of the time, I might make a smart remark back.

I couldn't forget about what happened the previous game or the previous day. My food tasted bad and my beer tasted flat. My salads tasted awful. I was really watching my weight at the time, and I was mostly eating salads. My waist was shrinking and so was my future.

I began calling friends, especially Jack Lasater, Pete

Lazetich and Jim Kauffman. All three have strong, positive attitudes. Lazetich's humor is something else; he has played the pro game too, so he has a feel for what goes on. They made fun of my situation, trying to boost my spirits. All three talked about the good times we had at Stanford. I always felt better after talking to them. They were able to assuage my depression—at least until the morning.

"During the season I would get calls from Jim. I knew he wasn't calling to say 'hi.' He was down or worried or depressed. He never asked me what to do, but by his calling that's what he was saying."

—JACK LASATER

At about this time, Gerry Lavelle moved from Boston to San Francisco to take a job as a buyer. We began dating again. Gerry seemed to enter my life when times were bad. She is a terrific person with a big heart and a willingness to listen to all my problems. We became Doubting Thomases together.

Thomas spiced his two-year turbulent stay in San Francisco by nearly coming to blows with a 49er beat reporter in a disco at the hotel in which the team was staying before a game with the Redskins in Washington.

The sportswriter had excoriated Thomas in an article. Thomas had to be restrained from attacking him.

"I'll get you," Thomas screamed at the writer while being dragged from the disco.

Ken Meyer was fired after one season. It wasn't unexpected. Thomas alibied that he had been rushed into hiring a coach his first year and had grabbed Meyer at the last minute. Now Thomas was free to hire his "own man," which turned out to be McCulley, the one assistant coach in Baltimore who backed Thomas in the Marchibroda embroglio. Thomas hadn't forgotten.

Meyer hadn't helped himself by screaming at his wife

on the plane home from a 49er away game, and by asking reporters after a defeat: "What plays would you guys have used?" Getting McCulley wasn't much of an improvement.

McCulley was big on physical fitness. He claimed: "I've found the Fountain of Youth in the weight room." He was 46, looked 35 and was proud of it. But he aged the players 10 years with some of his ideas.

He installed hydraulic lift systems at the 49er practice field. He was completely in reverse on how they should be used. McCulley wanted the players to lift weights before practice, thereby tightening up their muscles and making them more susceptible to pulls on the practice field. Smart thinking.

McCulley sincerely believed lifting weights meant a winning season. If a player improves from 350 to 500 pounds on the bench press, this will make him stronger. But not necessarily a better player.

John Brodie once said something that makes considerable sense: "There are a lot of impressive-looking bodies in the locker room that are nothing more than pieces of meat. There are also a lot of funny-looking bodies in the locker room who are great players."

The size of the heart is more important than the size of the bicep in football. So is the size of the mind. At our quarterback meetings, I felt I knew more about defenses than Pete McCulley.

The '78 season started out with more veterans being given their walking papers by Thomas. We were now so young and inexperienced that I couldn't see myself making this team a winner. Not for at least two seasons, if then. I was 30 years old. My No. 1 enemy had changed. It was no longer Thomas, but the calendar.

I really began to miss Monte Clark. I didn't agree with all the things he had done as a head coach, but he had made the players confident.

Al Cementina dropped by training camp in '78.

"Jim, are you healthy?" he asked.

"Physically, yes," I replied. "Mentally, no."

McCulley told the 49er press corps: "I've never been around a quarterback who worked any harder than Jim. And he's whistling the ball. I've always thought that he was a good passer."

McCulley was my fourth head coach in four years, which meant my fourth new system. My fourth straight losing season (the Patriots were 7–7 in 1974) was all but assured.

McCulley is a man of little imagination. He had coached at Baltimore and Washington, and now merely incorporated parts of both systems as his own. The 49ers used a lot of quick slants, quick outs, throwing to our backs. The idea was to create the big play by sucking the secondary in to stop the short play. McCulley wanted me to sprint out like Joe Theismann. My style is dropback, not sprintout. Hadn't I been through this somewhere before?

I played well in the pre-season opener against Dallas, completing 9 of 14 passes for 160 years and 2 touchdowns, with no interceptions. We were ahead, 24–21, when the veterans came out. We eventually lost, 41–24, but I was pleased with my first performance.

Two weeks later, it all came undone in Oakland. Eleven passes, 11 incompletions. I was more afraid than ever to make a mistake. I wish I had only thrown 1 pass in the pre-season finale at Denver, because that was all I completed—and even that one depended on a great catch by Freddie Solomon.

One didn't have to be a mystic to know that I wouldn't play again for the San Francisco 49ers. There were rumors that Gene Washington and I were on the trading block. Thomas liked what he had seen of a young quarterback, Steve DeBerg, and Thomas was satisfied with Bull. Why shouldn't he be? Keeping those two and getting rid of me would save Thomas $100,000.

The 49ers are honored before each season at a Cham-

ber of Commerce luncheon in San Francisco. The team
practiced that morning, put on coats and ties, then bused to
the luncheon. I was a featured speaker. After we got back
to the practice field, McCulley said he wanted to see me.

I knew what that meant. It was standard procedure.

The 49ers had released me. I had gone through waiv-
ers, McCulley said, and no one claimed me. My friends,
especially Jack Ditz, were not only incensed later on to find
out that I was cut, but how I was cut. Thomas allowed me
to talk to a luncheon group about the upcoming season,
knowing all along that he would release me that same afternoon.

"That's unforgivable," Jack told me.

"That's Joe Thomas," I told Jack.

Thomas wasn't around when I was cut. He didn't
have the guts to tell me himself. He left it up to McCulley,
who also told Gene Washington he was cut.

Thomas later told the press that DeBerg was the
starter. The biggest choice Thomas said he had to make was
who would be the backup: Bull or me?

"Scott was about the same as Jim," Thomas said, as if
that explained his decision.

I got in my car and drove away. My initial reaction
was one of relief. I was happy to get out from under Joe
Thomas. God, how good that felt! My time with Thomas, and
the 49ers, was the worst experience of my life.

Then reality set in. Cut! I was humiliated. I wasn't
good enough to play for anyone. What had happened to me?
I was a nobody, a nothing.

I called my mom so she wouldn't hear it on the news
first. I opened up a beer, took a deep swallow and sat down.

I took a good look at myself and what I saw was an
ugly mess. The best quarterback in the NFL? Sure thing.
The best ex-quarterback, maybe. I was really down, lower
than I had ever been. My confidence was shot. I was a disaster.

There was only one thing to do: change professions. I couldn't stand any more heartbreak. I would get out of the game.

Big deal. I was already out of the game. No one wanted me.

Friends heard the news. They rushed over, tried to console me. "It's not your fault," they all said. "It's the situation." They tried to lift my spirits, but couldn't. There weren't enough of them.

I felt bad for my friends. No one wanted me to succeed more than they did. I wanted to do well for them. But now it was over. My Super Bowl dream was dead, buried with my football career. My friends could read my epitaph in the next day's sports section on the NFL waiver list. My career had gone from headlines to agate type.

Bob Moore came over the next day. He had just been cut by Tampa Bay. His career looked over too. We spent the next two weeks together, playing tennis, drinking beer, talking. Bob said he was going to write a book. He wasn't being realistic. It was a hard time for both of us.

"Jim and I were suffering pretty badly, like two lost souls. He kept saying, 'It's all over. I've got to think of doing something else.' It's a real empty feeling, rock bottom, when you're suddenly out of football and nobody's terribly interested. For some strange reason, while Jim repeated that he was through with football, I kept thinking that what he really wanted was one more shot."

—BOB MOORE

Chapter Six

THAT LEFT-OUT FEELING

"Al Davis works with a Pygmalion syndrome. He takes players who haven't made it elsewhere, for whatever reasons, but who have ability. Then he rehabilitates them . . . exactly like he did Jim Plunkett."
—WAYNE HOOPER

Hoop called.

"Jim, the Oakland Raiders phoned. They'd like you to come over for a tryout."

"The Raiders? You've got to be kidding. They've already got Ken Stabler."

"They just want to watch you throw the football. I get the feeling, Jim, that they're really interested."

"What about the other clubs?"

"Well, I've talked to the Colts, Packers and Giants. Those are the only three interested, and they all need quarterback help. But you know Bert Jones is going to play in Baltimore if he's healthy. I told the Colts that. The thing you have to decide, Jim, is whether you're going to get a legitimate chance to start. It may not be worth traveling all that distance just to be a backup."

"What more of a chance would I have in Oakland?"

"They've got a great offensive line, for one thing. You've never played behind a line like Oakland's. This is what you really need to get your confidence back."

"I know that, Hoop, but what difference does it make? Obviously, I'm not going to play there."

"I'm not so sure, Jim. I have a feeling Kenny may not be around. It may not be this year or next year, but I've got a hunch. . . ."

Lawyer's intuition. Al Davis isn't going to get rid of Stabler, not after The Snake won him a Super Bowl two years before. Even if Hoop is right, why would Davis want me? Nobody else seems to.

Then again, I'm tired of playing on bad teams. The last thing I want or need is to pack my bags again and sail off into the unknown. Oakland does have stability and pass protection, even if it doesn't offer playing time.

To be a backup in Baltimore or a backup in Oakland, that is the question. To travel 3,000 miles when the same predicament is 50 miles away, that is the answer.

"OK, Hoop, I'll do it. Where do I go, how do I get there and what time?"

I never wanted to play for the Raiders. I never even liked them. The 49ers were my team. The Raiders dressed in black, the Hell's Angels of football. Their owner had a ducktail, for crying out loud.

I had heard all the Al Davis stories and believed them: He was devious. Besides his 45-man roster, he had 20 other players stashed somewhere in Oakland, paying them, working them out on the sly.

He was commissioner of the American Football League and tried to steal all of the NFL's top quarterbacks. Before that, as a USC assistant coach, he got the Trojans in trouble with the NCAA over recruiting violations.

The man is trouble. He comes from Brooklyn and talks like Dixie. He dresses in black and white, with blousy shirts and baggy pants. Who is his tailor, the Fonz? Davis must be the worst-dressed millionaire now that Howard Hughes is dead. The last place you'll find Al Davis is in *Gentleman's Quarterly.* The first place you'll find him is in trouble with the NFL.

And the football team he owns, if it isn't a halfway house, it's just down the road. Do I want to get involved in all that? Yes. What choice is there? But I'm not going over there alone. I'll call Kauffman.

"The worst I ever saw Plunk was on that drive over to Oakland. He was really low. It had been a miserable two weeks. The Raiders have an arrogance, a spitefulness that no one is going to beat them. Plunk needed to assume that kind of attitude."

—JIM KAUFFMAN

I wasn't sure what would happen at the tryout because I had never been to one. I hated to drag Kauffman along because the day before he'd lost one tooth and half of another diving into my swimming pool. When he talked, he whistled. That didn't bother him, but nothing ever does. He went over and stood next to Al Davis while I threw passes. The two of them talked. Well, Davis talked and Jim whistled.

Two Raider assistant coaches, Tom Flores and Lew Erber, watched me throw; John Madden, the head coach, wasn't there. I felt nervous and awkward. I threw to Larry Burton, who was cut by the Saints after they drafted him No. 1. He didn't catch on with Oakland, but wound up later in San Diego.

Kauffman whistled with excitement all the way back to Atherton. He thought I looked good and he believed Davis thought I looked good. I wasn't sure until Hoop called.

"Jim, be in my office at 1 P.M. tomorrow. Al Davis will be here."

We met in the law office library. Hoop smoked a pipe and listened. Davis said he always liked me as a player and that Joe Namath and I were the two best quarterbacks he had seen come out of college. Davis wanted to sign me to an Oakland contract, but he had to get rid of a quarterback before I joined the team.

I mentioned the other clubs interested in me. I wasn't the least bit interested in them, but I didn't tell Davis that. He was miffed, regardless.

"Look, Jim, you'd be crazy not to sign with the Raiders. You'll never play behind an offensive line like the one we got in Oakland. You understand what I'm saying?"

I knew exactly what he was saying. But what was Davis's motive? Everyone thinks I'm a 30-year-old washout and he wants me. Why?

"Stabler has bad knees and we need backup insurance. Look, Jim, I still think you can play. You follow me? You were a great quarterback in college. Your pro career hasn't turned out the way you wanted. We still think you're good enough to play for the Oakland Raiders. Wayne and I have got to work out a contract first."

Davis looked over at Hoop.

"Wayne, you've known me a long time. Have I ever been unfair to the players you've represented on the Oakland Raiders?"

Hoop took the pipe out of his mouth.

"Absolutely not. In fact, Al, you've been very fair."

Davis smiled. He then got into X's and O's, explaining that the Raiders ask their quarterbacks to hold onto the football longer than other teams on passing downs. Oakland quarterbacks, Davis pointed out, don't throw the football when the receiver makes his break, but when the quarterback can see the numbers on the receiver's chest.

A 3-year contract was worked out in a few days. Davis

was a fair man: I would make $135,000, $150,000 and $180,000 a year plus a $25,000 bonus if the Raiders made the Super Bowl. Oakland traded Mike Rae to Tampa Bay, leaving Stabler, David Humm and Jim Plunkett as the three Raider quarterbacks. In that order.

Head coach John Madden called me in for a meeting.

"Sit down, Jim. Got everything you need, your playbook? Good. Now this is going to be a different situation for you. Every place you've been, you've been expected to be the savior. Here, you can come in, learn the system, be one of the guys. There is no pressure on you to perform right away."

Madden didn't mince words. The message was crystal clear: I wasn't going to play, possibly the entire season. I was to drop my burdens by the door, relax, and become Humpty-Dumpty, i.e., to put all the pieces back together again.

I met with the Oakland press corps. Later, one writer told me privately that I handled my first interview as a Raider well.

"Yes, but I haven't thrown my first interception yet," I reminded him.

As it turned out, I wouldn't get the chance in 1978. Though I suited up for every game, I didn't step on the playing field once for Oakland that fall.

After eleven years, I had regressed to my redshirt days at Stanford, running the opponents' plays in practice. Instead of impersonating Gary Beban, I was now Jim Zorn. A right-handed Jim Zorn.

I wasn't at all inspired in 1978. I wasn't going to play, so there was no reason to prepare mentally for games. Lethargy took over. I didn't feel any zip, and my passing showed it. I was nothing more than a camp follower.

My depression increased. I was a Raider in body, but not in spirit. Idleness only made things worse. The 49ers— a bad team—had cut me. Then I had to go through the further embarrassment of a tryout. I felt like some bum who had wandered in and asked the Raiders for a handout. I was ready to chuck my career.

I didn't know it at the time, but John Madden was considering the same thing for his own career.

Madden's best friend in 1978 was a bottle of Maalox. It was a bad year for him. Although he would pass the 100-victory mark after just 10 years—Madden's career record of 103–32–7 (.763) is the highest percentage of any coach who has won at least 100 games—he acquired an ulcer in the process as the Raiders failed to make the playoffs for the first time in 7 years.

Madden was a coach who got heavily involved with his players. He enjoyed sauntering into the locker room, sitting down and chatting with the team. John was a players' coach and it showed. He didn't work the players all that hard in practice and many times let them go in without running their laps and sprints.

John was a softy.

Those who've watched him jump and shout and turn various shades of red on the sidelines may find this hard to believe. The game officials called him "Big Red," out of fear, but also respect. They knew he wasn't grandstanding, that he intensely wanted to win. His ulcer was a testimony to that intensity.

Madden's heart was much bigger than his temper. John and his wife Virginia spent a lot of time with Darryl Stingley and his wife Tina in an Oakland area hospital where Stingley learned he was paralyzed following Jack Tatum's tackle. Madden would fly in from a Raider away game and drive to the hospital to see Stingley. When it came time for Darryl to leave, the Maddens showed up with gifts for the Stingley family.

That's the real John Madden.

John's a very funny man. At the Wednesday night quarterback meetings, he'd run the film back and forth.

Then he'd turn off the projector and say, "All we've got to do is block and tackle against those SOBs and we'll win." John believed in getting down to the basics.

We later canceled some Wednesday night meetings because John wasn't feeling well. He'd throw up before games, after games, at halftime. A sportswriter saw John with a Maalox bottle in his hand and told him that he might be better off retiring.

"How can I leave those guys?" Madden replied, gesturing toward the locker room.

Madden is an interesting man, but not nearly as interesting as the Oakland players and owner. Resting and rehabilitating, I had time to sit back and observe the Raiders goings-on. It was worse than I ever imagined. No football team could be like this. No group of men could be like this.

These guys are crazy!

Al Davis's history is that of finding society's incorrigibles and dressing them in football uniforms. Warren Wells ran picturesque pass patterns, even with an attempted rape charge over his head. John Matuszak nearly OD'd one night as a Kansas City Chief, has spent time in a straightjacket and was stopped by police near Oakland with a .44 pistol and a bayonet in his car. Tooz's real life is far more dramatic than his off-season movie roles.

The Raiders frequent bars—the kind you drink in and the kind they lock you up behind. Warren Wells experienced both. Marv Hubbard loved a bar fight as much as he enjoyed beating up the Chiefs. Marv's now the singing fullback; he has cut some records, made the local country charts. Then there was "Loose Wire" Chip Oliver, the Raider linebacker who left football to join a commune.

When I came to Oakland, it wasn't a typical day if someone wasn't arrested or the police didn't call up looking for a player. The Raiders ran their own missing persons bureau. Cliff Branch missed a 1979 game against Atlanta. The team said he was excused with an ankle injury; he "slept" through the game. Stabler and Matuszak missed a practice because, supposedly, their car broke down at Lake Tahoe. Skip Thomas plowed into a parked car one night in a residential area. The car belonged to an *Oakland Tribune* sportswriter. Phil Villapiano was beaten up by a motorcycle gang. George Atkinson was acquitted on a charge of bank embezzlement and larceny.

These "All-American" types made the Raiders—and Al Davis—winners.

The Raiders have had lovable as well as unlovable characters.

George Buehler, an offensive guard, loved the game of football—when he had his mind on it. The trouble was, George's mind was often somewhere else. Teammates would have to yell to get his attention in the huddle because he was staring at the stands, or at airplanes flying overhead. When he wasn't daydreaming, George loved to build these little radio remote cars. At training camp, he would guide the cars from his room to the camp office, where his mail would be placed in the car. George would then guide the car back to his room.

George Blanda played in Oakland, making the Raiders the darlings of senior citizens everywhere. Ben Davidson played in Oakland, twitching his handlebar mustache and burying Joe Namath every chance he got. Big Ben also had a role in a porno movie—with his clothes on. Jim Otto played in Oakland too; he has a Pro Football Hall of Fame bust and an artificial knee as proof.

Fred "The Hammer" Williamson, one-time cornerback and now a movie-and-television actor, played for Oakland. Don Manoukian, the only Stanford graduate to become a professional wrestler, played for Oakland.

The most lovable of all Raiders was Dan Birdwell, a defensive tackle. Birdwell stories are part of Raider lore. Here is just one:

The Raiders were leaving for an away game and everyone was aboard the flight but Birdwell. Oakland officials searched all over the airport for an hour without success. As the team was about to take off without Birdwell, someone spotted a plane off in the distance. Sure enough, sitting in the plane all by himself was Dan Birdwell.

"Danny," the official said, "we've been looking everywhere for you. What are you doing here?"

"I found the plane," a nonplussed Birdwell answered. "It's not my job to make sure you guys get on."

Oakland has a player of more recent vintage who was as unpredictable as Birdwell. His name was Charles Philyaw, a 6–9 defensive lineman who wasn't a very good player. He drove the coaches and trainer crazy—practicing when he shouldn't, not practicing when he should—and sending teammates into hysterical fits.

Philyaw cornered fullback Mark van Eeghen one day.

"How come you get your first and last name on the back of your jersey?" Philyaw demanded to know.

"I don't," van Eeghen said.

"Yes you do. Van Eeghen."

Philyaw was convinced Mark was lying to him and insisted on betting him. Another time, Philyaw was late for practice. He pulled into camp in a tow truck, his car hitched to the back.

"What happened, Charles?" a coach asked.

"I ran out of gas. No money."

"Then how did you get your car back?"

Philyaw reached into his wallet and pulled out a plastic card.

"Master Charge," he said, proudly.

Philyaw had a lot of injuries—sometimes real, more often imagined. On a road trip, he went to see trainer George Anderson about his latest fictitious injury.

"I don't have anything to help you," George growled. "Go see the doc."

Philyaw knocked on Skip Thomas's door. Thomas opened it.

"Yeah, what do you want?"

"George says I should come see you. My ankle's bad."

"See me? You've got to be kidding."

"No, he said to see the doc, and you're the doc."

Thomas's nickname was Dr. Death.

Philyaw later complained to Anderson at halftime of a pre-season game that his left foot was hurting. Anderson discovered the problem: Philyaw had worn two right shoes the entire half.

Our most celebrated character, of course, was Ken Stabler. The Snake loved to party and have a good time, and he made no bones about it. He was the only player I knew who could play just as hard off the field as on and keep right on going. He claimed he only needed an hour or two of sleep a night and that he saw nothing wrong with reading the game plan by the light of the jukebox. At times, Stabler's lack of sleep did catch up to him and he started throwing interceptions.

The Snake never let anything bother him, though. Not game plans, pass rushes, Wild Turkey or the ladies. He saw himself as the second Bobby Layne, only at a slightly faster tempo. Snake's like the guy Waylon Jennings sings about, who has always been crazy to keep from going insane.

Other guys tried to imitate Stabler, but couldn't keep up the pace. I've played hard at times too. I've got such a guilt complex that after I do it once, I cool it and settle down. The Snake never slowed down.

When it came to throwing a football, Stabler had every kind of delivery you could think of and a few you couldn't. Three-quarters, sidearm, underhanded . . . even a bouncing forward roll, tuck position.

Houston had Oakland all but beaten in 1978 when Stabler and Dave Casper were Raiders, not Oilers. Stabler rolled out and threw the ball as hard as he could into a group of Oilers. The ball ricocheted off three of them like a pinball and Casper somehow grabbed it for the game-winning touchdown.

Another time in San Diego, Stabler was being sacked when he pitched the ball forward underhanded, making it look like a fumble instead of what it really was—an incomplete pass. Pete Banaszak batted the ball into the end zone and Casper recovered it. The officials called it a touchdown, and the Raiders won, 21–20.

The Snake knows how to win, even if it isn't always by the book.

Stabler's biggest strength is accuracy. He has great zip on hooks and comebacks. He knows where everyone is supposed to be and he'll get the ball to them. He can do it blindfolded.

He isn't your Arnold Schwarzenegger look-alike, with pipestem legs and a bulging middle. But Snake is all courage and guts. He has to be because he isn't mobile, which is asking for trouble in this age of big, fast defensive linemen. Stabler has been pounded on a lot, but he'll still get up and win the game in the last minute—sometimes the last second.

Snake and I are alike in one respect: we aren't receptive to game plans. Snake would go down the list of passes the Raider coaches wanted him to use, shake his head up and down at each suggestion, knowing full well he wasn't going to use all of them.

I'm like that too, the impromptu type. However, I have this theory about play-calling. Snake may think the same way; I'm not sure. A coach will send in a play he believes has a high-percentage chance of succeeding. I might want to call a low-percentage play. My theory then is that the low-percentage play has a better chance of working because I believe in it.

The 1978 season was especially rough on Madden and Stabler. Madden went through a 6-week period where he wasn't talking to Davis. Stabler went through a 12-week period where he wasn't talking to the media. This was surprising because Stabler always had been cooperative with reporters. The year before, he threw 7 interceptions against Denver, then endured 90 minutes of interviews, refusing no one. Then he stopped talking altogether. His reason, which didn't come out until later, was that he didn't want to knock teammates.

Oakland was slipping from dominance, and Stabler felt that silence would be the smart approach. The team was heading for a 9–7 season and Stabler was upset about something else: Fred Biletnikoff, his clutch receiver and good friend, was benched after the second game and replaced by Morris Bradshaw, a younger player. Biletnikoff seldom played until the last two weeks of the season, when Stabler consciously threw him the football and Biletnikoff scored twice.

The Snake wound up with a career-high 30 interceptions, though many weren't his fault. There were a number of tipped passes. Nevertheless, the interceptions hurt Oakland. So did the lack of defense against the run. We gave up a lot of yards on the ground. It wasn't so much the points scored against us as time of possession: our opponents played keep-away from our defense.

Topping off Stabler's season was Davis's comment to the press that The Snake was like a 21-game winner in baseball who was having a 13-game season. Davis may have tried to appeal to Stabler's sense of character, getting him to think more seriously about physical conditioning. Whatever Davis's ploy, it failed. When Stabler drove away toward his off-season home of Gulf Shores, Alabama, his resentment for Al Davis was almost strong enough to burn a hole in the windshield.

Madden resigned after the season, citing the ulcer as the main reason. Flores, the receivers coach, replaced him. Some players felt Davis forced Madden out because their owner-coach relationship had deteriorated. Davis wants his head coaches to be subservient, or at least receptive to his coaching ideas. And he has lots of ideas.

I have no doubts that Davis coaches the Raiders. I'm not saying he is the only coach, but he does a lot of the coaching and demands that the staff do things his way. Madden fought this intrusion, because he wanted to prove that he, and not Al Davis, was the head coach of the Oakland Raiders. Many football people really believe that Davis is the Raiders' head coach. Flores is more receptive to Al's ideas than was Madden.

Al calls the coaches and asks if they have this play or that play in the game plan. After I became a starter, Al would approach me after practice.

"Jim, did Tom or the other coaches tell you to run this play?" he asked, then diagramming the play.

"No."

"Well, I'll remind Tom."

Al's very much into that kind of thing. If you're going to work for Al, you're going to have his input. Flores and Davis have talked offense since the days when Tom quarterbacked the Raiders and Al was the head coach. They have a good rapport, although Flores told me he has resisted Davis on certain plays because Tom felt they wouldn't work. But that doesn't stop Al from making more suggestions.

The Raiders have an unusual situation. On every NFL team except Oakland's, it's the head coach you fear, whether it's Shula, Landry, Noll, Grant, etc. In Oakland, it's the owner.

Davis doesn't deny that he runs a dictatorship. He feels it is a benevolent dictatorship. He pays his players well and they respect him. I'm not sure they trust him, but they pay close attention when he talks.

Many head coaches couldn't work for Davis, which is irrelevant because he wouldn't hire them anyway. There have been only four head coaches in Oakland since 1963—Davis and the three men he hired: John Rauch, John Madden and Tom Flores. All three were Raider assistants before-hand and all three have coached a Super Bowl team.

When a new coach takes over an NFL team, he generally puts in his own system. Not in Oakland. Coaches change, but the system—Davis's system that he learned from Sid Gillman in San Diego—remains the same. Davis's system has produced more victories over the last two decades than any other system in football.

Al knows what he wants—big offensive linemen and talented defensive backs. His first two picks in the 1981 draft were a cornerback (Ted Watts) and an offensive tackle (Curt Marsh). Davis wants big linemen to give his quarterbacks longer protection so Raider receivers can run deeper routes. He wants cornerbacks who are fast enough to stay with the speed receivers and strong enough to come up and stop the run. Lester Hayes is a perfect example. He led the NFL with 13 interceptions in 1980 and he can handle Earl Campbell one-on-one on the sweep play.

Davis has a job description for all his athletes, then he goes out and looks for them—in the draft, on waiver lists, through trades. Eight of his 22 starters in Super Bowl XV started their NFL careers elsewhere. Two more started in Oakland, went elsewhere, then came back. Only 6 starters were No. 1 picks.

I don't know if Davis is "The Genius" (which he enjoys being called), but he is intelligent about football. He has been associated with the game all his life, which separates him from other NFL owners who purchased a team after making their millions in other enterprises. They don't know the game as Davis does; few people do.

After awhile I realized that Davis didn't match the image I had of him prior to my joining the Raiders. Well, not completely anyway. Maybe he hasn't always done things on the up and up. But, he has been fair with me. Our interactions have always been friendly.

Ken Stabler feels differently about Davis, I'm sure.

After the '78 season, *Sacramento Bee* sportswriter Bob Padecky traveled to Stabler's birthplace, Foley, Alabama, to do a series of articles on Stabler. Padecky's idea was to interview people in Foley without talking to Stabler. The Snake's reaction was that Padecky was "digging up garbage."

After the series ran, Stabler phoned Padecky and invited him to Gulf Shores. Stabler's explanation later was that Padecky broke the story of Davis criticizing his No. 1 quarterback, and that Stabler wanted to know what Davis had said—even though the story ran in two newspapers a full week before the NFL season ended. Padecky said the reason for Stabler's invitation was that Snake was ready to "spill his guts" about what happened to Oakland in 1978. Padecky returned to Alabama and was arrested in a drug setup in Gulf Shores. Stabler emphatically denies that he was involved. Snake feels his friends might have gotten carried away and tried to scare Padecky. That sounds like a logical explanation to me.

The Gulf Shores incident made sure the Raiders—and Stabler—were front-page news throughout the off-season: football's longest running soap opera.

During this time, I thought even more seriously about retirement. My desire to quit after the 49ers waived me was motivated by despondency. My desire to leave the game a half-year later was spawned by neglect, which hurt worse. The Raiders didn't want me; I was just a forgotten name on the roster. You could find me every Sunday on the statistics sheet, under "Did Not Play"—16 J. Plunkett. If I slipped out the back door and called it a career, no one would notice or care.

I told my friends that this was it: I was getting out. The football money was good, but there was a ton of things I could do well in the outside world. My friends were wor-

ried about me, I know. My biggest faults are lack of patience
and a hidden temper, and both were hard to control after
the 1978 season.

*"Between Jim's first two seasons in Oakland—that
was the lowest I have ever seen him. It was like he was being
kicked around. I even saw a change in his personality. He
became short and negative. He began snapping at people,
which he never did before."*
—NICK VLASOFF

*"There must be a hundred and fifty Stanford athletes
who have worked for my construction business during summer vacations. Two or three have stood out, and Jim was one
of them. I don't know what it was about him, but I knew
here was a kid that was going to do things. If he hadn't been
able to throw a football, he undoubtedly still would be
working for me. I would have given him an attractive opportunity to make damn sure that I didn't lose him. Jim would
make it in the business world. He would be successful, kind
and honorable. He is both bright and street-smart. But it is
his dedication that makes him what he is. I don't think
people realize the fire that burns inside that kid. If he didn't
have it, he wouldn't be in football today."*
—JACK DITZ, alumnus and active supporter of Stanford

I had already planned my future after football, although I hadn't contemplated that the future could be now.
Work-wise, I still want to find something that I enjoy and can
dig into, find meaning in. I'm still growing as an individual,
trying to learn more about the world and myself. I wouldn't
want to be like some of my old high school friends from San
Jose, who have settled down with or without families and are
just taking it day to day, not doing much about anything. Just
existing isn't for me. I need to be continually stimulated, and
that includes my choice of profession.

I could also see settling down and raising a family someday. I'm thinking of moving to Reno, Nevada, or some place in Idaho. It's quieter there, pretty country, and I just want to get away and be comfortable. I have some friends who live in the Reno area. John Sande, my center at Stanford, is an attorney in Reno, which is just a 4-hour drive from the San Francisco Bay Area. I might even take up skiing— if my knees can stand it.

But in 1979, I went back to camp like I said I wouldn't. What helped change my mind was the July edition of *Sport* magazine, which ran an exclusive—and explosive—interview with Stabler.

Al Davis, while in Alabama to watch the Blue-Gray Game, contacted Stabler's attorney to arrange a meeting with Snake. Supposedly, Davis wanted to bury the hatchet.

"I'd like to bury the hatchet," Stabler was quoted, "right between Al Davis's shoulder blades."

Oooh!

Stabler proceeded to knock some teammates, doing exactly what he said he wouldn't do. He criticized wide receivers Morris Bradshaw and Cliff Branch, saying Morris "doesn't play very well and I don't know how consistent Cliff can be over a long period."

Snake saved his strongest attack for offensive tackle Henry Lawrence: "Our right tackle didn't play very well, and sometimes when I went back to pass it felt like I was standing in the middle of a freeway. He got me banged around a little."

Stabler said he never would play for Davis again. Henry Pitts, Stabler's attorney, received permission from Oakland to try and make a deal for his client with another NFL team.

After reading that, I thought to myself, "Jim, you better get along to camp and see what happens." David Humm was thinking on the same wavelength.

Humm had been with the Raiders five years. He

threw the ball well and had a strong arm for his size, but had little experience because Stabler seldom came out of the lineup. When he did, Mike Rae replaced him. David Humm was an excellent holder on placekicks. Errol Mann, the Raider kicker at the time, said David was the best he ever worked with.

With Stabler late for camp, Humm and I were prepared to battle for the starting job in case Stabler wouldn't show up.

"I don't know if this is a transition year," Humm told the press, "but I want the job. I know I have to work for it, but I want it."

So did I, but both our chances faded when Stabler rolled into camp in his new Porsche. Pitts hadn't made a deal. Status quo resumed.

Humm felt differently toward me, however. When there had been three quarterbacks in camp, I was the backup to the backup. When Snake hadn't reported on time, there were just two of us. David now saw me in a changed light.

When Stabler showed up, that feeling intensified. David thought Snake was the greatest anyway; he might have idolized him. He'd do things for Snake, like getting him footballs to warm up with, then warming him up. They laughed together, joked together. I wasn't made a part of the fun.

They were friends. I was the odd man out.

Stabler broke his silence with the media, minus one reporter: Padecky. When Padecky walked up to Stabler at training camp for an interview, Snake gave him a 2-word reply—something you won't find in a first-grade reader. Stabler was available for interviews with everyone else the rest of the year.

Snake felt lost at camp in 1979. The people he was closest to—Madden, Biletnikoff, Banaszak—were gone. Snake and Freddie used to lie on their backs in loosening-up drills, never moving. They just joked and kidded around. Without Biletnikoff and the others, Stabler felt lonely.

I was having just the opposite experience. Camp had become fun. I had known John Vella before, so I wasn't exactly around strangers when I reported to Oakland in 1978. I got to know Villapiano, Dave Dalby, Steve Sylvester, Rich Martini. It was fun drinking beer and having a few laughs with Double D (Dalby) and Syl, getting involved in the crazy things the Raiders do. Like the air hockey tournament, an arcade game that has become a training camp ritual.

Carol Doda, a famous San Francisco topless dancer, was the air hockey queen one year. Stabler later posed with her in a magazine photo layout, both unclad to the waist. Al Davis must have loved that! Maybe that's why Stabler did it. I couldn't do something like that. Dan Pastorini posed for *Playgirl,* and I have nothing against it, but I wouldn't do it. Besides, who would want to look at me?

I've never had more fun in football than summer training camp with the Oakland Raiders. This is where I learned about the Raiders camaraderie that holds the team together. You've got blacks and whites, crazies and straights, yet they rally together and defend one another both on and off the field. It's hard to explain; you have to live it to understand. There is a uniqueness about Raider football.

Even the coaches get involved. They show up at the air hockey tournament and even such bizarre things as the rookie party. They'll share some beer with the players. There is a closeness between Raider coaches and players you may not find on other teams.

Training camp is supposedly the Spartan ethic for five or six weeks. But the Raiders live like Romans just before the fall of the empire. You never know what is going to happen from day to day or night to night with Oakland, football's happy hedonists.

I try to separate my personal life from my football,

however. It is good having Gerry to confide in. Kindness is one thing I want in a companion, and Gerry is that. She is a beautiful person—both inwardly and outwardly. She is a very special person to me now. Our relationship has grown into something more serious.

Yeah, love.

"Our relationship had nothing to do with football. I didn't know who Jim Plunkett was, or if he was a quarterback. The one quality about him that attracted me is that he is a caring person. He would call sometimes three times a day in Boston just to see how I was. He would come over for a date, ask to use the phone, and call his mom in California. I felt guilty because I wouldn't even pick up the phone and call my parents in Cleveland. Another quality I admire in Jim is his ability to handle people. He treats everyone, no matter who they are, the same way. Working in retail sales, I had to have things done right away, in a particular way. When they weren't, I became hypersensitive. I talked to Jim about the problem. We worked it out together. He told me that it isn't important to always think I'm right. I calmed down a lot after that. Jim's kind of unique."
—GERRY LAVELLE, Jim Plunkett's fiancée

Gerry and I like to go to plays and movies. I'm a movie buff and see as many as I can. I even watch the old movies on late-night TV. I like Cary Grant: he's so perfectly suave and debonair. I like Clark Gable movies. He wasn't a handsome guy, but he made himself appealing on the screen. The movie *It Happened One Night* with Claudette Colbert is a classic. And I love those old Humphrey Bogart movies like *Casablanca* and *Treasure of the Sierra Madre.*

I can hear Bogey saying: "The name's Dobbs. Fred C. Dobbs." Recently I saw Irene Dunne in a war-time movie on TV. She was great, quite a comedienne.

I've gotten into movie trivia. I like movies from thirty

years ago, when Hollywood had the star system. You don't see that as much anymore. How many actors can you name from *Star Wars?* I enjoy reading books, magazines, anything I get my hands on. But movies are my hobby.

I could feel myself coming on as a player again in 1979. I hadn't taken any lumps for a full season. There had been no stress, no pressure other than my own indecision on whether to continue playing. I might be coming back, like the summer after my freshman year at Stanford when I worked myself back into top throwing condition. However, like that long-ago summer, my prospects for playing in the fall appeared just as remote. I called my attorney in Oakland.

"Hoop, I'm thinking of quitting again."

"Hang in there, Jim. Just hang in there."

Tom Flores made me feel somewhat better. He continually asked me how I was doing, told me to keep working hard. John Madden was entrenched with certain players and Flores wasn't. Tom had more problems to worry about than I did, though.

Tom had a tough time his first year as Raiders head coach. The team wouldn't make the playoffs for the second straight year. Because he wasn't a vocal, cheerleader-type coach, people thought Tom couldn't get the job done. He had a tough act to follow.

Madden was so visible on the sidelines, pulling his red hair, bellowing at the officials. Flores was invisible, standing passively, arms folded, staring. When he talks, it is closer to a whisper than a shout. People interpreted this as a sign that Tom wasn't a strong leader. Those people were wrong.

Tom never gets rattled. He remains cool regardless of the situation. The team found out he was knowledgeable about defense as well as offense. He spent his years as a coaching intern, observing the entire system. He has a temper too, we discovered. Tom will hold it back until he can hold it back no longer, and then the players feel its lash. Tom is a tougher disciplinarian than Madden was, but on the Oakland Raiders there can only be so much discipline.

The Raider practice field is the antithesis of a Marine training camp. Al Davis's philosophy isn't to win football games on Wednesday or Thursday. He wants to win on Sunday. The Raiders save for one big burst a week. The rest of the time, anything goes.

Ted Hendricks has practiced in a German World War II helmet painted in silver and black. Other times, he has worn a Three Musketeers hat—the D'Artagnan of linebackers—and even a pumpkin hat on Halloween. Other players tape feathers to their helmets. The highlight of the day, however, is who wins the "tip" drill before practice. The players get in a circle and tip the football to one another. Those who let the ball fall to the ground are eliminated. This drill is often more heated—and interesting—than what follows at practice.

Raider players have problems with punctuality. It's a rare day when everyone is on time for a film meeting. Cliff Branch is late more than anyone else. Flores will have to switch off the projector, turn on the lights and wait for Cliff to take his seat. Tom really gets angry when this happens, but he is helpless to stop this kind of behavior.

Davis knows that Branch can catch the long pass, so Al is willing to put up with anything Cliff does. Cliff caught 2 touchdown passes in Super Bowl XV; he wouldn't have if the Raiders had tired of his shenanigans long ago and got rid of him.

There's a method to Al's madness.

Winning is the end result in Oakland, regardless of how many rules are bent along the way. And the Raiders win, in their zany, madcap, crack-brained, singular way.

I will say this about Tom Flores: he is the head coach. Even though Davis interferes, Tom formulates the game plan and makes the final decisions. On the field, it is Tom's team and he runs it with an even disposition and a firm hand.

In a playoff game at Cleveland, Flores sent in a running play. The offensive linemen grumbled that it wouldn't work. I called time and went to the sidelines.

"You still want this play?" I asked Tom. "The line wants something else."

"I want that play," Tom said.

We used it and got a first down. Tom is often succinct, but he can be adamant and—the players have learned—right. The man knows his trade.

One thing I learned quickly about the Oakland Raiders is that the offensive line makes the quarterback. Stabler is a strong leader and a deadly thrower. Yet he wouldn't have been effective if the Raider line wasn't as good as it is, because he isn't that mobile. Snake could sidestep the rush and he could drift and throw, but Al said that it was important for a quarterback to run, especially inside the 20 when things break down and a first down is needed.

Stabler has been a great quarterback, but because of his immobility, he might not be able to play for a number of NFL teams. Snake owed a big thanks to Upshaw, Dalby, Art Shell, Mickey Marvin and, yes, Henry Lawrence.

The Raiders call Upshaw the "Governor." He does all the speaking for the team, considers himself the team spokesman. I'm not sure the rest of the players think of him as such, but that doesn't stop Uppy from speaking. Nothing goes on around the team without his knowing it.

The "Governor" title isn't entirely a joke. Upshaw has lofty political aspirations. He is involved in all kinds of civic and charity work. Upshaw has taken notes at Oakland City Council meetings. He serves on the board of governors of California's community (2-year) colleges and is president of the NFL Players Association.

Upshaw was a great football player who has slipped

some in recent years. However, that's to be expected with advancing age. Remember, Uppy has played in three Super Bowls in three different decades!

Shell and Upshaw have played side-by-side for more than a decade. Art is a good athlete, a former college basketball player, and the gentle, quiet type. He is extremely sensitive about his weight. Art had a deal with Madden that he would never be weighed. The Raiders list Art at 280. He has weighed more than 300.

Shell was phenomenal in Super Bowl XI. Jim Marshall, the Minnesota defensive end who played across from Art that day, didn't have one tackle. Not even an assist! Doug Sutherland, another Viking lineman, said after the game that Upshaw and Shell were so big, "they blocked out the sun."

Dave Dalby and Jim Otto are the only centers in Raider history. Dalby is like a little kid. He can't walk by an electronic game or a pinball machine without playing it. Dalby's a good football player and a fast dresser. After the game, he is the first player showered and gone from the locker room. There are two reasons why: he is the club's premier beer drinker, and that way, he isn't quoted much. He never rocks the boat. You never hear any criticism from Double D.

Mickey Marvin is a big, strong country hoss with an easy smile and friendly manner. He'll meet a stranger on a plane trip and that person will tell his life's story to Mick. Marvin's got a good story too: he married a Raider cheerleader—Lisa Conway. The Raider and the Raiderette.

Marvin hasn't yet heard of the invention of the forward pass. All he knows is run, run, run. If its third-and-fifteen, he'll say, "Let's run it in, let's run it in." I'll say, "Calm down, Mick." He'll say, "OK."

Henry Lawrence is another extremely nice person. Madden thought of him as a son. Lawrence became involved with an ailing child through a charity. When the youth died, Henry cried for days.

Henry loves to sing in the locker room, though no one likes to listen. And he is by far the worst dresser on the team. He will wear plaids, stripes and polka dots—at the same time!

Lawrence is big, strong and a hustler. After he completes his block, he'll run upfield in case there's a fumble. Henry's problem is that he psyches himself out by talking a lot. Before a game with Kansas City, he said that if Chiefs defensive end Art Still "is all-pro, then I am all-world." Still had a great game against him the following Sunday. Henry's problem is inconsistency, though he has become more consistent each year.

I would have given anything in the summer of 1979 to work behind that line. I usually played behind rookies, reserves and guys who would be gone by the end of the week.

Operating under such conditions, I beat out Humm for the No. 2 quarterback spot that summer.

Humm and I worked the Pro Football Hall of Fame Game against Dallas in Canton, Ohio. Stabler sat this one out because of his late arrival. David and I threw well, except that I just missed a couple of bombs to Rich Martini. We beat the Cowboys, 20–13.

The next week in Los Angeles, we were down 14–0 in the fourth quarter. On third-and-fourteen from our 15-yard line, I threw a 38-yard pass on which Larry Brunson made a tremendous leaping catch. We scored, stopped the Rams, then on third-and-eighteen from our 48, I hit Brunson again for 39 yards. From the Rams 5, I passed to Derrick Ramsey all alone in the end zone to tie the score.

The Rams won the toss in sudden-death overtime and scored right away to win, 20–14. Pre-season games, like popularity polls, don't mean anything because things change radically from week to week. I looked upon that Rams game as a turning point in my career; only this time it was positive, not negative.

Al Davis came up to me in the dressing room after the game and thanked me. By that, I think he meant that I had vindicated him for signing me.

My old form *was* back. I could feel it. I was staying in the pocket instead of fleeing from it. I was holding onto the football with confidence, not fear. I was no longer gun-shy.

But there was no way to beat out Stabler as No. 1. He had been with the Raiders so long that he knew their system in his sleep. And Stabler is an acclaimed master of the come- back finish. I was the apprentice quarterback with little or no chance of advancing further.

The Raiders played the Patriots the next week in Foxboro, my first trip back to New England since the 49er trade. The Patriots handled us that day, 35–14.

I told a Boston writer that leaving New England possi- bly "was a bad decision on my part. I look around now and see Dan Pastorini and Archie Manning doing well. They were able to stick things out until those teams got turned around. When I left New England, the offensive line was just coming into its own . . . I made a decision. Maybe it was an unfortunate one because I left all that talent behind. The nucleus was there when I left."

There were times—and I didn't believe that I would even think this way—that I missed the option play. At least when I was running the darn thing, I was playing. Now I'm not running it and sitting. I hated the option, really, but hated not playing even more. My mind was confused. I wanted to start in Oakland, not New England. But I was downcast and liable to say anything.

One thing Davis likes even more than big linemen and fast corners is a quarterback who can throw the football 60 yards. Stabler could throw the bomb at one time, before he lost some arm strength as he got older. When that happened, he broke his 60-yard passes into fragments, 15 here, 8 there. . . .

All Stabler had to do to make up for the aging process was to throw the bomb a little sooner. He didn't do it. Stabler changed the Raider offense to suit his shortcomings. In other words, shorter passes. Davis's offense was designed for longer passes. He didn't want to move from sideline to sideline, but from end zone to end zone. Don't punch to the body, go for the jaw! He taught this philosophy to Tom Flores and then to Daryle Lamonica, "The Mad Bomber." Davis and I shared the same philosophy.

Now, finally, I saw Davis's motive for signing me. It wasn't Stabler's knees, but his arm. Davis could see it before anyone else, possibly before even The Snake. Al signed me because I had a stronger arm than Stabler and Humm. Perhaps, in time, I would get a chance to prove Davis was right.

It was a matter of waiting for my chance. When would it come? I ran four or five miles before practice every day in '79. I was in shape, my arm and legs felt great and I could help this team.

Flores knew this too. A couple of times in '79, he turned on the sidelines and looked at me. I looked at him. I could tell Tom wanted to put me in, but he was committed to Stabler. How could a first-year head coach bench the player who had taken the Raiders to their greatest success? He couldn't.

Tom confided in me once: "I can't pull out Snake. He's the guy who has gotten us here so many times before."

Flores was right, I guess. I sympathized with his thinking even though it was hard for me to accept. Stabler was still winning football games, as much with his fierce competitiveness as with his left arm.

This was plainly evident in a Monday night game in New Orleans. The Saints cuffed us around badly for more than a half, grabbing what looked like an insurmountable 35–14 lead. Stabler was buried by a bunch of Saints in the third quarter and got up slowly. Flores could see that he was dizzy.

"All right, Jim, get warm. You're going in."

I warmed up until my arm felt ready, then ran onto the field. I was really excited. My first real chance after nearly two years of vegetating. There's still time left, I told myself, we can get these guys. I clapped my hands together and the other ten players in the huddle turned toward me. I started to kneel down to call the play when . . .

I felt a tap on my shoulder.

It was Snake.

"I'm OK."

That's all he said. But, in essence, he was telling me to take a hike. He replaced me even before I had a chance to replace him.

I jogged back to the sidelines, keeping my head down, trying to disguise the anguish on my face. Everyone on the sideline knew. They looked away. Rebuffed again.

Snake then did the impossible, leading the Raiders to 4 touchdowns, including 2 passes to Branch, who didn't start the game because he missed a practice the week before. The Raiders won, 42–35, in the biggest turnaround ever on Monday night. It was vintage Stabler. He hadn't lost the master's touch.

We played Cleveland six days later and Stabler smashed his hand. Flores told me to warm up again. Uh uh, not so fast. I found Stabler on the bench.

"Hey, Snake, you going back in or not?"

He was. I just didn't want to be embarrassed again. Once is enough.

We missed the playoffs by losing at home to Seattle, 29–24, on the final weekend. My season's output was 15 passes, 7 completions, 89 yards and 1 touchdown over my mothballed year of 1978.

I didn't interpret that as progress. It was just one more wasted year. I was 32 and not getting any younger or happier. What did I have to look forward to at 33, 34 . . . ?

Five months later, Hoop's hunch came true. Oakland traded Stabler to Houston for Dan Pastorini. Straight up, a No. 1 for a No. 1. In the NFL you don't trade one starting quarterback for another and put either on the bench. Flores made that clear right away.

"We traded a starter for a starter," he said. "Pastorini is the starter for us and Plunkett is second. It's Pastorini's job to keep or lose."

It made sense. I had been cut by my former team. Pastorini had taken his former team to the playoffs. He should be the starter in Oakland.

Nevertheless, I felt more confident now about my own situation. Stabler was gone, which was a gigantic load off my back. I can compete against Pastorini. I knew it. Just give me half a chance.

Pastorini has a strong arm, one of the strongest in football. Davis liked the way Pastorini could stand in against the blitz and still get the ball off. Dan is a tough guy who was beaten up badly his early years in Houston, just as I had been in New England. Only it was rougher on Pastorini because after he was sacked three straight times, he had to get up and punt.

I had two advantages over Dan. I knew the Raider system and I could run. Pastorini wasn't much better running with the football than Stabler was. And Dan was instructed to pass the football within four seconds at Houston. In Oakland, the quarterback sometimes holds the football as many as six seconds before releasing it.

Pastorini had one advantage over me, though—the all-important advantage. He was the starter.

Dan wasn't the only new quarterback in town in 1980. The Raiders used their first-round pick in the draft to select Marc Wilson from Brigham Young University. Flores emerged from the drafting room and faced the media. He smiled.

"We think Marc Wilson will be our quarterback of the future."

Distant drums pounded in my head. Hadn't I heard that same refrain long ago in another time, in a faraway town? A nauseous feeling gripped my stomach. If Pastorini is the Raider's quarterback for now and Wilson is their quarterback for the future, where does that put me?

Left out, if you ask me.

No one asked.

I saw Pastorini for the first time after he became a Raider at a veterans mini-camp that May. We said hello, but both of us knew that our relationship would be strained at best.

A mini-camp is football without pads, punishment or pressure. The players and coaches get together for three days. The coaches get to see what shape the players are in, how they care coming off an injury or surgery. The players run around in drills, listen to philosophical changes the coaches are planning to make for the upcoming season. The players tell one another a few off-season stories.

Some players complain about attending mini-camps, but there is a valid reason for having them: players start thinking about football again.

I've tried to help out various charities over the years. Let's face it, there are people who are handicapped and can't always help themselves. But I never thought I would get involved in a fund-raising event that would benefit two bars.

It's the annual Nuts to Zots race, which originally started from one bar—the Peanut Farm, and finished at another—the Alpine Beer Garden, or Zots. It is a hilly run, and the course had to be altered for that reason, but it is still seven miles.

Part of the entry fee goes for a quart of beer at Zots

at the end of the race, and the entrants get a great-looking Nuts to Zots t-shirt too. About five of us came up with the idea of the race, and we lose money every year. But the run is for people to have a good time, so it's worth it.

I've barbecued for people at my place after a couple of runs. One year, we had two hundred people eating chicken and shishkebab. I flew in that same morning from Dallas at 4 o'clock, I completed the run, but my time naturally wasn't so hot. That's okay. The idea is to have fun, and for two years Nuts to Zots was a lot more fun than playing on the Oakland Raiders, where I wasn't starting *or* finishing.

I showed up for training camp thinking that if I outplayed Pastorini, and the job remained his, then I would consider leaving. Remaining in the Bay Area was no longer the prevailing thought in my mind. Time was running out and I would go anywhere to get a legitimate chance to start.

I started to feel old. A rookie quarterback in camp told me that I had always been his idol, and that he had to resist the urge to call me Mr. Plunkett.

"If you do," I said, "I'll kill you."

"Plunk was away at camp when the water heater went out in his house. I picked up a new heater, got my dad, and we went over and installed it. The next day we came back and did a little more work. A month later, I'm at Plunk's house and he hands me this brown paper bag. You have to know Plunk; he's not a showy person. 'Here, this is yours,' he said. Inside the bag is the watch he received as NFL Rookie of the Year. He had sent it back to New York and replaced the back plate with a new one, on which was engraved: 'To Phill, TE [tight end], from Jim, QB' with the date. Both of us couldn't talk."
                                        —PHILL PASSAFUIME

Pastorini opened the pre-season in San Francisco. The Joe Thomas tragi-comedy had played itself out and Bill

Walsh was in his second year of trying to get the 49ers back to the point of respectability. The 49ers looked respectable against Oakland that night, cutting through us like the fierce Candlestick wind in a 33–14 thrashing. The fourth-quarter quarterback—me—threw 2 touchdown passes to tight end Todd Christensen.

One week later, Wilson showed the future might even be sooner than Flores expected. Marc tossed a 17-yard touchdown pass to halfback Terry Robiskie with nine seconds left to defeat New England 31–29.

Pastorini and I each played one quarter against the Patriots behind the starting offensive line. Dan completed 5 of 8 passes for 109 yards, including a 65-yard touchdown pass to Branch. I connected on 8 of 9 passes for 93 yards and a 21-yard scoring strike to Branch.

"I'm still No. 2, I suppose," I told the media after the game. "All three quarterbacks played well, no question about it."

Upshaw told a reporter: "Our best quarterback is the Mormon [Wilson]."

Upshaw grinned. Did he mean it?

It became apparent the next week that I wasn't being given a fair chance to compete for the job. I didn't get into the Washington game until late—with the other reserves— when we were way behind. I got my butt kicked. After the way I played the first two weeks, I didn't think it was fair. When we got back to training camp, I knocked on the head coach's door.

"Tom, I've got to get something off my chest. I think I'm playing well, but at my age and making the money that I am, if I don't get a chance at a starting job soon, I may never get another opportunity. I don't think I'm going to start here. You've got Dan and you're thinking about Marc in the years ahead. It doesn't look like I'm in your plans. Going to another club would mean scrambling and taking risks again, but I'm willing to take that chance. If you can trade me, go ahead."

"Jim, it would be silly for us to trade you and not have an experienced backup quarterback. I'm happy with the way you are playing. We stayed with Dan longer in Washington because he is our starter, it's a new system for him and we have just one more pre-season game left. But you're throwing the ball well. Just keep working hard. I know you're not the kind of player who would walk out of training camp or create any trouble."

"You're right. I'm not that way. But if things don't change, I may come back and talk to you about the same thing."

"I understand what it's like, Jim, to be a backup quarterback. I went through the same thing. Once again, we're pleased with your performances. I'll relay to Al what we talked about."

I couldn't have done anything more to win the starting job the following week against Philadelphia. Pastorini completed 8 of 22 passes for 111 yards and no touchdowns. Playing less than a half, I completed 9 of 18 passes for 136 yards and 2 touchdowns. Dan had 2 interceptions; I had 1.

The Eagles had us beaten on the scoreboard, 23–10, and we were pinned back on our 6 with eight minutes left. The big play of the drive was my 40-yard pass to Ramsey at the Eagles' 28. On fourth down from the 5, I threw high again for Ramsey, who jumped up, pulled the pass in and it was 23–17.

There were 58 seconds left when we got the football back on our 43. I looked deep for Martini and he made a 39-yard catch at the Eagles' 29. A roughness penalty moved us to the 14. I threw incomplete to Raymond Chester, then Christensen. Ramsey then faked to the corner, broke across the middle and I drilled a touchdown pass against his chest. With four seconds left, we had won, 24–23.

"This game will make an old man of me yet," Flores said afterward.

The growing quarterback controversy might make him older sooner.

"You'll have to talk to Tom about who is No. 1," I told every reporter who asked. "I feel confident about myself. I feel I did the best job I could do under the circumstances. It may not be enough."

Dressing next to me, Pastorini was even more middle-of-the-road in his comments to reporters.

"You can't take anything away from Jim's performances. But you have to remember, I'm not working against him. I'm working with him. It's a coach's decision."

The decision was Pastorini No. 1, Plunkett No. 2 and Wilson No. 3. David Humm was traded to Buffalo. Pastorini would later say that I outplayed him that summer.

Oakland opened the regular season in Kansas City. The temperature was ninety-four degrees, a muggy heat with little or no wind. Some high school band members collapsed from heat prostration before the game. Pastorini was icy cool, however, completing 19 of 37 passes for 317 yards and touchdown passes of 16 and 32 yards to Bob Chandler, whom we picked up from Buffalo in the off-season. The Raiders won, 27–14.

Pastorini hit Branch on a 48-yard touchdown pass the next week in San Diego, but the Chargers fought back to lead, 24–17. With a minute left to play, Gary "Big Hands" Johnson broke through on third down and sacked Pastorini for a 7-yard loss. Dan couldn't get up. He had to be helped off the field.

Suddenly I was in the game with little time left and possibly just one play to either put us back in the game or knock us out. Well, 50–50 odds are better than anything I've had lately. I drew the Chargers offside, which moved us to their 18. This made it fourth-and-twelve. Thirty-nine seconds were left.

Chester lined up to the left. He ran a post pattern and I hit him in the back of the end zone. Chris Bahr, who had missed 4 of 5 field goals, was accurate on the conversion and we went into overtime.

Teammates mobbed me as I came off the field. One pass, 1 touchdown, tie game. You couldn't ask more from a quarterback. I really felt good. Now it was sudden death. I wasn't worried. I had just found sudden life.

Flores came over to me.

"Jim, wait and see what happens."

"What do you mean?"

"Dan might go back in."

Go back in! Dammit, Tom! Pastorini's carried off the field, I save the game, now he's going to play? It's just not right. This is my game to win or lose. Don't take it away from me.

Why in the heck was I telling myself all this and not Flores? Sure he had a game to win, but he has feelings. You don't treat people this way. I've got to say something, make him see. What good would it do, anyway? He's not going to change his mind.

I held my rage inside. One-Play Plunkett.

Pastorini threw an interception on his first pass, but so did Dan Fouts and we got the ball back. Bahr's 50-yard field goal was partially blocked, then Fouts threw a 24-yard touchdown pass to John Jefferson. San Diego won, 30–24.

Flores told the media afterward that Pastorini twisted his knee, but Dan said he could still play. Pastorini called the injury a "little hyperextension," but admitted to a San Diego writer that the knee was stiff.

If it was stiff, why did he come back in? He's helped off the field and then he runs back on. His leg got well very quickly. Heck, it's possible. The initial shock passes, the adrenalin is going, and you never feel the pain anyway until later. Maybe I would have tried to come back too.

I tried to think things out rationally, but I was confused, hurt and mad. How else should I feel?

I was interviewed on a sports talk show a few nights later and told the listeners that I should have played in the overtime period. The media were sympathetic and in my corner from their comments after the game.

Raider executive Al LoCasale, on his weekly "Ask the Raiders" call-in show, said the media had distorted what happened in San Diego, that no one on the Raiders was upset about the quarterback situation.

You have to understand that LoCasale is extremely faithful to the Raiders and worships Al Davis. I once mentioned to LoCasale that the Davis Cup finals would be held in San Francisco.

"It was nice of them to name a tennis tournament after Al," he replied.

If LoCasale thought that no one on the team was upset by the quarterback situation, it was because he hadn't asked me. However, even if he had, I'm sure he would have said the same thing on the radio.

Pastorini had a rough time the following week against the Redskins. Early in the fourth quarter, they narrowed our lead to 17–14, and Flores told me to warm up. Tom clearly indicated that if we didn't score on our next series, I would replace Pastorini.

Kenny King, our new halfback from Houston, broke off a 30-yard run to keep the series moving and Pastorini closed it out with a 5-yard touchdown pass to Chandler. I never got in as we held on to win, 24–21.

I snapped at Gerry after the game. I didn't mean to, and apologized the next day. But not getting a chance to play—warming up was beginning to leave me cold—really got to me and I took it out on her unfairly.

My other friends were encouraging as usual. Everyone felt my time was coming. Everyone, that is, but me.

The following week in Buffalo, I didn't play or even warm up. Our offense failed to score as King fumbled the ball away twice inside the Bills' 20. We lost, 24–7, and looked bad in the process.

The Raiders were 2–2. Our performances had ranged from fabulous to flat. Things seemed to be deteriorating as fast for the Raiders as they were for Jim Plunkett. My 33rd birthday was two months away and I was still playing second-fiddle.

Should I go see Flores again? What good would it do? What good did it do the last time? I was a man running on a treadmill—a few steps forward, a few steps backward. Getting nowhere.

The nowhere man? I knew it wasn't true.

I had something to give. I could take this team somewhere.

My spirits sagged further after Buffalo. What the heck am I practicing for anyway? I'm working hard like Tom asked, running extra miles, lifting weights, preparing mentally for each Sunday. And for what, to be the healthiest, most game-ready unused quarterback in the league?

Al Davis must have recognized the depths of my dejection. He grabbed my arm one day after practice.

"Be prepared, Jim. You never know what's going to happen."

Prepare for what? Nothing has happened in two and a half years. What could possibly happen now?

A few days later, I found out.

Chapter Seven

OPPOSITES DON'T ATTRACT

"I watched Bellarmine High play and told my wife: 'You won't believe this, but I just saw a player with probably more physical ability than Plunkett. Jim's stronger, but this player is quicker, has a quicker release. He punts and kicks off too.' My wife said: 'Who is it?' I told her: 'A kid named Pastorini."

—AL CEMENTINA

Dan Pastorini and I are not friends.

We do a good job of hiding it. We are careful to say all the right things about each other so the public won't suspect anything.

Yet the two of us seldom speak unless it is through common courtesy. When we do talk, it is usually about football or inconsequential stuff. You know, small talk.

It was predictable that our relationship would turn out this way. We were high school athletes from the same town who have competed against each other far too long—

195

first for recognition as quarterbacks and later as competitors on the Oakland Raiders.

Our careers first crossed in San Jose, California, in the mid-1970s. Pastorini attended Bellarmine, a Catholic high school with a number of students from upper-crust families. I went to James Lick, a public school from the poor side of town.

We were both heavily recruited. I decided on Stanford, a major university, and Pastorini selected Santa Clara, a small college, twenty miles away. I was one year ahead of Pastorini in school, but my redshirt season at Stanford put us in the same class in terms of athletic eligibility.

Stanford plays major powers like USC. Santa Clara schedules predominantly Division II teams like Chico State. So it was inevitable that Stanford would draw the greater media focus.

Pastorini was named Small College All-America. I was chosen University Division All-America and received the Heisman Trophy. Stanford played in the Rose Bowl. Santa Clara didn't play in any bowls. Then came the NFL draft: I was the first player taken, Pastorini the third.

Because of this entire series of events, it is easy to see why we don't get along all that well. Perhaps if our lives hadn't intersected as often as they have, we might feel differently about each other. But, then again, maybe not.

We're two diverse personalities.

Pastorini travels on a faster track. He likes fast boats and racing cars. I get seasick and prefer freeways over speedways. He is good-looking and knows it. His temper flares in public; just ask a Houston sportswriter. I'm more controlled; I grin and bear the criticism. He is flamboyant and likes to be seen. I'm more reserved and don't care if I'm seen. His life is public, mine is private.

Total opposites.

Pastorini and I would never be drawn together except for the unexpected. The Raiders picked me off the

NFL's junk heap. Two years later, they traded for Pastorini. Now we were teammates and forced to co-exist, our lockers side by side.

We have made an effort not to open old wounds or create new ones. We have succeeded in creating an air of amiability, though it is only thin air.

But even if we aren't friends, is this so abnormal? There are other Raiders who don't like one another and who camouflage their true feelings so the media won't know. Not everyone in society gets along. Rozelle doesn't like Davis. Mailer doesn't like Vidal. Dean doesn't like Nixon. And vice versa. These are the complexities of life and easier left alone than explained.

However, one thing Pastorini said about me I found very amusing. He told a reporter that I wasn't the kind of guy he would go out with and have a few beers. Like there was something wrong with me, that I'm not one of the boys.

And I've drunk with Pastorini before!

"Pastorini's statement casts Jim in the same light as Steve Garvey, some guy you wouldn't go out and have a hoot with. I think of the innumerable number of beers I've had with Plunk, which are some of the best times of my life. It just shows you to what extent Pastorini knows Plunk. That's the problem: he doesn't know Plunk. There's just some bad blood between those two."

—JACK SCHULTZ

Regardless of how I feel about Pastorini as a person, I respect him as an athlete. He will go to the wall to win a football game and he won't spare life or limb to get there. Unfortunately, in Dan's fifth league game as an Oakland Raider, one of his limbs was broken.

It happened in the first quarter of our division home-and-home rematch with Kansas City. The Chiefs grabbed a quick 7–0 lead when Pastorini was hit, fumbled and linebacker Gary Spani scooped up the ball and ran 16 yards for a touchdown.

On Pastorini's next pass attempt, he threw incomplete to Chandler just before Chiefs lineman Dino Mangiero dropped his 265 pounds on Dan's right leg, cracking the tibia.

I didn't see it happen because I was looking at our receivers. When I saw Pastorini on the ground, my first thought was the injury isn't serious. The San Diego game still was on my mind. I was ready to ask Dan how badly he was hurt.

Then I realized he was in great pain. I felt especially sorry for Dan because he had worked hard to win over his new teammates and fans, the majority of whom were still carrying on a love affair with Ken Stabler.

Pastorini's homecoming hadn't turned out well either. In fact the moment the fans saw he was hurt, they began cheering.

Poor Dan was writhing on the turf, his face contorted with pain, and the fans were cheering his misery. It was disgusting. Sickening. I've been injured enough times in my career to dread seeing others get hurt. I couldn't believe the cheering. It wasn't all of the 40,153 fans, but the noise was loud and unmistakable. Those who cheered wouldn't have if their own sons, not Pastorini, were on the ground.

The whole scene—ridicule on top of injury—left a bitter aftertaste for all the Raiders. Marc Wilson, the rookie, was in disbelief. He had never witnessed this kind of fan behavior. He said he would never feel the same about football again.

I warmed up quickly. This is it. "Be prepared," Davis had said. The man must be psychic. I didn't want to become No. 1 this way, but I had no time to think about it. I was in the game.

I didn't exactly start off with a flourish. On my first play, Art Still sacked me. The tone was set for the rest of the game. I threw 52 passes, a Raider record, but completed only 20 for 238 yards. I was sacked 4 more times, threw 5 interceptions and fumbled the ball away once.

I was cold all afternoon. My passes were high; I wasn't stepping into my throws. One of my completions was torn out of Dave Casper's hands by Whitney Paul and returned 32 yards for a touchdown. It was that kind of day. Kansas City led 31–0 and it was just the second quarter.

Oakland made it a battle in the second half. I hit Branch and Chandler for fourth-quarter touchdowns. Branch almost had another touchdown, but he couldn't get both feet down in the end zone. If he had, the score would have been 31–24. We still would have had time to tie it up. However, Kansas City's early cushion held up for a 31–17 victory.

I finally get my chance and then blow it. I really felt terrible. I saw Lew Erber, our receivers coach.

"I don't know what happened, Lew."

"You haven't played for two and a half years, Jim. That's what happened."

The players had confidence in me, I thought, from the pre-season and that one play in San Diego. The linemen had been unhappy with Pastorini's play-calling. He threw a lot of deep passes the first few games. The guys up front were getting tired of pass-blocking. I'm more conservative than Dan. I like to throw deep too, but I'm more selective.

If I was to keep my teammates' confidence, I had to make them believe in me. I had to produce right away.

However, there was a team matter to take care of first.

Upshaw, the offensive captain, called a players meeting after the Kansas City defeat had dropped our record to 2–3. We were in danger of blowing the season right there. The players read that Flores was in trouble with Davis and in danger of losing his job. I'm not sure what effect that had on us because you never know about rumors.

Regardless, something had to be done to turn the

team around. Maybe a team meeting would help; it couldn't
hurt. Upshaw got up and said that we could turn the season
around if we worked harder as a team, dedicated ourselves
to the all-for-one, one-for-all concept.

Then one stood up against all.

Dave "The Ghost" Casper is anything but inhibited.
He is a bright guy with an economics degree from Notre
Dame. He has an opinion on almost everything and isn't
afraid to voice it.

Casper maintained that if everyone was trying as
hard as he could, he didn't have to worry about anyone else.
In other words: Look inside yourself instead of looking to
others.

Needless to say, Casper's comments were unap-
preciated by Upshaw, and others too. Casper may have been
right in what he said, but he had gone against the grain. It
wasn't a very good time for The Ghost anyway. He was kind
of lost. Things weren't going well financially and at home.
Casper was really caught up in country music. His real desire was to become a singer like Willie Nelson.

There was criticism of Casper's practice habits. He
practiced, though not diligently. He played great on Sun-
days. Ghost argued that his chronic back problem and bad
hamstrings prevented him from working hard in the middle
of the week. He was saving his one big burst for Sunday.

I didn't agree with everything Casper said at the
meeting, but I didn't totally agree with what others said
either. This is what team meetings are for: to air out griev-
ances. We used to have a meeting a week in New England
and San Francisco. It is difficult to judge what effect they
have, unless you look at the outcome.

The one in Oakland must have been a success. We
began to win.

Pastorini's leg was placed in a cast and he was put on
injured reserve. The job was mine, if I could keep it. The
coaches were high on Wilson. He is tall, 6′ 5″, and feisty for

THE PROS: Before Oakland — The Agony
(New England Patriots and San Francisco 49ers)

The option-play coach, Chuck Fairbanks, and me, heading for the locker room after beating the Miami Dolphins in 1974. *(Wide World Photos, Inc.)*

New England cheerleaders and fans sing "Happy Birthday" to the Stanford Connection — Randy Vataha and me — in 1971. *(Wide World Photos, Inc.)*

Socking it to Baltimore before the Colts sock it to me. (*New England Patriots*)

Running for my life in New England. (*New England Patriots*)

Hitting from the real rough — a gravel access road — in Harrah's annual Celebrity Golf Tournament at Lake Tahoe. *(Jim Plunkett)*

With coach Monte Clark, at the press conference announcing that I had become a 49er. *(Wide World Photos, Inc.)*

Give me some time, men! *(San Francisco 49ers)*

Joe Thomas (right) — the man I love to hate — and Eddie DeBartolo as they take control of the 49ers. *(Wide World Photos, Inc.)*

The man who replaced me:
Scott Bull, No. 19. *(Russ Reed)*

Rams defensive end Fred
Dryer won't let go. *(Wide
World Photos, Inc.)*

Another bad day with the
49ers. (*Robert Stinnett*)

With my fiancée, Gerry
Lavelle. (*Jim Plunkett*)

With the Oakland Raiders — The Ecstasy

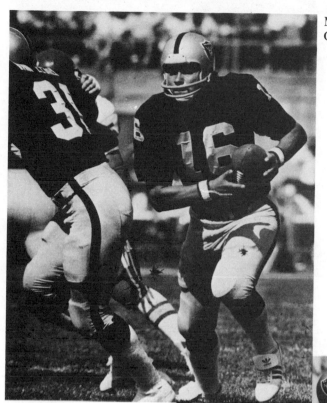

Making things happen in Oakland. *(Ron Riesterer)*

Nose tackle Dino Mangiero of the Chiefs doesn't want me to pass. *(Ron Riesterer)*

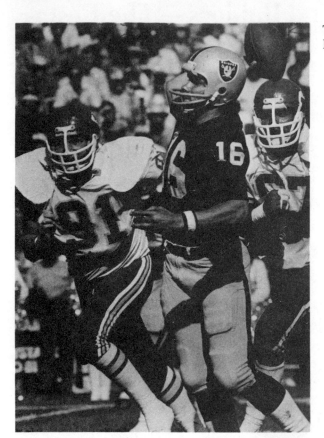

Throwing on the move against
Kansas City *(Ron Riesterer)*

Get those knees up, Plunkett!
(Ron Riesterer)

Wearing my Stanford ring in Oakland, following a victory over Seattle. *(Wide World Photos, Inc.)*

Denver's Rob Nairne makes me wince. *(Wide World Photos, Inc.)*

All smiles before the 1980
Houston playoff game. (*Wide
World Photos, Inc.*)

Running for daylight against
Houston in the NFL playoffs,
1980. (*Ron Riesterer*)

Everything's A-OK with the Raiders. *(Howard Erker)*

Raiders' owner Al Davis: devil or angel? *(Wide World Photos, Inc.)*

Tom Flores and a Super Bowl victory are near at hand.
(Russ Reed)

The ecstasy of winning the 1981 Super Bowl. (*Wide World Photos, Inc.*)

Tom Flores and I celebrate our
Super Bowl victory. *(Wide
World Photos, Inc.)*

Mr. Interception — Rod Martin
— with me at Oakland Airport
reception following the Super
Bowl. *(Howard Erker)*

WORLD CHAMPIONS OF PROFESSIONAL FOOTBALL

A happy team photo of the Oakland Raiders, Super Bowl XV champions. *(Norm Fisher)*

The post-Super Bowl party at the 4141 Club. Up front: Phill Passafuime, Ron Kadziel and Jim Kauffman. Back row (l. to r.): Randy Vataha, me, Jack Schultz, Jack Lasater, Jack Alustiza. In the middle, Jim Collins. *(Nancy Ditz)*

Cooling-off time in Hawaii after the 1981 Super Bowl. *(Jim Plunkett)*

his size. Usually it's the short players who are feisty, but Wilson gets very upset at practice if he does something wrong. He is determined. He wants to succeed badly, and he will someday.

I knew, then, if I didn't come through, it would be my last chance. I would be a backup quarterback for the rest of my career. Football's longest comeback, two and a half years, was over, yet it was just beginning, really.

Al Davis gave me some sound advice before my first start.

"Look, Jim, it's not important that you have a good game. It's important that we win. You get what I'm saying?"

I knew exactly what he meant. If I had a good day statistically and we lost, the critics would say, "See, he still doesn't have it." If I didn't pass too well and we won, they'd say, "Plunkett showed great leadership."

A full week to prepare for my first start as a Raider after forty-six games as a reserve (including pre-season) was exactly what I needed. I ran all the plays in practice—the Raiders', not the opponents'—and I was ready.

We jumped out early against San Diego, which meant I only had to throw 14 times, completing 11 for 164 yards. The protection was great, just 1 sack. The running game was even more explosive—214 yards. We really took it to the Chargers.

Usually after a new quarterback takes over, the next week's score is low, like 13–12. This happens because there is a feeling of unfamiliarity with a new quarterback. I was older and more experienced, so I was able to avoid that problem. I used mostly short passes that day, taking the pressure off our overworked linemen. I threw under the zone and used the quick out more than the Raiders had done in three years. The change at quarterback had a positive effect.

My first touchdown was picture-perfect. We were on San Diego's 43. We had the proper situation working because of all the short passes. I called a formation that tied up the Chargers underneath and sent Branch toward the left corner. Branch faked to the post, drawing the cornerback in that direction, then turned toward the flag. Cliff had two steps on his man as the ball left my hand. I watched it spiral off into the distance against a clear blue sky. Branch looked back over his shoulder, picked up the ball's descent, stretched out his arms and clutched the brown leather at the 5 without breaking stride. Six!

I don't remember a whole lot after the third quarter. I was running for a first down when Woodrow Lowe, a Charger linebacker, caught me with a forearm and turned off my lights. He was called for unnecessary roughness as I wobbled off the field. Wilson replaced me for 4 plays. I returned on third-and-six and everything looked fuzzy . . . the scoreboard, my teammates. I managed to hit Chandler—he's No. 85, right?—for 14 yards and a first down at the six. We scored and I returned to the bench for more oxygen.

This game brought Kenny King to the forefront. King was the blocking back for Billy Sims at Oklahoma and a backup to Earl Campbell on the Houston Oilers. Davis thought Kenny had the speed to play halfback, a position he hadn't played since his high school days in Clarendon, Texas. King turned out to be faster than any of us thought.

He broke off 2 big touchdown runs against the Chargers, a 31-yarder to open the game and a team-record 89-yarder after San Diego tied the score, 24–24. On the ensuing kickoff, Todd Christensen recovered Chuck Muncie's fumble in the end zone to put the lid on a 38–24 victory.

Special teams players are a special breed. They are reckless and play without fear of bodily harm, which is amazing when you think that they have a 30-yard running start before a collision. If you want to know who the faint of heart are in football, put them on special teams. You will find out in a hurry.

It is a thankless job handled by those who should be

thanked every day by their coaches and teammates. Oakland usually has fine special teams. Christensen and Derrick Jensen are two of the best special teams players to be found in the league. They are always there to make the tackle, even though people try to double-team them. Special team players are football's stunt men, and they love the challenge —and even the danger—of the job they do.

Morris Bradshaw has logged more minutes on special teams than he has at wide receiver in seven years with the Raiders. Morris can catch the deep bomb and he can also catch the fast return man. So can Jeff Barnes, who is a linebacker with a receiver's speed. Both would like to play more than they have in recent years, but neither grouses over lack of playing minutes. They just do their job, whatever it is.

Christensen, Jensen, Bradshaw, Barnes and others on the Raiders are more than special team players. They are *team* players.

I told someone after the San Diego game that I had a lot of good passes stored up. After all, December 18, 1977 to October 12, 1980 is a long time to go between starts. The Raiders now believed in me and I believed in myself.

"I think everyone was surprised by Jim's performance. We knew he had the ability a long time ago, and he had the great pre-season, but he hadn't done much for awhile. The team tried to play better when he came in, to help him. But he has to have a lot of inner strength to do what he did. He has a lot of confidence in himself and, though he's a modest person, he spreads this confidence to others through his playing. I'm sure he's proud of what he accomplished in 1980 and we are just as proud of him. It was a storybook season."
—DAVE DALBY, Oakland Raiders center

After the San Diego game, Casper was traded to Houston for a first- and second-round pick in 1981. The Ghost is one of the finest tight ends in football, an all-pro his first four years as a starter. He has a knack for catching the football that is hard to explain; he just has it. Maybe it was inevitable Davis would trade him, not just because of Casper's stance at the team meeting, but because of their contract haggle from the year before. Davis may have done Ghost a favor, too, by giving him a change in environment.

We would miss Casper, but we still had three other tight ends. Raymond Chester had a great year in 1979, just like Casper. Each one made one all-pro team and both made the Pro Bowl: an unprecedented double for tight ends from one team. Chester is a sincere individual who works hard all the time; he is a great physical specimen. Raymond is in his thirties, but he can still get deep. Derrick Ramsey was a college quarterback at Kentucky who switched to tight end in Oakland. Derrick is going to be a fine player. He can run like a deer. Todd Christensen, our special teams captain, also is a converted player. Dallas drafted him as a running back and Oakland made him a tight end. He is a Mormon kid who's on the borderline of being a crazy. A typical Raider.

I had never beaten Pittsburgh before the Raiders played them on Monday night TV. The Steelers dominated football in the 1970s, but Oakland doesn't fear them. On Monday night, Oakland fears no one. Through 1980, the Raiders' record on Mondays is an amazing 16–1–1.

Teams tend to play well on Monday night. There is the extra day's rest and, of course, the national exposure. You want to look good. I had a special reason for playing well: I wanted people to know that I was still around and not bartending somewhere.

They probably thought a bartender was quarterbacking the Raiders as I completed only one of the first 8 passes. The Steelers jumped into a 10–0 lead. King scored on a 27-yard sweep for us, but the Steelers came right back to make it 17–7. Then Oakland exploded for 3 straight touchdowns, including Rod Martin's 34-yard fumble return and Morris Bradshaw's 45-yard catch. The Steelers had a double zone on our outside receivers. Bradshaw lined up in the slot in our 3-receiver offense, split the middle of the field and was wide open.

Pittsburgh narrowed our lead to 28–24 at halftime. It wasn't a night for defense.

Steeler Coach Chuck Noll used the blitz a lot, thinking he could shake me up because I hadn't played in a long time. The blitz is a play in which players other than defensive linemen rush the quarterback, and the Steelers tried to surprise us by sending both safeties and the right cornerback, Mel Blount, in various combinations.

We were prepared for the blitz. We had seen on film how the Steelers blitzed Cincinnati the week before. Bengals fullback Pete Johnson wasn't covered on a 28-yard touchdown pass that cost Pittsburgh the game, 17–16. Fortunately, we had the right play called when Pittsburgh blitzed. There is an old saying: when preparation meets opportunity, you wind up with success. We were very successful that night.

Despite the added defensive pressure, I wasn't sacked once and didn't throw an interception. I was throwing with Steelers hanging on my arms and attacking me from all sides. I felt invincible.

Branch caught a 56-yard touchdown pass and then a 34-yarder as the Steelers blitzed everyone but owner Art Rooney. I was excited by football again. I really let my emotions show after each touchdown pass.

We beat the Steelers, 45–34. San Diego and Pittsburgh . . . that's an impressive 2-game winning streak. A writer asked me after the Steelers game if I wanted to say "I told you so." I didn't. Those who didn't believe in me could see for themselves on the football field. I'm not one to hold a grudge.

Pittsburgh's Mean Joe Greene said: "I wasn't surprised by Plunkett's play. He never has had the fortune to be on a good team. I've always been a fan of his. Tonight, he just got a chance to prove it."

So much of football is time and location. With the right combination, you've got a winning football team. With the wrong combination, you've got the situation Archie Manning has dealt with for so many years in New Orleans. Put Archie in a winning situation and he'll be "discovered" like I was in Oakland.

I was deluged by interview requests after the Pittsburgh game. Only this time I was prepared. I had put things into perspective during the down years. Now if something great happened, it wouldn't be earth-shattering. If the bottom fell out, it wouldn't be catastrophic. I was conditioned. Having been to hell and back once in my life, I couldn't be burned anymore. It didn't make a damn bit of difference what people thought of me. I was Jim Plunkett, for better or worse, and better most of the time. I wouldn't be destroyed again.

The Seattle Seahawks had been a problem for 2 years, beating the Raiders 4 straight times. We couldn't stop Jim Zorn's passing or his running. He would just kill us. Our defense caught up to him in 1980. Zorn was sacked 6 times, threw 2 interceptions and rushed for zero yardage in Oakland.

This game did more for my confidence than even Pittsburgh. I now felt comfortable in the pocket. I'd drop back, set up and hit whomever was open. That particular afternoon it was Bob Chandler. He caught 3 second-half touchdown passes of 5, 12 and 23 yards. I can't say that all 3 were perfectly thrown.

Chandler told me the whole game: "I'm open on the corner." I finally throw him a pass in the corner and he's covered. I had no choice; I was about to get sacked. So I threw the ball and said a prayer. Bobby leaped up between two defenders and made a spectacular one-handed catch in the back of the end zone. He later told the press: "It was pretty routine."

We beat Seattle, 33–14. Three in a row.

Everything was going well. The protection was outstanding and I hadn't thrown an interception in three games. I was no longer scared to make a mistake. In Oakland, you make a mistake and the defense will get you the ball back. Make a mistake in San Francisco and we'd fall behind, or further behind. The kind of club you play on determines the sizes of the holes you dig. Confucius.

The prospect of being booed didn't even frighten me anymore, and that's a tough mountain to climb. If you're an entertainer or athlete, you are going to be booed. What would it be like to read Shakespeare and hear boos? Has Olivier ever been booed?

Another thought hit me after the Seattle game: we can make the playoffs.

The whole team had the same feeling as we left the Oakland Coliseum for the post-game party, which the Raiders hold after every home game. From what I hear, Oakland is the only NFL team that does so. There is food and drink, but the main thing being offered is togetherness. The front office cares about the players and we care about one another. Togetherness and talent is a hard combination to beat.

When I wasn't playing, it was difficult for me to attend these parties, which are held in banquet rooms reserved by the Raiders at an Oakland hotel. Everyone was friendly toward me, but I felt awkward because I didn't feel a part of the team. I'm quiet anyway, and people didn't know how to approach me. But they tried their best to make me feel better. The other players introduced me to their family, parents and friends.

But now that I was playing—contributing—I felt like I belonged. I looked forward to the parties. I felt happier and people responded more to me. Each player is assigned a table for himself and his guests, and there now seemed to be larger crowds around my table. My life had undergone an 180-degree turn in a matter of weeks. I felt in control.

Bring on those Miami Dolphins!

I've always wanted to play for Don Shula. I would have liked to play for Vince Lombardi and George Allen for the same reason, to find out what made these men successful. I'd like to know the way they think, how they plan, what they teach, what methods they use. I may not agree with all their methods, but I'd be interested nonetheless.

Shula always has been tough on me. I really admire the man. New England only beat him twice in 10 tries while I was there. Whether Shula's Miami teams make the playoffs or not, they are well disciplined. He is the epitome of the word: coach.

And my 1980 run-in with Shula was almost a replay of my previous encounters—3 interceptions and 3 sacks.

The gods were smiling on us, however. Vern Den Herder almost sacked me once, but I ducked under his rush and throw to Raymond Chester, who scored only because Dolphin linebacker A. J. Duhe fell down covering him. Then Chandler made a Houdini reception. Safety Glenn Blackwood was about to intercept my pass when the ball disappeared right in front of his eyes. Chandler had flashed in front of Blackwood, tipped the ball and made it reappear in his hands for a touchdown.

We hadn't played our best football, but we won, 16–10. Four in a row.

By now it was apparent to anyone who knew a football from a tennis ball that the Raiders were coming on. Especially on defense.

This was a new catchword in Oakland: defense. The Raiders always have been known for high-octane offense. Defense was something the other guys did while the offense caught its breath between touchdowns. No longer. Defense was carrying the team.

It was a gradual transition that required the firing of one Raider coach and the hiring of Charlie Sumner, who had been fired by Oakland ten years earlier.

After Denver defeated Oakland for the 1977 APC championship, Al Davis hired Myrel Moore, the Broncos' linebacker coach, to perfect the 3–4 defense in Oakland— 3 defensive linemen and 4 linebackers. After 2 straight seasons of failing to make the playoffs, Moore complained that Davis hadn't furnished him with enough talent to run a successful 3–4. Davis didn't invite Moore back for the 1980 season.

Sumner, who was let go by Davis in 1968 only to be brought back to Oakland in 1979, took over the defense and things began to happen. Sumner's best idea was to let Ted Hendricks play every down. Moore spot-played Hendricks, whose performance level then dropped. With more playing time, Hendricks was voted all-pro linebacker in 1980 at the age of 33.

The defense became known as the Boys of Sumner, a group of oddballs playing an "odd" (3–4) defense.

Hendricks is one of the lead crazies. You never know what he is going to do or say, and he may not either.

Madden once tried to break up a fight between two rookies in training camp, but was knocked off his feet in the process. John got up, his face flushed. "Hey, John," Hendricks said calmly, "did you take your salt pills today?"

Hendricks plays hard on and off the field. On the bus trip to a celebrity tennis tournament in Arizona, Hendricks made the driver stop in front of a liquor store. Hendricks bought a case of beer and some bottles of vodka and tonic, then got back on the bus. "OK, driver, let's go," he said.

Hendricks and Lester Hayes were the Raiders' defensive leaders in 1980. When I first got to Oakland, Hayes was just a jive guy trying to be cool rather than a good football player. The next year, I noticed a marked change in his attitude. He was determined to be the best cornerback in the NFL. In 1980, he not only became the best corner, but the best defensive back in the league. He had an incredible year. In addition to 13 interceptions during the regular season, he had 5 more in the playoffs and another 4 nullified by penalties. That would have made it 22 interceptions, which would have been an unfathomable year.

The biggest person on the defense—and the biggest character—is Tooz. John Matuszak has led a turbulent life. Paul Wiggin, the Stanford coach who previously coached Matuszak in Kansas City, pounded on Tooz's chest one night in an ambulance to get his heart pumping again. Tooz would walk into Chiefs team meetings with his portable radio blaring. One night his wife tried to run him over in a car at Kansas City's training camp.

Matuszak was lauded by film critics for his role in *North Dallas Forty.* He had a supporting role in *Caveman,* which featured Ringo Starr. At 6′ 8″, 280 pounds, Tooz is an awesome display of musculature, whether in a caveman's suit or a football uniform. It takes two men to block him, and even that usually isn't enough.

Tooz isn't one of my favorite people, however. He's somewhat condescending and treats me like a little kid. He tells me things like "We're real proud of you." He treats me like he's my father, and I'm older than he is! What gets me even more, he doesn't mean what he's saying anyway.

Dave Browning, our other defensive end, is 6′ 5″, but weighs only 245 pounds. He's not very physical, but he never lets up. Dave fights off blocks by much larger offensive linemen because he is more intense than they are. I don't know of anyone on the team who plays with more intensity than Browning.

Dave lives in Washington state in the off-season. He missed a Raider mini-camp right after Mount St. Helens had its famous upset stomach. Dave started toward Oakland, but his car filled up with ash. It is the only time in NFL history that a player was excused from a camp because of a volcano.

We have two more ends who are pass-rush specialists: Willie Jones and Cedrick Hardman. There is no telling how good Willie will become once he stops jumping offside. Hardman, like me, was paroled by the 49ers and found new life in Oakland. Cedrick's a funny guy. He told me: "I didn't think I would like coming in on just passing downs. Now I'm liking it as I enter my second decade of football."

Our nose tackles, Reggie Kinlaw and Dave Pear, are as different as pâté de foie gras and pepperoni pizza. Reggie was a last-round draft pick in 1979. Because of his 6' 2", 240-pound frame, pro scouts couldn't determine whether he was a lineman or linebacker. Oakland stuck him in the line and he made some big plays because of his extraordinary quickness. Reggie's very quiet, but Pear is an off-the-wall guy. He once used a teammate's helmet for a toilet. Pear was Tampa Bay's first Pro Bowl selection, but his weird behavior made him unwelcome with John McKay, the Tampa coach. Pear is one of the strongest Raiders: he once bench-pressed 350 pounds 17 times in succession.

Linebacker Rod Martin has a voice like a basso profundo and hands made out of oak. He weighs only 210 pounds, but he has quick tackling instincts and surprising strength. Oakland picked Rod in the last round of the 1977 draft, then cut him. The 49ers also cut him and he wound up back in Oakland. Rod plays his best in big games.

Bob Nelson is quite a comeback story. He was cast off by Buffalo, Oakland and San Francisco before resurfacing with the Raiders. He played for the 49ers against us one year after attending the Raiders training camp. I asked him afterward: "Which training table did you sit at today?" If it hadn't been for Sumner, who spotted Nelson on some old film footage and liked what he saw, Bob would be in the ice cream distributing business in Minnesota. Bob came through on his fourth chance and played great football for us in 1980.

Our other inside linebacker, Matt Millen, was a defensive tackle at Penn State. He has an unusual build for a linebacker—6′ 2″, 260 pounds—but Matt can really play. He gave the Raiders two things they needed: enthusiasm and someone who can close down the middle of the line. Matt jumps up and down on the field, thrusts his fist in the air like Thor after a tackle. He talks to opponents all the time and they don't like it. But Matt is a sweetheart of a guy. He doesn't even drink. You wonder, What is he doing on the Raiders?

Dwayne O'Steen, the cornerback opposite Hayes, calls himself "The Duke." Some writers think it is because of John Wayne. O'Steen does have "Wayne" in his first name and he does wear the kind of cowboy shirts that the real Duke wore in *Stagecoach*. But that isn't the reason. O'Steen is the best dresser on the team. I've never seen him in the same clothes twice. And he drives an expensive car. He is . . . The Duke.

Oakland obtained free safety Burgess Owens from the Jets for a sixth-round draft pick. The Jets should check their pockets to see if they weren't robbed. Burgess became a defensive leader in Oakland and a stabilizing force on the team. He is a bright person from a family of college educators. Burgess majored in marine biology and he's an off-season stockbroker in New York. You won't find many nicer people in football.

Mike Davis, our strong safety, is a tough kid. Some opponents might say overaggressive, because Mike occasionally shoves an arm into someone's face longer than he should. Mike wants people to know that he plays mean, which he does every game—elbow or no elbow.

The defense came through again when Cincinnati came to town. The Bengals' running game was shut down with 70 yards (2.7 yards per carry) and their quarterbacks threw 4 interceptions. We were even more careless with 5 turnovers—2 interceptions, 3 fumbles—and 12 penalties.

One thing the offense did right—a perfect 7-for-7 on third-down conversions in the first half. And I missed only 6 times out of 25 pass attempts as we totaled 244 yards in the air.

We needed something extra against Cincinnati, however, and we got it on Arthur Whittington's 90-yard touchdown return of the opening second-half kickoff.

Whittington's not a big guy, but he is gutsy with good speed and the ability to catch the football. He plays behind King because he doesn't have Kenny's size. All our backs are alike in one respect: they can block.

Al Davis told me that he drafts running backs who can block for the quarterback. That's the first criterion. The second is whether he can catch the ball and the third is whether he can run. Davis's thinking is just the reverse of that of most teams.

Fullback Mark van Eeghen is an excellent blocker. He has rushed for 1,000 yards 3 times even though he doesn't have outstanding speed. His longest career run is 34 yards. Mark is a super cutback runner who always finds a hole. He generally leads the team in rushing and humility. He is shy and says "gosh" and "gee" a lot. Mark acts like a scared rookie.

With 9 minutes left against Cincinnati, we led 21–17. We couldn't run 3 times, punt and then rely on the defense. We had to force the issue. I had to pass.

Branch caught a sideline toss for 9 yards, but King fumbled the ball to Cincinnati on the next play. Rod Martin —the big-play man—got us back in gear with a 19-yard interception return to Cincinnati's 49.

Whittington scooted through tackle for 5 yards. Van Eeghen ran a delay route over the middle and caught a 19-yard pass. Branch got loose for a 9-yard reception on the left sideline and Chandler found room on the right sideline for a 7-yard catch at the Bengals' 9. Whittington swept left end for 5. I dropped back, looking for the kill, and saw nothing but white jerseys in front of black jerseys. So I headed straight for the end zone and just made it. We got out of there alive, 28–17. Five in a row.

"Plunkett's got a big butt; it must be from eating all those tacos," a grinning Upshaw said. "But his running takes a lot of pressure off the line. He did another good job for us today."

I forgot to vote that season. Well, I ran out of time to vote. I was too busy trying to keep our winning streak going. I slept late, went to practice, and by the time I got home on election night, the polls were closed. I normally register as a Republican, but in 1980 I had signed up as an Independent. That doesn't necessarily mean I would have voted for John Anderson, though I feel he is a good man. It would have been Anderson or Ronald Reagan. I always vote for the man, not the party.

I can tell you I wouldn't have voted for Jimmy Carter. I didn't in 1976. But I do think Carter did the best possible job of handling the hostage situation in Iran. I approved of his attempt to fly in and evacuate the hostages. The mission failed—miserably—but how could we know what was going to happen to the hostages if no effort had been made? There was a lot of criticism of Carter from around the country after this. But I wonder how an outsider could tell the president what he should or shouldn't do without being involved in the day-by-day, sometimes minute-by-minute develop-ments of the crisis. At the time our country felt, in effect, that we were being held hostage by a smaller country. It really got to us. I thought about it a lot during that 1980 season.

It is hard to keep a winning streak going in the NFL, because there will be games where you can't do much of anything right. This is how it was against Cincinnati and again the next week in our second Monday night game of the season, at Seattle.

The Seahawks were just the opposite of the Raiders that evening, doing little wrong. Seattle is a colorful team with a placekicker, Efren Herrera, who is also a punter and a pass receiver. You just never know what the Seahawks might do, which makes opponents nervous. Sure enough, the Seahawks faked a field goal against us and Zorn passed to Herrera for a first down at our one. Lawrence McCutcheon scored on the next play and we were down, 7–0, at halftime.

This is the game where Oakland introduced a new blocking back. Whittington started a sweep right at the Seattle 10, reversed direction and started left. I was just standing there, watching the play, and suddenly here comes Little Arthur back my way, trailed by all these Seahawks. I got in the way of one—it was nothing more than a shield block—and Whittington made it into the end zone.

The Kingdome never has been the Raiders' favorite place in which to play. We never had scored more than 10 points inside that building prior to 1980. And in the fourth quarter, we had only 7 points to Seattle's 17.

Hendricks increased our total to 9 by blocking a punt that rolled out of the end zone for a safety. Time was slipping away. I had to make something happen fast.

Ramsey streaked down the left side and I just missed him. On the very next play, Derrick flew down the center of the field and this time we connected for 58 yards to the Seahawks' 1. Van Eeghen cracked over on his third try and we were just a point behind, 17–16.

Hendricks tipped a Zorn pass and Hayes intercepted, returning the ball to our 39 with 4:20 left. Dame Fortune was on our side. On third-and-seven, I fumbled but Art Shell recovered. On fourth-and-three, I gained 4. Whittington picked up another first down before Ramsey caught an 18-yard pass at Seattle's 17.

Ramsey played more that night for a reason. Raymond Chester's depth perception isn't as good in night games or in domed stadiums. Raymond dropped 2 passes earlier that evening.

Chris Bahr kicked a 28-yard field goal with 56 seconds

left and we flew out of Seattle with a 19–17 triumph. Six in a row.

I couldn't walk after the game. Well, not very well. Someone had driven a helmet into my groin. There would be two more injuries within the next thirty-four days. My left shoulder gave out the following Sunday in Philadelphia.

Eagles coach Dick Vermeil said before the game that he tried to trade for me before the season, but that Al Davis refused. Vermeil needed a backup for his quarterback, Ron Jaworski. Because Dick coached me for two and a half seasons at Stanford and was familiar with my play, he attempted to get me. "Al Davis was too smart to let him go," said Vermeil. "Davis is the brightest football man I've ever heard speak."

Before the Philadelphia game, Pastorini was interviewed on national television. He said the broken leg was mending faster than anticipated and there was a good chance he would return to the Raiders before the season was over. He added that it would be as a backup quarterback, and that he expected to fight for the starting job in 1981.

That interview may not have endeared Pastorini to Davis, who prefers to make his roster revisions more quietly. Pastorini didn't help matters by coming up to Davis in the Philadelphia hotel where the Raiders were staying and throwing his arm around Al's shoulder.

"When are you going to activate me, Al?" Pastorini asked. "I'm the best damn quarterback you've got."

Davis, who was in the company of friends at the time, walked away without saying a word.

Our 6-game roll rolled to a stop in Philadelphia. The Eagles worked me over: 8 sacks. Claude Humphrey had 4 of them. Here it was 9 years later and Humphrey is still knocking me around and telling me he'd be back on the next play. And he was. Claude may have been 36 at the time, but he certainly wasn't ready for the burial grounds for defensive ends.

My statistics were embarrassing—36 attempts, 10 completions, 2 interceptions. I overthrew Chandler on one touchdown pass and underthrew him on another. Chester caught a pass at the Eagle 5, then fumbled the ball away. Bahr's 45-yard field goal attempt bounced right off the right upright. You couldn't say we didn't have our chances.

The one time we did connect, it was in a big way. Branch lined up in the slot and ran an out-and-up. No one saw Cliff until it was too late, and I hit him on an 86-yard touchdown pass. We now led, 7–3, in the fourth quarter.

It didn't stay that way for long. Randy McClanahan had Ron Jaworski nailed on a linebacker blitz, but Jaworski ducked underneath and came up throwing—43 yards to Leroy Harris. Wilbert Montgomery then scored from 3 yards out and Philadelphia had a well-earned 10–7 victory.

The Eagles were Super Bowl potential. They had an excellent defense, they were disciplined and they didn't make mistakes. In other words, a Dick Vermeil team. Another thing about the Eagles: they wouldn't be pushed around. Philadelphia and Dallas were the most physical teams we played all year. One Eagle grabbed me and threw me down on the hard carpet at Veterans Stadium. The tendon in my left shoulder was torn.

One thing was certain now.

If I was going to play the rest of the season, I would have to be shot up.

Purists will react with alarm that I received shots to keep playing. I took Xylocaine, which deadens the pain, and cortisone, to reduce the swelling.

It is very difficult for football players to go through a season without taking something. Players get banged around, especially in the joints, which then swell up. Anti-inflammatory drugs are taken to keep the swelling down. Most of the drugs I have seen in pro football are of this kind, or antibiotics.

I don't see a lot of pill-taking. I know it exists, but I

haven't seen much of it done. You're always going to find those who feel they need something "extra" to get ready to play. You find the same thing outside of sports. Football players are part of humanity, not above it. I've never taken drugs to get "high." That's not my way and I couldn't function if I did.

Drugs are a dirty word, but medication is a part of football. So is pressure. If you're hurt and you don't play, someone might replace you and you won't get your job back. More football jobs are lost through injury than anything else. It's the name of the game and that is why players will continue to perform even though parts of their anatomy may resist.

However, there is a limit to everything. I won't let anyone shoot up my knees, for instance. I don't want to walk the rest of my life with a limp or an artificial knee. When I was younger and naive, I played no matter what. Not anymore. Older veterans tend not to play as much if they are hurt.

If I feel I can play without the risk of permanent disability, I will. I'll let the team know that I have to be shot up. It is like this on every team, I'm sure. You have to understand football players to know why they would continue playing with an injury that would lay up a businessman for days.

We love the game. For all the pain, the agony, the frustration, the coach's chewings, the media's lambasting, the fans' booing . . . we love it. The excitement of being on the field, seeing a packed stadium, joining in a single, unified purpose with the rest of your teammates—to win . . . we love it.

There's a special attraction about football that draws us to it like a giant magnet. It's hard to explain, but leaving the game for good can be a painful withdrawal. Some players never recover. They still feel the urge to play in their fifties. They have pictures in their minds that won't go away.

One of the most beautiful things to watch in football

is the sweep play. To see the guards pulling out, the backs following them around end, cutting off the guards' blocks . . . that's a pretty picture.

My knees and shoulders will likely pay me back someday for all the pain I've put them through. It is almost certain that I will have arthritis in my joints. I chose my career and I'm prepared to live with the consequences. My friends and family are concerned about my health. I know that. I'm aware of what could happen if I take too much punishment. Joe Namath is talking of getting a fiber-glass knee. That won't happen to me. I know the danger signs. And at the moment, there is no red light flashing in my mind.

I could play with a bad groin and a torn tendon in my shoulder. Other football players do, why couldn't I? And I was motivated by something else: the playoffs. I had waited ten years to get there and I wasn't going to pass up this opportunity.

Art Shell, our offensive left tackle, was mad. Both at Bob Trumpy and me. Trumpy, a former Cincinnati tight end, was the TV color analyst for our game in Philadelphia. Trumpy told viewers during the game that Shell was tipping off the Raider plays. If Shell's feet were squared, Trumpy said, the Raiders were going to run. If Shell placed one foot behind the other, the Raiders were passing.

"What does Trumpy know?" Shell responded afterward. "Who did he ever line up against?"

Shell said that he always lined up this way. And if he was tipping off plays, why don't the Raiders have the fewest wins in football the last twenty years instead of the most?

Art complained that I was dropping back too far in the pocket so that when he drove his man to the outside on pass blocking, it wasn't far enough.

"It's a minor adjustment Jim will have to make," Shell said. "When a guy takes an outside rush, you've got to drive him wide. I did, but Jim was standing there. I get a little upset when something like this happens."

I was upset too. At Art. He was more concerned about looking bad. I told Art that I didn't feel any pass-rush pressure, so saw no need to move. I had dropped back the same distance all year and we won. Then I get sacked a few times, we lose and people point the finger. That's not fair or right.

I respect Art as a football player. And I respect the rest of the offensive line. I didn't accuse them of poor protection in the Eagles game. I didn't accuse them of being responsible for my injuries. Humphrey had a great game against Henry Lawrence, but I didn't say anything bad against Henry. I expect the same respect.

The Raider defense criticized the offense toward the end of the season, because we weren't scoring a lot of points at the time. But when the defense gave up 89 points to the Chargers and Steelers back-to-back, no one criticized them. That's because we won. You can overlook the same problems when you're winning that you can't when you're losing. Winning is a miracle salve that soothes all ailments.

Even though there is tenseness at times on the Raiders, the team gets along very well. We've got that great camaraderie. We're basically one happy family—though no one in the NFL wants to live next door to us.

"Jim wasn't sharp against Philadelphia. Tom Flores didn't criticize him. Tom wrote it off and went on to the next game. I've always said that the key to Jim Plunkett is how he is handled by his head coach. Jim has days when he isn't going to do well. Just pat him on the back and he'll come back and perform well the next week. Jim needs continual reassurance. Maybe it's because he is super-sensitive. Tom Flores is the kind of guy who doesn't rant and rave. He is the ideal kind of coach for Jim Plunkett and deserves a real pat on the back for the season Jim had."
—JOHN RALSTON

Our third Monday night game was at home against Denver. It was the only game in probably 60-plus years of the National Football League where the fans drew more attention than the players.

The Raider fans staged a 5-minute boycott at kickoff of the Denver-Oakland game as a protest to Al Davis's attempt to move the Raider franchise to Los Angeles.

Oakland's fans are intensely loyal. They supported the franchise through some very lean years in the early 1960s. Davis came along and the franchise took off. There was an unbroken string of sellouts at every Raider home game in the 1970s.

The Raider rooters were unique in that they never booed their team, not even when Seattle knocked Oakland out of the playoff picture in 1979. The fans' attitude changed after Davis decided to move the team 500 miles south. Pastorini innocently got caught in the middle of the fans' wrath the day his leg was fractured.

The boycott was successful. The Oakland-Alameda County Coliseum was half-empty at kickoff. By the end of the first quarter, the Coliseum was filled near capacity. At the 2-minute warnings, the fans held up signs which had been passed out: "Save Our Raiders." The entire stadium looked like one big card stunt.

The Raider players were sympathetic to the fans. We couldn't fault them for their frustrations. The Raider fans deserve a team—not necessarily the Raiders.

It would be a good business move for the Raiders and their players if the team were allowed to move to Los Angeles. I'd prefer to stay in Oakland, but there might be a few more business opportunities in Los Angeles. If the other Raider players were compensated for the move, I'm sure they'd be for it.

The whole thing is a real dilemma. Two guys are at odds: Davis and NFL Commissioner Pete Rozelle. One man wants to move a football team and the other man wants to stop him. It is important for the NFL to have rules governing the move of franchises. But rules can be changed.

I don't foresee dirty play in the NFL if the Raiders do move to Los Angeles. The league will continue to function as it always has.

But as the Godfather said: "It's business."

The Raider offense nearly boycotted the Denver end zone that night: we scored only one touchdown for the second straight week.

And I had reverted to old habits.

I was no longer comfortable in the pass pocket. After catching heat from my teammates and the press for not scoring more points, I became afraid to make mistakes and I lost my aggressiveness. Once more, I was the Jim Plunkett of New England and San Francisco. The ghost of seasons past.

I bootlegged 8 yards for a third-quarter touchdown that gave us a 6–3 lead. Chris Bahr missed the PAT kick. But instead of building on the lead, I was content to sit on it.

The defense held us together with 3 interceptions and 3 fumble recoveries. Bahr kept us from opening the score further by missing 4 of 5 field goals—2 wide lefts, 2 wide rights—for the second time that season.

It is a terrible feeling to drive 80 yards and then come away with no points. It is unfair. You've worked and sweated to get down there. Then your kicker, whose only job is to kick, misses the field goal. I'm not trying to be critical of Bahr, because when I overthrow a wide-open receiver in the end zone, I feel bad and people are mad at me too. I wouldn't want them to ignore me. This is why I react the same way to a kicker whether he makes or misses the field goal. I pat him on the back.

Failure is as much a part of sports as accomplishment. It is important to remember that athletes are not perfect, though their fans demand that they be and almost revolt whenever they aren't.

It wasn't pretty, but we edged Denver, 9–3, to keep our playoff chances alive. But we needed to get the offense moving, which wouldn't be easy because Dallas was coming to town.

The Cowboys are the opposite end of the spectrum from the Raiders. Dallas has a cold, computerized image; the Cowboys approach the game of football as a computer print-out. Oakland is ad-lib, draw-from-the-hip football; the Raiders approach each game as a gun fight. The Cowboys are like a society out of Orwell's *1984* compared to the Raiders, who are Dodge City, 1892. However, it isn't the method, but the results. Both Dallas and Oakland are eminently successful franchises.

We gave signs of offensive life 5 minutes into the game when Chester ran a crossing pattern and caught a 6-yard touchdown pass to make it 7–0. Then before we could say Tony Dorsett, the Cowboys moved into a 16–7 lead and that was the last we saw of them. We had one final chance late in the game, but Dallas's Dennis Thurman ruined it with a safety blitz. With one second more, I would have hit Cliff Branch for the touchdown. With Thurman in my face-mask, I had to throw before Cliff came open and cornerback Aaron Mitchell intercepted in the end zone to lock up Dallas's 19–13 victory.

The Raider defense began muttering and making strange faces at the offense across the locker room after the game. A reporter showed me some statistics he had compiled. In my first 5 starts, I was sacked 4 times, completed 65.5 percent of my passes, 9 for touchdowns. In my last 5 starts, I was sacked 18 times, completed 39.9 percent of my passes, 2 for touchdowns. The interceptions in each breakdown were 5.

The reporter's contention was that my protection had fallen down, thereby creating problems for the offense. My reply was that I needed to be more aggressive, sacks or no sacks, so that the offense would improve. We had 2 road games left against Denver and the New York Giants, and we could make the playoffs by winning both.

My theory proved right. I was sacked 3 times in each of the last 2 games and it didn't hurt the offense because I came out firing again. If you can complete 2 touchdown passes against Louis Wright in 1 game, you've got to be firing and confident, and maybe lucky too.

Wright isn't beaten too often. He plays corner for the Broncos and he is an excellent pass defender—quick instincts, good reflexes and fine athletic ability. Chandler scored twice on Wright that day, coming back beautifully on an 11-yard pass and then catching a 38-yard reception.

Another day, the outcome might be just the opposite: Wright could have 2 interceptions. However, we had to try everything against the Broncos that afternoon because their offense piled up 507 yards. Our defense hadn't given up that much yardage in 2 games!

The Broncos threw 42 passes, which is about a 2-game output for them. But they were out of the playoffs for the first time in 4 years and decided to open up their attack and have some fun. Burgess Owens returned an interception 58 yards for a touchdown and we struggled to a 24–21 victory.

"It's never easy in this town," Dave Browning said.

One to go.

"I'll tell you when I got the ultimate confidence in Jim Plunkett. It was after that Philadelphia game. He took a lot of punishment and a whole lot of criticism. A lot of players couldn't pick themselves up from all that, but Jim did, and came back. That has to tell you something about the man. There's something inside Jim that drives him, makes you believe in him. He held our team together."
—RAYMOND CHESTER, Oakland Raiders tight end

The Giants looked like "General Hospital." They had lost so many players with injuries, teammates had trouble recognizing one another. New players arrived every day while others were carted to the hospital. Linebacker Harry Carson was placed on injured reserve twice with unrelated injuries. Giant players were literally shaking hands and introducing themselves to one another in the huddle on game days. You definitely needed a program to tell the Giant players.

Games like this are worrisome because they can look so easy just before they backfire. It was extremely cold in The Meadowlands, which could work against us too. Not this day. We couldn't feel the chill. We knew what was at stake. By game time, we were so warm we almost ran a fever.

Branch caught a 31-yard touchdown pass to give us a 20–10 lead. Things looked good. Then just before halftime, I twisted my left knee. Not another injury! That makes 3. I hope I can get up.

I couldn't, not by myself. Wilson took my place for the rest of the half. I hobbled to the locker room.

Long ago I told myself that I would never play with a knee brace. However, there was no way I wouldn't finish the Giants game. I put on a knee brace and came out for the third quarter.

We needed another touchdown, just 1 more. Chester got 2 steps on his man and caught a 37-yard pass in the end zone. That's it! We've got them!

The Giants scored in the last minute, then tried an onside kick. The ball has to travel 10 yards for either team to recover. The Giants kicked 2 that didn't make the required 10. Then, on the third, which did, Derrick Jensen picked it up for us and ran 33 yards for a touchdown. We won, 33–17.

Hello playoffs! I've been looking for you.

Chapter Eight

VINDICATION

"*Jim Plunkett's comeback is one of the great stories in football history.*"
— TOM FLORES, Oakland Raiders coach

"*It is one of the great sports stories of all time. Imagine getting waived out of the league and then coming back to be the Most Valuable Player of the Super Bowl.*"
— JOHN RALSTON

"*If ever a person has a right to tell people to shove it up their rears, this is it. But I've never heard Jim say this once.*"
— DAVE OLERICH

The Snake is coming back.

My first challenge in my very first playoff game is to outplay the quarterback I couldn't beat out in Oakland: Ken Stabler.

The Ghost and The Assassin—Dave Casper and Jack Tatum—would be here too.

227

It will be old home week in Oakland.

The Houston Oilers are the southwest branch of the Oakland Raiders. Stabler, Casper, Tatum and Mike Rein-feldt are former Raiders who wore the "Luv Ya Blue" of Houston in 1980.

Kenny King and Dan Pastorini are former Oilers who joined the Pride and Poise boys in Oakland.

The Oilers and Raiders set up a hot line in 1980. Stabler was traded for Pastorini. King came to Oakland in a swap for Tatum and a seventh-round draft pick. Casper went to Houston for two high draft choices.

Now the two teams were about to do business again in the first, or wild-card, round of the NFL playoffs.

Wild-card teams are comparable to runners-up in beauty contests—not good enough to finish at the top, but still a pretty good package.

In Pete Rozelle's post-season party, the six division champions are invited along with the two best noncham-pions—or wild-card teams—from each conference. This means ten invitations.

The wild cards square off—NFC versus NFC, AFC versus AFC—with the winners playing on the road for the duration of the playoffs or until they are eliminated.

Oakland and Houston finished with identical 11–5 rec-ords. The Raiders became the home team against the Oilers through the NFL's complicated formula for determining such matters. No one—not even the NFL—understands the formula. If explaining it were the final requirement for grad-uation from American universities, there would be few graduates. It is rumored that the NFL formula actually was Einstein's last mathematical equation, and even he didn't understand it.

Stabler hit Houston with a bigger splash than any athlete in history. He did more TV commercials in his first three months than Pastorini did in nine years. The Snake got his own television show, marketed a diet cola—"Snake

Venom"—represented a big furniture outlet and opened a country music night club appropriately called "Diamondback." Even with his busy off-the-field commitments, Stabler still found time to lead the Oilers into the playoffs.

Casper also found happiness in Willie and Waylon land. Bum Phillips ran as loose a football operation as Tom Flores, so there was little adjustment for any of the relocated Raiders. Casper paired with Mike Barber in Houston's double tight-end offense that contributed to Earl Campbell's career-high 1,934 yards rushing.

Tatum may be, pound for pound, the hardest hitter ever to play in the NFL. He had lost some speed by the time he got to Houston, where he played a backup free safety to Reinfeldt but still led the team with a personal-high 7 interceptions.

Jack wrote a controversial autobiography, *They Call Me Assassin*. The book's contents upset the league office, but that didn't stop the book from selling or the Oilers from making the deal with Oakland for Jack.

Houston released Tatum in May, 1981. Jack was 32 and his knees were bad.

Of all of Oakland's playoff games during the 1980 season, the one against Houston was the most emotional. We didn't want to lose against our former teammates. It was doubly emotional for me, and not just because of Stabler. My body was malfunctioning and I was worried about how much longer I could last.

Both of my shoulders bothered me now. I had the rotator cuff problem in the left shoulder, which would require off-season surgery. My right shoulder began to stiffen up. I had tendinitis and would need additional shots later on to loosen the muscles and allow me to throw the football.

The groin was even a bigger problem. The doctors couldn't determine what was wrong. Since the Seattle game, I hadn't been able to run at practice and my weight zoomed from 218 to 230, the highest of my career. Now I had a sprained left knee on top of everything else. I was rapidly getting out of shape.

Contrary to popular belief, you don't have to be in great shape to play quarterback. To drop back and occasionally scramble, what shape do you need to be in? A number of my former critics exclaimed: "Look at Plunkett. The reason for his success is that he's the slimmest he has been in years." What were they saying three years earlier when I was 30 pounds lighter and the 49ers cut me?

Nevertheless, even with all my physical problems, the playoffs was an exciting time for me. I may have been falling apart, but I wouldn't have missed it for anything.

For Pastorini, the playoffs would be a time of depression and near-disaster. The Raiders didn't activate him. Tom Flores said he didn't want to break up a "winning combination." Flores said that Pastorini's extracurricular problems did not influence his decision one way or another. You'd have to believe Tom, because the Raiders have suited up players who were less law-abiding than Dan.

At any rate, what Pastorini interpreted as a snub from the Raiders left him in a bitter mood and ripe for trouble, which is exactly what he found.

Dan dropped by the Coliseum the day before the game to visit with the Oilers and watch them work out. Pastorini wound up back at the Oakland hotel, where the Oilers were staying. Houston sportswriter Dale Robertson, whom Pastorini had shoved through a locker room door the previous year in Houston, was in the hotel. Pastorini saw Robertson and accosted him, according to witnesses. Dan left the hotel and drove a 1980 Scirocco into a tree, cutting his face and banging his ankle. He was lucky to escape with just those injuries.

It was one rough season for Pastorini. Meanwhile, Oakland was starting the playoffs with just two quarterbacks, Jim Plunkett and Marc Wilson. If both of us were hurt, who would play quarterback?

Probably our punter.

Ray Guy is a tremendous athlete who is not only the best punter in football, but the strongest thrower on the Raiders. He can wing a football 80 yards. He can actually sit on the sidelines at the 20-yard-line and throw a football between the uprights. That's a tough throw and a tougher angle. Guy can kick off, kick field goals and he's a deadly tackler. He would like to play safety—he intercepted 18 passes in his college career—but the Raiders prefer to use him just as a specialist. Guy hasn't given up hope, however.

Casper hadn't forgotten that October team meeting. In the Sunday morning *Oakland Tribune/Eastbay TODAY* he called Upshaw "the Michelin man who never gets his uniform dirty." Upshaw was asked for his reaction to Casper's remarks and said he would reply after the game.

A few hours before kickoff, Stabler came into the Raider dressing room. I told him that I was glad he was having a good year—but in Houston, not Oakland. Snake grinned. He said that I might be playing in Oakland even if he were still a Raider. I don't think he meant it, but it was nice of him to say it anyway.

Snake wouldn't have been so relaxed if he knew what Charlie Sumner had in mind for him: a blind-side blitz executed by the left corner, Hayes, and the strong safety, Davis. Lester and Mike sacked Stabler twice each, and Hendricks, Browning and Jones had 1 sack apiece.

Earl Campbell scored on a 1-yard run in the first quarter. However, our defense did a great job stopping Earl, who rushed for 91 yards, but only a 3.4 average per carry. It was very emotional, aggressive football. We had outprepared the Oilers too.

Our offensive game plan was to beat Houston's linebackers 1-on-1 with our running backs in passing situations. Whenever it was second or third down and long yardage needed for a first down, Houston's defense shifted into man-on-man coverage. We exploited their defensive design with 2 big, big passes.

Oakland had a second-and-eight on Houston's 39 in the second quarter. The Oilers switched to 1-on-1 coverage as expected and Kenny King made a great over-the-head catch at the 2. Bum Phillips's jaw dropped 6 inches. Bum said later that the reason he traded King was that Kenny couldn't catch the football. "I could have cried when he caught that one in Oakland," Phillips said.

We caught the Oilers by surprise again 2 plays later. Todd Christensen caught his first pass of the regular season for a touchdown. Todd lined up as an extra tight end at the 1. He broke to the left, I threw low and to the outside, and he made a sliding catch.

We held that 10–7 lead into the fourth quarter, when we struck again with a long pass. Whittington slipped out of the backfield and took off down the right sideline. I led him perfectly on a 44-yard touchdown throw.

Many football people believe I throw a better deep pass than short pass, but this isn't true. If the distance between a quarterback and his receiver is shorter, it has to be an easier pass to complete. I am partial to the long pass simply because I have belief in it and the damage it can cause. The bomb is like the 3-point shot in basketball. You won't hit it as consistently as a 12-foot jumper, but it can win games for you.

You only give a football defense confidence when you throw 3 completions and don't get a first down. Any defense would be glad to give up 70 percent completions, if they only meant 5 first downs. But you really can see the frustration on the defense faces when you get behind them with the big one. The back-breaker.

I had a low-percentage passing game against Houston —8 for 23 and 168 yards. But the ones I hit paid off. Twenty yards a completion.

Lester Hayes played possum in the flat all afternoon

until Stabler tried to complete one in his direction. Lester jumped like basketball's Dr. J, intercepted the pass and ran 20 yards for a touchdown.

We won convincingly, 27–7. Then Upshaw fired back on Casper. "I wish I could have played some defense today," Uppy said. The Raiders, picked for last place in our division, had just knocked off the team that had played in the last two AFC championship games. We had a few more surprises left too.

The defeat cost Bum Phillips his coaching job. All Bum had done wrong was direct the Oilers to 3 straight playoffs. And for this, he was fired. Obviously, it was a personality conflict between Bum and Houston owner Bud Adams. Six weeks later, Bum was hired to coach the New Orleans Saints. He must like coaching indoors.

"Jim and I are close, but he never has said, 'Gee, Schultzie, this is the greatest thing in the world.' He's more excited for us and our excitement. People love an underdog. Jim's story has captured the hearts of the American public. For people to persevere and end up on top, as Jim has, appeals to everyone's sense of fair play."
—JACK SCHULTZ

I'm a Californian, but I know what it's like to be cold. Foxboro in December isn't Jamaica in July, you know. I've never been as cold, however, as I was January 4, 1981, in Cleveland, Ohio, when the Raiders met the Browns in Round Two of the NFL playoffs.

The thermometer read 1 degree at game time. A 16-mile-per-hour wind whipped in off Lake Erie through the north, open end of Municipal Stadium. Lake Erie looked more like a frozen tundra in the Arctic. The chill factor had brought the temperature down to minus 36 degrees. Browns fans dressed in two and three layers of clothing as if they were about to accompany Admiral Byrd on a polar expedition. This was weather more suited for Bigfoot than football players.

Brrrrrrrrrrrr.

When it is this cold, the football feels like a brick. It is no longer a game of the fittest, but who slips the least. One "Ooops!" by a defensive back on pass coverage and it's good-bye ball game. Most of the playing area was as hard as a rock, like a highly waxed linoleum floor. Therefore, the Raiders and Browns wore Astroturf shoes. Down around the goal lines, the field was slushy. Snowshoes might have been the best footwear in those areas.

I wouldn't want to make a living in this kind of weather unless I owned an obedience school for Yukon trail dogs. Cleveland has it bad enough already, being known as Pittsburgh's ugly sister and Buffalo's homely niece. I kid Gerry a lot about Cleveland, telling her she likes it well enough to live in California. I do like Cleveland, however. In the summer.

The Browns tried a pre-game snow job on us as a psychological ploy, talking up how the adverse weather conditions would favor them, the Nanooks of the North.

We were concerned more about the Browns than the thermometer. Their season virtually bordered on fiction, so spectacular were their last-minute victories. Their nickname, the Kardiac Kids, wasn't as novel as the ways they discovered to win football games. Brian Sipe was the Kardiac Kid with 30 touchdown passes, only 14 interceptions out of 554 attempts and a 61.4 completion percentage. Sipe was the unanimous all-pro quarterback and received NFL Player of the Year honors as well. We felt we had the best defense in the playoffs, so let the (snow) chips fall where they may.

Ron Bolton had played with me in New England. Halfway through the second quarter, I wished Ron were back in Foxboro. Chandler ran an out-pattern of 10 to 12 yards; I was going to be clever, first looking left and then throwing right. Bolton saw me set up short, then watched Chandler make his break. I let the ball go just before I said "Damn!" Bolton cut in front of Chandler, grabbed the brick-ball and sped 42 yards over the icy field in Eric Heiden time to put Cleveland ahead, 6–0. Hendricks blocked the PAT attempt.

We took the ensuing kickoff and set off for the Browns' end zone. Chandler returned to the same sidelines where Bolton picked me blind and made a tremendous catch for 15 yards. Bob planted 2 feet just inside the sideline, caught the ball and then fell over like an axed tree. We call this our "Timber!" pattern.

I ran for one first down and van Eeghen another to keep the drive alive. Then came an important play, third-and-thirteen at the Browns' 28. Chester found an open area down at the 2 for a 26-yard reception. We held our breath as van Eeghen fumbled on the next play, but Mark recovered the ball himself. Two plays later, he hid behind massive Mickey Marvin at right guard and pushed into the end zone. Chris Bahr's kick made it 7–6.

Don Cockroft's two third-quarter field goals of 30 and 29 yards in the south, closed end of the stadium lifted Cleveland into a 12–7 lead.

Neither offense would score this game at the north end, where throwing footballs into the wind was the Siberian version of Russian roulette. Out of 70 passes thrown by Sipe and myself that miserable day, only 6 were completed toward the north end, and two of those were screen passes.

We waited until the fourth quarter before making another move in a southerly direction. Once again, it would be a pass to Chester that led to the go-ahead touchdown. The Browns' secondary concentrated on Branch and Chandler, so Chester was unguarded down the middle and caught a 27-yard pass at the 15. On third-and-four, King caught a 6-yard pass at the 3. Three plays later, van Eeghen hitched onto Upshaw at left guard and sloshed in for 6 points. Bahr's kick made it 14–12.

When Sipe fumbled and Odis McKinney recovered for us at the Browns' 24, we thought the game was over. Van Eeghen had two chances to pick up a first down, but couldn't get the final yard, and Cleveland took over at its 15 with 2:22 left.

Plenty of time for the Kardiac Kids.

Sipe's first pass was incomplete to Reggie Rucker. Tight end Ozzie Newsome caught Sipe's next throw for 29 yards. Sipe appeared stymied after 2 incompletions and a running play that went nowhere. But Dwayne O'Steen was called for defensive holding and Cleveland had a first down on its 49 with 1:19 left.

Sipe was on the move. Every one of the chilled 77,655 fans inside the rickety old stadium could sense it. How will Brian win the game this time, they wondered. Greg Pruitt slipped out on the left sidelines and Sipe hit him for 23 yards. Mike Pruitt, no relation to Greg, swept left end for 14 yards for another first down. Cleveland called its second time out at our 14-yard line with 56 seconds left.

Sipe walked over some snow patches on his way to the Browns' bench. Head coach Sam Rutigliano, quarterback coach Jim Shofner and Sipe talked among themselves.

What are they saying?

Sipe pointed toward the north end, Shofner adjusted the headphones connecting him with the Cleveland coaches on the roof of Memorial Stadium. Rutigliano put a hand to the side of his face, reflectively.

My heart was thumping. I didn't know how we were going to do it, but we were going to stop them. No more Ron Ayalas. Those days were gone. The Browns will miss a field goal, they'll fumble, they'll do something wrong. They won't pass, not in that end of the stadium, not into that wind. The back of the end zone is caked with ice. No receiver can stay upright on that stuff.

What will they call?

Rutigliano and Shofner each put an arm on Sipe's shoulder. Three heads less than a foot apart. Three heads moving up and down. They'd decided on something.

What was the play?

Sipe started back toward the huddle. He turned back to the sideline as Rutigliano cupped his hands around his mouth and shouted one last instruction. I could see only the vapor coming out from between Rutigliano's hands. Sipe moved his head affirmatively. He knew what to do.

A run. It has to be a run. The Browns have 1 time-out left. Run the ball up the gut, get it closer for Cockroft, stop the clock, try the field goal.

You don't chance a season on anything but a field goal. "Don't come out of there without something," Lombardi once said. He meant down by the goal line. Don't go for 6 points if all you need is 3. And all Cleveland needed was 3.

I watched Sipe lead the Browns out of the huddle and to the line of scrimmage. He looked both ways, barking signals, vapor blowing in two directions, grabbed the brick-ball on the snap and started back.

He's going to pass!

It seemed impossible. Going for the jugular. The Kardiac Kids. They are unreal!

Dave Logan, a Brown wide receiver lined up on the left, took two steps upfield, then crossed over the middle. Oh my God! He's open. Sipe didn't see him. Hendricks was blitzing, blocking Sipe's view of Logan.

Sipe threw. To whom? Geez, it's Newsome! He's behind Mike Davis. He's by himself!

Newsome got a step on Davis. But Burgess Owens, moving over from free safety, forced Newsome slightly off his pattern, enabling Davis to make up the ground he had lost.

Davis moved between the spiraling football and Newsome, turned toward the ball and caught it against his belly, one leg in the air. Newsome reached in from behind with his right arm, trying to pry the ball loose. He failed.

Davis fell to the turf, with the ball, as Newsome tumbled away. Sipe kicked at the sloppy turf. Rutigliano put both hands alongside his face, just before one long stream of mist left his mouth.

Why did he call that play?

We didn't care. We had the football and the game. It wasn't long before a mass of Raider humanity was piled in the north end zone. Davis was somewhere on the bottom. It was the warmest Mike felt all afternoon. It was the warmest we all felt. Millen kicked the goal-line flag five yards in the air. Flores and the other coaches hugged one another.

Sipe walked dejectedly off the field and Rutigliano hugged him.

"I love you, Brian. Forget it," the coach said.

"I should have thrown it into Lake Erie," Sipe said later.

If he had, it would have bounced.

We ran out the clock. "I was baffled by the call," Mike Davis told reporters. We all were. "I was confident," Cockroft said. "I would have liked the opportunity." We were grateful he didn't get it.

Rutigliano explained that he went for the pass because conditions were too risky for a field goal. Cockroft had already missed 2 field goals at the north end, Sam added. He gambled that a pass would be the safest course because passing is what the Browns did best.

Rutigliano was asked if the defeat was the hardest thing he had ever accepted.

"Only death is hard to accept," he replied.

Years ago, Rutigliano fell asleep at the wheel of his car. His little daughter was killed in the crash.

Losing a football game is nothing.

The weather hadn't beaten the Oakland Raiders, and

neither had the Cleveland Browns. Had the game been played in warm weather, we still would have won, something like 35–34. Ron Bolton agreed.

"The game would have gone the same way in any conditions," he said. "Give Oakland credit. They came up with the big plays all day, including the biggest play at the end. They deserved to win."

Cleveland was the roughest game for us in the playoffs. But we came through again. Our team is peaking. We can feel it. We'll be even better next week.

The Kardiac Kids. Dead of cardiac arrest.

Next up: the AFC championship game, and Air Coryell.

"The American hockey team in the 1980 Olympics started low and gradually worked up. Jim started at the pinnacle, then got knocked all the way to the bottom. It is tougher to come back than it is to start at the bottom and work your way up the first time."
                                        —RANDY VATAHA

Don Coryell believes the football was designed for throwing, not running. Coryell has had just 1 losing season out of 23 through 1980 with his pass-minded offensive. The man's philosophy works.

Coryell never has had more firepower than in San Diego, where quarterback Dan Fouts passed for a pro football-record 4,715 yards in 1980 to Pro Bowl receivers Kellen Winslow, John Jefferson and Charlie Joiner, who finished 1–2–3 among AFC pass catchers with a combined 242 catches, good for 26 touchdowns. Bespectacled Jefferson led NFL receivers in yards (1,340) and touchdowns (13), proving that quarterbacks do throw passes to ends who wear glasses.

The Chargers made it to the championship game on the strength of their passing theatrics. Fouts threw a 50-yard touchdown pass to Ron Smith with little more than 2 minutes left to give San Diego a 20–14 comeback victory over Buffalo the week before.

Though the game would be played at San Diego's Jack Murphy Stadium, and Super Bowl fever had sent temperatures rising in Bordertown, we were confident. We played well against the Chargers and they knew it. Match-ups are so important in football, and our offensive line matched up well with their defensive front four, three of whom—Gary "Big Hands" Johnson, Louie Kelcher and Fred Dean—started for the AFC in the 1981 Pro Bowl. We moved the football against San Diego, and they can move the football against anybody. This would be a game where the defenses take a holiday. It was very possible that 60 points could be scored, because the 2 teams had combined for 54 and 62 points in our 2 previous games.

When the Oakland Raiders are playing, there are always pre-game distractions that divert attention from the game itself. Before we played Houston, it was Casper-Upshaw and Pastorini's driving habits. Before the Cleveland game, it was the Browns' hype job about the elements.

These incidents were like a Daughters of the American Revolution cake bake compared to what took place three days before the Oakland-San Diego game.

Chargers owner Gene Klein is not one of Al Davis's biggest fans. He dislikes Davis's vanity. "He can't walk past a mirror without stopping to comb his hair," Klein once said. Davis's attempt to move the Raiders to Los Angeles rankled Klein even more.

Klein has chastised Davis more than once over this issue. However, at a press conference on the Thursday before the championship game, Klein began by stressing that he would say nothing about Davis and reporters should keep all questions relative to the football game. Somewhere in the middle of the interview, Klein forgot about his opening remark and began to rage once more at you-know-who.

"Al Davis practices the big lie . . . like Hitler and Goebbels," Klein roared, starting a 20-minute dialogue on the man he refused to discuss 20 minutes earlier. Charger players said the next day it was amusing that two grown men should act like this. However, Davis never responded to Klein's barrage. Klein would suffer a heart attack the following May after testifying against Davis on the Oakland-Los Angeles matter.

Davis has been accused of many things, but never of having a divine influence on weather conditions. It hadn't rained in San Diego in five months before the AFC title game. Around sunset on Saturday night, dark clouds suddenly appeared over San Diego and there was a rain shower.

"Damn you, Al Davis!" a Charger supporter yelled at the Old Town Mexican Cafe, a popular hangout in San Diego.

By kickoff, the football field was wet and slippery. Air Coryell wasn't grounded, but it would have trouble taking off.

Something divine—the Immaculate Deflection— happened to us in the game's opening moments. I threw across the middle to Kenny King, who deflected the ball right into the hands of Raymond Chester, who ran off from 2 flat-footed Chargers to complete a 65-yard scoring play.

Nothing fazes the Chargers, however. Fouts threw for our end zone and Joiner made an acrobatic, falling 48-yard catch to even the score at 7–7.

You don't stop San Diego. Tom Flores told us the best way to contain the Chargers was to outscore them. So we didn't wait around. We went after them as often as we could.

Branch caught a 48-yard pass. Then the Chargers were called for pass interference to move us to their 12. Two plays later, I dropped back to pass, saw no one open and took off for the end zone, sliding home safely on a 5-yard run.

On our next series, I passed for 16 yards to Chandler, 9 to Chester and, finally, 21 to King to put us up by 21–7.

The Chargers believe their pass rush can't be held out all day, or even all quarter. They send those four horses loose, double-zone the outside receivers and dare the quarterback to find other receivers before the pass rush lowers the boom. San Diego even changed up its defense in order to confuse us. We were well prepared and guessed right along with the Chargers, hurting them with our running game to the "weak" side, the side opposite to where the tight end lines up.

We also took the Chargers out of field position with Ray Guy's stratospheric punts. There are days when Guy is great, and there are days when he is greater. January 11, 1981 was one of his greater days. Guy averaged 56 yards a punt, a record for championship games. His longest punt was 71 yards, an AFC title game mark. Maybe Guy brought the rain the day before in practice.

Two plays after his 71-yarder, John Matuszak squeezed the air out of Charger halfback Mike Thomas, the ball popped loose and Ted Hendricks recovered at the San Diego 29. We were penalized back to our 39, but Branch grabbed a 24-yard pass. On third-and-three, Whittington caught a 5-yard pass at the 3. Van Eeghen broke up the middle on the next play and we led, 28–7.

This might seem an impossible deficit to overcome for most quarterbacks. Not Dan Fouts. He only grows more determined. Fouts is the master at dropping back 3, 4 yards and drilling passes into the seams, or openings, of a zone coverage. It's a difficult pass to stop anyway, but even more so against Fouts and his quick receivers. Before we knew it, the Chargers were breathing on our necks.

Fouts threw an 8-yard scoring strike to Joiner. Rolf Benirschke kicked a 26-yard field goal. Chuck Muncie rushed around left end with the force of a dam bursting open and scored from our 6 to make it 28–24. It had taken the short span of one quarter for the Chargers to turn a runaway into anyone's game again.

I blew my cool on the next series. I handed off on a running play to van Eeghen, then stepped back to observe the action. The play was almost over when Big Hands Johnson hit me across the same knee I had injured against the Giants.

Pain ripped through my body as I slid on the damp turf. I'm out of the game! I'm out of the playoffs! No Super Bowl!

I could only think the worst. Then I saw Upshaw walking nonchalantly back to the huddle. Upshaw's job was to block Big Hands. I jumped all over Uppy.

"Goddammit, you son of a bitch, keep that bastard out of here!"

I was mad. Screaming mad.

I don't lose control, generally. But I can get angry. I would throw my helmet when things went bad in New England. Another time, John Hannah, one of the Patriot guards, kept after me to run the ball when we were having success throwing it.

"Look," I snapped at him, "if you don't like it, get out of here." That was the end of that.

I can also be stubborn. The coaches will send in a play and I might say, "Dammit, I don't want that play!" I'll refuse 2 or 3 a game out of stubbornness. Coaches let you drive the team down the field to the 10, then send in a play. What were they doing when I was back on my 30?

However, I have never exploded like I did at Upshaw. You *don't* scream at Gene Upshaw. He did a great double take, then said something back. Not even the element of surprise keeps Upshaw quiet for long.

I made it back on my feet and stayed in the game. Shakily. We didn't score on that drive, and Hendricks came up to me on the sideline. He grabbed me by the jersey. He had fire in his eyes.

"You've got to keep scoring," he virtually ordered. *"We can't stop them."*

Somehow our defense did, on the Chargers' next drive. We moved down the field twice for field goals of 27 and 33 yards by Bahr. Our lead was now 34–24. Fouts, driving passes into the chests of Joiner and Winslow, moved to our 8, where Benirschke's 27-yard field goal made it a 7-point game, 34–27.

There was 6:43 left in the game—or the season. Everything hinged on what would happen next. We couldn't give the ball up. We couldn't give the Chargers another chance to do to us what they did to Buffalo. Fouts glared at us from his sideline, pulling at the hairs on his beard.

Van Eeghen blasted up the middle behind Dalby's block for 5 yards to the 30. Van Eeghen followed Shell through left tackle for 10 to the 40. Van Eeghen hammered a third time for 4 behind Marvin at right guard. King squirmed for 2 straight ahead.

Third-and-four at our 46. First crucial play of the drive. Whittington caught a 6-yard pass. First down. Four minutes left.

Derrick Jensen replaced Whittington. The bull backfield: Jensen and van Eeghen, both fullbacks.

Jensen drove behind Upshaw, Dalby and Marvin for 4. Van Eeghen got another yard behind Shell. Third-and-five at their 43. Second crucial play. I tried to get a Charger to jump offsides. Wilbur Young compiled. The measurement showed we were a foot short. Van Eeghen plowed behind right tackle Henry Lawrence for 4. First down.

Two-minute warning. We had chewed up 40 yards and 4 minutes and 43 seconds worth of time. We still weren't safe.

Jensen powered for 3 behind Dalby. Van Eeghen churned for 3 behind Marvin. Third-and-four at their 29. Third crucial play. I looked for an open receiver, was forced to run. Kelcher tripped me up, but after 5 yards. First down, Charger 24. San Diego called its first time out.

Tom Flores told me what I already knew: keep it on the ground. Back in the huddle, I looked at the Charger faces. Despair. They had sacked me 6 times. Kelcher was awesome: 20 tackles, 10 unassisted. But it didn't matter. We were executing. *They* couldn't stop *us*. It was a great feeling.

Van Eeghen squirmed straight ahead for 4. Second time out. I took a 2-yard loss. Third and final time out. I took another loss of 2 and the lights on the scoreboard blinked down to 0:00.

Fouts found me after the game.

"You were the difference, Jim. You ran for that early touchdown and you got the key down at the end. Great game. Good luck at the Super Bowl."

The Super Bowl.

Hey, he's right! We're the AFC champions.

We're in the Super Bowl. *I'm* in the Super Bowl!

The dressing room was pure chaos. Someone thrust a statistics sheet in my face: 18 attempts, 14 connects, 261 yards, 2 touchdowns. No interceptions and we didn't fumble once. In 3 playoff games, we had only 2 interceptions and 1 lost fumble. In all kinds of weather, too. We are a championship team!

Upshaw awarded the game ball to Al Davis. Who else! Davis made the moves—King, Chandler, Owens, Hardman, O'Steen, Nelson, Martin, Bahr, Christensen, McKinney, Pear, Plunkett—which brought the Raiders back to the Super Bowl after a 4-year absence. Only 11 Raiders were left from that Super Bowl XI team.

"Plunkett was our General Patton," Branch told reporters. "He came to win. You don't become no Heisman Trophy winner without being a winner. He used his receiving corps today; he used his backs. He had total command. He directed our army and we won. He had the game in his hands."

"I would have hated to be in the San Diego secondary

facing Plunkett," said Burgess Owens. "We have shown everyone we are the Cinderella team . . . and Jim Plunkett is our Prince Charming."

"Plunkett's scrambling really hurt us," said Charger cornerback Willie Buchanon. "When it really counted, when we really had to get our offense the ball, we didn't do it. Plunkett throws better on the run than standing still."

Philadelphia defeated Dallas, 20–7, for the NFC championship. The Eagles will be tough in New Orleans.

New Orleans!

Barbecued shrimp at Manale's. Breakfast at Brennan's. Hurricanes at Pat O'Brien's. Oysters at Felix's. Powdered doughnuts (beignets) at Cafe du Monde. Jazz at Pete Fountain's. Real jazz at Preservation Hall.

Old Claude and the Eagles defense at the Superdome.

"In my book, Jim's sort of a great American hero. Here's a guy who is a legitimate celebrity, yet I've never known him to go out of his way to get recognition. Everyone seeks out the camera. Not Jim. He's anti-celebrity. He honestly believes in his heart that what happened to him in the 1980 season isn't an extraordinary story. This is the thing that is most unique about him."

—BOB MOORE

There is no city better than New Orleans in which to hold a Super Bowl. The city's many attractions and boisterous life style make the Super Bowl one big, around-the-clock party.

However, for me, it would be a job. As much as I wanted to visit Manale's and Brennan's, I wouldn't have the time. There was plenty of film on the Eagles I needed to watch at night in my room. I would only spend parts of two evenings with my friends. I pointed them in the direction of Manale's, etc.

I needed 56 tickets for family and friends. Somehow, I got them. Mary Ann and Veva came to New Orleans along with two of Veva's three children. Lasater and Schultz arrived from Los Angeles. Kauffman and Schultz's brother Bobby drove out from Palo Alto and ran out of gas on a foggy night in Texas. Vlasoff—Mr. Menlo Park—was there. So were Ron Kadziel from Denver, Terrell Smith from Salt Lake City, Vataha from Boston, Passafuime from Santa Cruz, Calif., Doug Adams from Modesto, Calif., Jack Alustiza from Stockton, Calif., Jim Collins from Los Angeles. Jack Ditz came from Atherton with his family.

These were friends—some great friends—and they deserved this moment. Hadn't I leaned on them enough over the years? They had come through for me time and time again. I owed them so much. If this was my time, it was just as much their time.

Super Bowl week is for the league, the media and the tourists. The two football teams aren't the show, but part of it. There are parties and more parties and even more parties. Dissipation is the name of the game and, by running an eyeball count of the tourists each morning, everyone seemed to be winning.

For three straight mornings, the two teams met separately at scheduled times with the media. Each player had his own table with his uniform number painted on a card. For three days, I heard the same questions over and over, almost all of them about my family and undulating career. One morning, every question but one dealt with these two topics. The other questions had to do with the game. Imagine, someone wanted to know about the game!

There were more reporters camped at the hotel when the team returned from practice. One cameraman from a wire service followed me for an entire week. Restaurant or rest room, he was never far behind. I couldn't see him sometimes, but I could hear the shutter. When my friends got into town, we met at this bar. The cameraman came inside.

"Not in here," I told him.

"OK," he said and scurried away.

The Raiders created more pre-game news. This time it was John Matuszak, the self-appointed team chaperone.

"I'm going to see that there's no funny business," Tooz told the media. "I've had enough parties for twenty people's lifetimes. I've grown up. I'll keep our young fellows out of trouble. If any players want to stray, they gotta go through ol' Tooz."

The next night, ol' Tooz strayed. He was dancing and having a good time four hours past curfew. Like I said, Tooz never means what he says anyway.

Eagles coach Dick Vermeil was asked what the punishment would be if Matuszak were playing for Philadelphia.

"I'd fine him $10,000 and send him home on the next flight," Vermeil replied.

Vermeil might lose his mind if he woke up one morning and found that he was the coach of Oakland, not Philadelphia. Dick believes in strict discipline and regimentation. Most Raider players would need a dictionary to look up those words, because they are never used in Oakland.

Flores fined Matuszak a flat $1,000 and forgot about the whole incident. Tooz wasn't the only Raider to violate rules that week. Oakland's trip to the Super Bowl cost some Raiders a total of $20,000.

"Tom doesn't say much," Upshaw told the media. "He just cuts off your wallet."

Flores grew up in Steinbeck country, the San Joaquin Valley, in California. Tom's parents picked fruit for a living in the tiny town of Sanger. Tom and his older brother Bob picked fruit too.

Annapolis was interested in Tom until the academy

discovered his eyesight wasn't 20–20. Tom went to the College of Pacific and quarterbacked the varsity for two years.

A square-jawed quarterback from California's wine country arrived on the Pacific campus one spring. The coaches wanted to make him a halfback, so he transferred to San Jose State.

His name was Dick Vermeil.

For two years, Vermeil and Flores quarterbacked against each other. Pacific won both games. Now Vermeil and Flores were competing against each other in the Super Bowl.

John Hannah was in New Orleans to accept an award given to the NFL's top offensive lineman. Hannah wins the award every year, it seems. He repeated to an Oakland sportswriter a remark that he has made several times:

"Plunkett isn't a winner."

I don't like to get on people much. And I certainly don't want to get down to Hannah's level, but I haven't seen him in too many playoff games. I suppose he blames Steve Grogan for New England's losing the 1976 playoff game to Oakland.

What is a winner? Is it walking out on your team just before the first game of the season? Is it making all pro every year? All that may be enough for Hannah, but his comment doesn't make him a winner in my eyes.

The most talked-about confrontation during Super Bowl week wasn't the Eagles against the Raiders, or ol' Tooz versus curfew, but Rozelle meeting Davis. If the Raiders won on Sunday, then Rozelle, as commissioner, would have to present the championship trophy to Davis.

Upshaw predicted that Rozelle wouldn't even show up if Oakland triumphed. Many players brought cameras along to record this momentous occasion; the players were convinced we would win.

At his annual pre-Super Bowl press conference on Friday, Rozelle called Davis a "charming rogue" who had turned into an "outlaw." This was Rozelle's strongest language yet in describing Davis. As was the case in San Diego, Davis offered no reply. Publicly.

By Friday, I had enough of the whole thing. I was tired of answering questions, tired of signing autographs, tired of the wire service photographer, who was a nice, if persistent, "bird dog." I was ready to play the game right then.

Schultzie, Ditz and Passafuime saw me early Saturday evening. They couldn't believe I was so calm with the biggest moment of my life less than twenty-four hours away. I told them that I was excited, but just fed up with all the Super Bowl hype.

I didn't sleep much that night. I kept thinking about the game and all the situations that might come up. Like that long-ago San Jose State game, I kept glancing at the clock . . . 1:15 A.M. . . . 2:29 A.M. . . . 3:35 A.M. . . . 5:12 A.M. . . .

My stomach was tied up in about a dozen Boy Scout knots. I couldn't fail now. I had gone through too much, suffered embarrassment and humiliation, to stumble now. People took their shots at me, gave up on me, called me a has-been. I was a nobody to almost everybody.

Now it was my turn. I may have lost some games in September, October, November and December, but I don't lose in January. I won at the Rose Bowl and I'll win at the Super Bowl. January is my month.

The big games are my games.

Three miles away from the Superdome on the team bus, I saw the yellow ribbon. It was hard to miss: 80 feet tall, 30 feet wide, with streamers 180 feet long. The American hostages were out of Iran and back home after their horrible 444-day ordeal. It was great of the league to tie that yellow ribbon to the outside of the Superdome and pass out tiny yellow ribbons to the spectators. The NFL, even at its one big splash event of the year, reminded itself and football fanatics everywhere that there were other things happening in the world. The hostages were on the minds of most Raiders, and we were happy to have them back.

We knew what had to be done to beat Philadelphia: get up on the Eagles quickly. They didn't have a big-play offense like San Diego or Cleveland. The Eagles were run-oriented, built around halfback Wilbert Montgomery. We didn't think Philadelphia could come back if we scored 2 touchdowns right away.

That November 23 game in Philadelphia was more of an advantage to the Raiders than the Eagles. We changed the things that cost us the game. Philadelphia refined the things that gave it the victory. Football is like that, which explains why one team can trounce an opponent one week and then get trounced by the same opponent in a rematch. Los Angeles humiliated Dallas, 38–14, on Monday night TV. Dallas humiliated Los Angeles, 34–13, two weeks later in the playoffs. This is what I mean.

We had another factor working for us: pride. Philadelphia pushed us around the last time. There was no way the Eagles were going to get 8 sacks and force me to throw 26 incompletions again. Our offensive line wasn't going to let that happen. Neither were Flores and his staff.

Our game plan was to throw crossing patterns underneath the Eagles' zone. Their secondary covers well, but crossing patterns would enable us to run away from the coverage. I would also throw more quickly, helping to negate the Eagles' pass rush.

The coaches also decided to keep Philadelphia's defense off-balance by throwing a first down and short-yardage situations. Something else the coaches told us: don't turn the ball over. Throw it away if you have to, but don't give the Eagles the ball near our end zone. Make them drive the length of the field; make them work for every point they get.

A reporter told me later that the Eagles looked

beaten in the pre-game introductions. As the TV cameras moved from face to face among the linemen, the fear of uncertainty was plainly evident.

The Super Bowl was something new to the Eagles. The confidence emanating from the Eagle camp all week was just pre-game puff. A team has to walk out on the field the day of the game to know what a Super Bowl is all about. Suddenly, you don't feel as confident. It was their first time, and only three teams—Green Bay, the New York Jets and Pittsburgh—had won the Super Bowl their first time. And the Packers won in the inaugural game.

The Oakland offense was introduced after Philadelphia's. The Raider linemen glared at the camera. Upshaw spit twice. Dalby's eyes could have cut through steel. They had been at the Super Bowl before. Oakland knew what it was all about.

All right, guys, the Raiders told one another, let's get even for November 23.

Ron Jaworski's first pass of the game was intended for wide receiver John Spagnola. Rod Martin cut in front, intercepted and ran 17 yards to the Eagles' 30.

Seven plays later, after Branch's 14-yard reception, we were 2 yards from our first touchdown. The game plan said: pass. Mickey Marvin said something else.

"Let's run it in. Let's run it down their throats."

Upshaw had something to say too.

"Back off, Mick. Let Jim call his game. He's the man who brought us here."

We passed. Branch cut over the middle. I looked at Cliff, but Eagles cornerback Herman Edwards was on him tight. I started forward as if I were going to run, freezing the Eagles. Branch moved toward me and caught the pass in front of his eyes.

Oakland: 7–0. Now let's get another one.

Late in the first quarter, we had a third-and-four at our 20. The play: a crossing pattern to Chandler.

Bobby was covered. I drifted to my left and saw King waving his hands near our bench. I barely lobbed the pass over Edwards to King at the 39. Kenny turned around and saw nothing but green carpet ahead. Chandler joined King on the sprint down the sideline. Eighty yards, a Super Bowl record. I looked around for flags, saw none, smiled. Bum Phillips, wherever he was, cried all over again.

Oakland: 14–0. This is what we wanted, a 2-touchdown advantage. Okay, Eagles, see if you can come back.

The barefoot boy, Tony Franklin, kicked a 30-yard field goal for Philadelphia's first points. Jaworski brought the Eagles back for more, but he threw 3 times into our end zone without success. Franklin lined up from 28 yards, but the 6'7" Hendricks—who else?—slapped away the kick with one hand. It was a deflating first-half finish for Philadelphia, and elating for Oakland.

A 14–3 lead isn't enough, I reminded myself. I kept thinking it would wind up a 20–17 or a 27–20 game. Oakland. But we needed more points.

The Eagle corners played so far off Branch and Chandler that we weren't going to burn them on the bomb. They hadn't forgotten Branch's 86-yard catch. It would take more crossing patterns, more short stuff.

My best pass of the game was a 32-yarder to Chandler on a crossing route shortly after the second half began. I looped the ball over corner Roynell Young at the Eagles' 33. If I didn't throw one to Bobby, he might never speak to me again.

Chandler really was upset in the first half because Branch had caught 4 passes and he hadn't gotten one. After one pass to Cliff, Bobby came back to the huddle and said, "Dammit, look at my side!" I was about to jump all over him, then thought better of it. Chandler isn't different from any other receiver.

They all want the ball. Branch really gets dejected if he doesn't get any passes. Vataha used to drive me nuts!

Chester wasn't getting any passes toward the middle of the '80 season, so I consciously went to him. Raymond made a number of big catches afterward.

That last pass to Chandler should keep him quiet—until the next series. Two plays later I came back to Cliff, only I had made a mistake. I thought the Eagles were in a zone. They weren't. Young ran downfield with Branch and was about to intercept the pass when Cliff cut in front to make a great leaping 29-yard grab on the goal line.

Oakland: 21–3. The game was over.

"It was an emotional time for all of us. Every time Jim threw a touchdown pass, Schultz started crying."
　　　　　　　　—JACK LASATER.

Jaworski aimed for Spagnola and Martin intercepted again to set up Bahr's 46-yard field goal. Oakland: 24–3 and coasting.

I let up at this point. Our defense wasn't going to give up 3 touchdowns. Jaworski threw an 8-yard pass to tight end Keith Krepfle for the Eagles' only touchdown. Bahr kicked a 35-yard field goal and we were up, 27–10, with eight and a half minutes left.

Jaworski then fumbled a snap and Willie Jones recovered. Jaworski had one chance left and committed his fourth turnover—Martin's third interception. Rod was fantastic, a one-man show. *The* one-man show.

The game ended and Tom Flores hugged me. The only Mexican head coach in the NFL embracing the only Mexican quarterback. We're almost gringos, though: neither of us speaks Spanish all that well.

"He's always operating with such courage. That's the key to Jim. He's as courageous a quarterback as I've ever seen. He always comes back."
　　　　　　　　—TOM FLORES.

I looked for Burgess Owens after the game. Teary-eyed, we hugged. We both had come from losing situations. This was my first winning season since Stanford. This was Burgess's first winning season since high school!

I missed the Davis-Rozelle confrontation, which wasn't even that. Reporters had me cornered. I felt something on my hand and looked down to see my wrist being measured.

"What's this for?" I asked.

"You're the Super Bowl MVP," came the reply.

They could have given Martin the watch and me the watch box. Rod had an unbelievable game. Three interceptions were a Super Bowl *career* record.

I was happy with the statistics sheet: 13 for 21, 261 yards, 3 touchdowns. We didn't have 1 turnover and came up with 4. I was sacked only once, for a yard loss as I was caught running behind the line of scrimmage.

Things seemed to move in a hurry after that. I went to the interview room. Questions, flash bulbs, microphones . . . It was all like a blur.

Hendricks and I were the last players to leave the dressing room. We climbed on the bus heading for the Raiders' victory party. Ted explained what the Super Bowl victory really meant to him.

"If we lost today, we'd have gone back to camp as Eagles. But we won. Now we can continue to be Raiders."

Hendricks was fearful that Flores might have brought some of Vermeil's rigid, militaristic coaching to Oakland. I'm not saying Dick's system isn't right, it is—for Philadelphia. The Raiders may not be choir boys, but everything seems to turn out well on the football field.

The Raider way beat the Eagle way.

The victory party was too crowded and I got tired of signing autographs. So a bunch of my friends met me at the 4141 Club, away from the French Quarter. That was the best time of all.

"There's a scene at the 4141 Club I'll never forget. Rich Martini's girlfriend is sitting in a funk at the end of the bar. I thought: 'What could she be mad about at a time like this?' It turned out she had lost a diamond earring. Plunk picks up on this eventually. He gets the manager of the club to turn on the lights and everyone starts looking for the earring. We didn't find it, but that isn't the point. Here is a guy on the greatest day of his life—the king of our culture—down on his hands and knees, looking for something someone else has lost. That typifies the kind of guy Plunk is."
—JIM KAUFFMAN

People have asked me what my story means.

I imagine it is about a young Mexican kid who learned from his parents that blindness and poverty aren't necessarily deterrents to happiness.

I also learned that not all tumors are malignant, that you sometimes have to be lucky in life.

My story? It's about a guy who could have become a defensive end, but through hard work and determination, was able to stay at quarterback. Maybe there is a message in this for young boys. I hope so.

I had a good college career, then I was lost for a while, almost forgotten. I could have quit and never made it, but I stuck it out. Then through an injury to someone else came an opportunity—and a challenge.

I could have stepped in and failed. Then where would I have been, out of football for good? Playing backup somewhere?

I came through. It was important to me.

I was also lucky enough to be in and help win a Super Bowl, accomplishing a goal I had set for myself ten years before. I was able to share the experience with people who stuck with me through some very hard times.

I'm happy for me and I'm happy for them.